Progressive

Complete Singing

Manual

By
Peter Gelling

Visit our Website
www.learntoplaymusic.com

The Progressive Series of Music Instruction Books, CDs and DVDs

CONTENTS

Introduction .... **Page 6**
How to Use the CD **6**
Approach to Practice **7**
Listening **7**
Recording Yourself **7**
The Metronome **8**
The Keyboard **8**

SECTION 1 .... **9**

BEFORE YOU BEGIN .... **Page 10**
Everyone Can Sing **10**
Matching Pitches and Rhythms 10
Vocal Range **11**
Timbre 11
The Ultimate Melodic Instrument 12
How We Sing 13
Breathing **14**
Posture 14
Posture and Movement 15
Learning to Sing 15
Pre-Hearing Notes **15**
Common Problems 16
Registers **17**
Working With a Teacher 17
Breath Control **18**

How to Read Music **18**
Music Notes 18
The Quarter Note 18

LESSON 1 .... **Page 21**
Note and Rest Values **21**
Bar Lines 21
Time Signatures **21**
The Half Note 22
A Word About Pitch **23**
When to Breathe 23
The Whole Note 23
Rhythm Training **24**

LESSON 2 .... **Page 25**
Rests **25**
The Half Rest 25
The Whole Rest 25
The Quarter Rest 26
The Importance of Timing **27**

LESSON 3 .... **Page 28**
Voice Types and Ranges 28
How to find Your Voice Range **28**
Referring to the Keyboard 28
The Bass Staff 29
The Grand Staff 31
Soprano Range 32
Mezzo Soprano Range 32
Alto Range 32
Tenor Range 33
Baritone Range 33
Bass Range 33
Leger Lines 34
Matching Pitches **35**
The Octave **35**

LESSON 4 .... **Page 36**
The Major Scale **36**
C Major Scale 36
Octave Displacement 37
Sol-Fa Syllables **38**

LESSON 5 .... **39**
Three Four Time Signature **39**
The Dotted Half Note 39
Chord Symbols 40
Slow Waltz **40**

LESSON 6 .... **Page 41**
The Eighth Note 41
Eighth Note Rhythms **42**
The Dotted Quarter Note 43
Singing Songs **44**
Cue Notes 44
Silent Night **45**

LESSON 7 .... **Page 46**
Sounds Used in Singing **46**
Vowels 46
Dipthongs 46
The Shaping of Vowels **47**

CONTENTS CONTINUED

Consonants 48
Language and Style 49
Comin' Home to Me 49

LESSON 8 .... Page 50
Dynamics 50
Musical Use of Dynamics 51
Tempo Markings 51

LESSON 9 .... Page 53
Slurs 53
The Tie 54
Imitating Instruments 54
Phrasing and Expression 56
Moving Between Registers 56
Vibrato 57

LESSON 10 .... Page 58
Tones and Semitones 58
Sharps 58
The Chromatic Scale 58
The Natural Sign 59
Flats 60

LESSON 11 .... Page 63
More About Major Scales 63
Scale Degrees 63
Major Scale Pattern 63
The G Major Scale 64
The F Major Scale 64
Other Major Scales 65
Moveable Sol-Fa Syllables 65
Key of C Major 66
Lavender's Blue 66
Key Signatures 67

LESSON 12 .... Page 68
Keys and Key Signatures 68
Sharp Key Signatures 69
Flat Key Signatures 69
The Key Cycle 70
Major Scales in all Keys 71

LESSON 13 .... Page 72
The Eighth Rest 72
Syncopation 72
In Sync 73
Syncopation Using Ties 74
Identifying Eighth Note Rhythms 75
Minor Melody 75
Jamaica Farewell 76

LESSON 14 .... Page 78
Transposing 78
Get to Know You 80

LESSON 15 .... Page 82
Minor Keys and Scales 82
Relative Major and Minor Keys 83
Scarborough Fair 84
LESSON 16 .... Page 86
The Lead-In 86
First and Second Endings 86
Greensleeves 87
Up On Stage 88

SECTION 2 89

LESSON 17 .... Page 90
Developing Your Sense of Pitch 90
Interval Qualities 90
Intervals Distances 91
Identifying Intervals by Ear 92

LESSON 18 .... Page 96
Enharmonic Notes 96
Accidentals 96
The Blues Scale 98
Singing Scale Degrees 98

LESSON 19 .... Page 100
The Triplet 100
Amazing Grace 101
Swing Rhythms 102
St James Infirmary 103
Call and Response 104

LESSON 20 .... Page 105
12 Bar Blues 105
Blues Singing 106

CONTENTS CONTINUED

Come Back Darlin' **106**
If It Wasn't For the Blues **107**

LESSON 21 .... **Page 108**
Sixteenth Notes **108**
The Sixteenth Note Triplet 109
Interpretation and Improvisation **110**
Repetition and Variation 111
Hangin' Out **111**
Swing Low, Sweet Chariot **112**

LESSON 22 .... **Page 114**
Phrasing and Rubato 114
Born to Believe **114**

LESSON 23 .... **Page 116**
Six Eight Time Signature ($\frac{6}{8}$) 116
House of the Rising Sun **116**
Simple and Compound Time **118**
Twelve Eight Time ($\frac{12}{8}$) 118
Grouping Notes in Compound Time .. 119

LESSON 24 .... **Page 120**
Harmony Singing **120**
Banks of the Ohio **121**
Harmony and Chords 124
Chord Progressions 124
Harmonizing Melodies 125

LESSON 25 .... **Page 126**
Writing Vocal Parts 126
Four Part Harmony **127**

LESSON 26 .... **Page 128**
Chord Construction – Triads **128**
Double Sharps and Double Flats 129
Understanding Chord Symbols 129
Accents **121**

LESSON 27 .... **Page 130**
Chord Inversions 130
Voice Parts on the Grand Staff 132
Chorale (Schumann) **132**
Arpeggios **133**

LESSON 28 .... **Page 134**
Scale Tone Chords **134**
More on Chord Progressions 134
Rhythm Notation 135
Writing Harmonies (Chord Charts) 135
Major Key Triad Pattern 136
Scale Tone Chords in All Keys **137**
Common Progressions 137

LESSON 29 .... **Page 139**
More About Harmony **139**
Primary Triads 139
Harmonizing Melodies 140

LESSON 30 .... **Page 142**
Secondary Triads 142
Chord Functions 142
Voice Leading **143**
Practice Progressions 143
Chorale (Bach) **144**
Melodies to Harmonize 145

LESSON 31 .... **Page 146**
Minor Key Scale Tone Triads **146**
Chords in Other Minor Keys 147
Transposing in Minor Keys 147
Harmonic Minor Scale Tone Chords 148
Melodic Minor Scale Tone Chords 149
House of the Rising Sun (A Minor) .. **149**

LESSON 32 .... **Page 150**
Harmonies in Relative Keys 150
Where Are You Now? **151**

LESSON 33 .... **Page 152**
Seventh Chords **152**
Scale Tone Seventh Chords 154
Extended Chords 155

LESSON 34 .... **Page 156**
Jazz Singing **156**
Jazz Blues in B 156
Which Notes to Use 157
Using Arpeggios **158**
LESSON 35 .... **Page 159**
Articulations **159**
Tenuto and Staccato 159
Accents 160

CONTENTS CONTINUED

Accents and Swing **160**
Ghost Notes 161
Developing Rhythmic Control **162**
Vocal Soloing 163
Leave This Town Behind **163**

LESSON 36 .... **Page 164**
Musical Forms **164**
Greensleeves **164**
Typical Blues Song Format 165
Learning Song Forms 166
Some Jazz Terminology 166
Rhythm Changes **167**

LESSON 37 .... **Page 168**
Form, Harmony and Dynamics 168
Nobody's Fault But Mine **168**
A Full Vocal Score – All My Trials **170**

LESSON 38 .... **Page 176**
Singing With a Band **176**
Bass 176
Drums 178
Guitars 180
The Whole Band 182
Two Guitars 183
Guitar and Keyboard 183

LESSON 39 .... **Page 184**
Performing in Public **184**
Overcoming Nerves 184
Eye Contact 185
Stage Presence and Stage Craft **185**
Developing Your Own Style **185**
Microphones 186
Microphone Technique 187
Warming Up **188**
Looking After Your Voice **188**
The Importance of Listening **189**
Recording **190**
Tell Me Blues **190**

Cycle of Fifths **190**
Notes on the Keyboard **192**
Major Scales and Key Signatures **194**
Minor Scales and Key Signatures **196**
Blues Scale Summary **198**
Glossary of Musical Terms **199**

LTP Publishing PTY LTD
Email: info@learntoplaymusic.com
Visit our Website:
www.learntoplaymusic.com

For recordings by Peter Gelling, visit: **www.bentnotes.com**

INTRODUCTION

Progressive COMPLETE LEARN TO SING MANUAL is the ultimate Singing manual. It assumes you have no prior knowledge of music or singing and will take you **from beginner to professional level**. It contains all the essential information on how to read music, learning songs by ear, correct breathing and posture, how to develop your own interpretation of a song, harmony singing, and valuable tips on performing in public and how to use microphones.

Each new technique is introduced separately and all the examples sound great and are fun to sing. They include well known popular and traditional songs in a variety of styles, along with specially developed exercises and original songs. On completion of the book, you will be well-prepared to perform solo, sing with a band, or join a choir.

The best and fastest way to learn is to use this book in conjunction with:

1. Buying sheet music of your favourite singers and learning their songs. This will help you build a repertoire and mean you always have something to sing on social or professional occasions.

2. Practicing and singing with other singers and musicians. You will be surprised how good a basic melody and accompaniment can sound.

3. Learning more about music and learning to accompany yourself on either piano, keyboard or guitar. This will help you relate to what other musicians are doing when they accompany you. It will also help you to write songs and arrangements without relying on someone else to provide the musical knowledge.

4. Learning by listening to your favourite CDs. Start building a collection of albums featuring singers you admire or wish to emulate. Try singing along with one of them for a short time each day. Many popular singers have learned a lot of their music this way.

In the early stages it is helpful to have the guidance of an experienced teacher. This will help you keep to a schedule and attain weekly goals. It will also help you develop good vocal technique and avoid straining your your voice. To develop a good sense of time, it is recommended that you use a metronome for part of **every** practice session..

HOW TO USE THE CD

The musical examples and exercises in this book have been recorded on the accompanying CD. In most cases you will first hear a female voice, then a male voice, followed by another version with no singing at all for you to use as a backing track. For each song you will hear a chord played by a piano to establish the correct key in your mind, followed by the starting note of the song. With most of the songs, only the first verse is sung on the recording. This is followed by a longer version without any singing, so you can practice any or all of the verses.

Each exercise has a CD symbol next to it.

CD 1 **2.** ← CD Track Number

APPROACH TO PRACTICE

Regardless of the style of music you sing, It is important to have a correct approach to practice. You will benefit more from several short practices (e.g. 20-30 minutes per day) than one or two long sessions per week. This is especially so in the early stages, because your muscles and your voice are still developing. If you want to become a great singer you will obviously have to practice more as time goes on, but it is still better to work on new things a bit at a time. Take one small piece of information and learn it well before going on to the next topic. Make sure each new technique is thoroughly worked into your singing. This way you won't forget it, and you can build on everything you learn.

In a practice session you should divide your time evenly between the study of new material and the revision of past work. It is a common mistake for semi-advanced students to practice only the songs they can already sing well. Although this is enjoyable, it is not a satisfactory method of practice. You should also try to correct mistakes and experiment with new ideas. To develop good timing, it is essential that you always practice with a metronome (or drum machine). Beginning singers are often particularly weak in this area. Your timing and all-round musicianship will also improve dramatically if you learn to accompany yourself on keyboard or guitar.

Apart from practicing your actual singing technique, it is important to spend time thinking about the lyrics of each song and how you can bring meaning to the song with your interpretation. From this point of view it is useful to learn a bit about acting. Maybe you could talk to an actor or take a few drama lessons.

LISTENING

Apart from books and sheet music, your most important source of information will be recordings. Listen to albums which feature great singers. Regardless of the style of music you prefer to sing, it is important to listen to many different styles, in order to hear a wide variety of interpretations and expressions. There is something to be learned from every style of music and singing. It is a useful exercise to listen to several different recordings of the same song performed by different singers. Listen to their phrasing, their timing, their note choices, the tempo they choose, and the style of accompaniment. By doing this with several songs, you will soon work out your own preferences, as well as get valuable ideas for how to approach other songs and the type of arrangements you prefer. When you are listening to albums, sing along with the songs and try to copy the sounds you are hearing. This helps you absorb the music and before long, it will start to come out in your own style. It is also valuable to sing along with albums sometimes imitating what you are hearing and sometimes improvising. This is good ear training and is also a lot of fun.

RECORDING YOURSELF

From time to time it is a good idea to record your performances or practice sessions. Unless you have studio quality equipment, the tone quality you hear on the recording may not be wonderful, but any recording will pick up timing and relative pitch accurately. As you listen back to yourself, pay particular attention to areas you think are particularly weak or particularly strong. Anything you think sounds good is worth developing further and anything that doesn't (e.g. timing, or pitching on high notes) should be the focus of your practice sessions until it is corrected.

THE METRONOME

A metronome is a mechanical or electronic device that divides time into equal beats by producing a ticking or beeping sound. The number of beats per minute is adjustable so that you can vary the speed at which you wish to sing or play a piece of music.

The metronome has three functions:

1. It indicates the tempo to sing at by sounding the number of beats per minute. e.g. ♩ = 60 sounds one beat (quarter note) per second.

2. It acts as a control for your timing so that you do not rush or slow down when singing a melody.

3. It is a good idea to learn new songs and choral works at a slow tempo. The metronome enables you to then gradually increase the tempo, keeping exactly the same rhythm, until you can sing the piece correctly along with the CD.

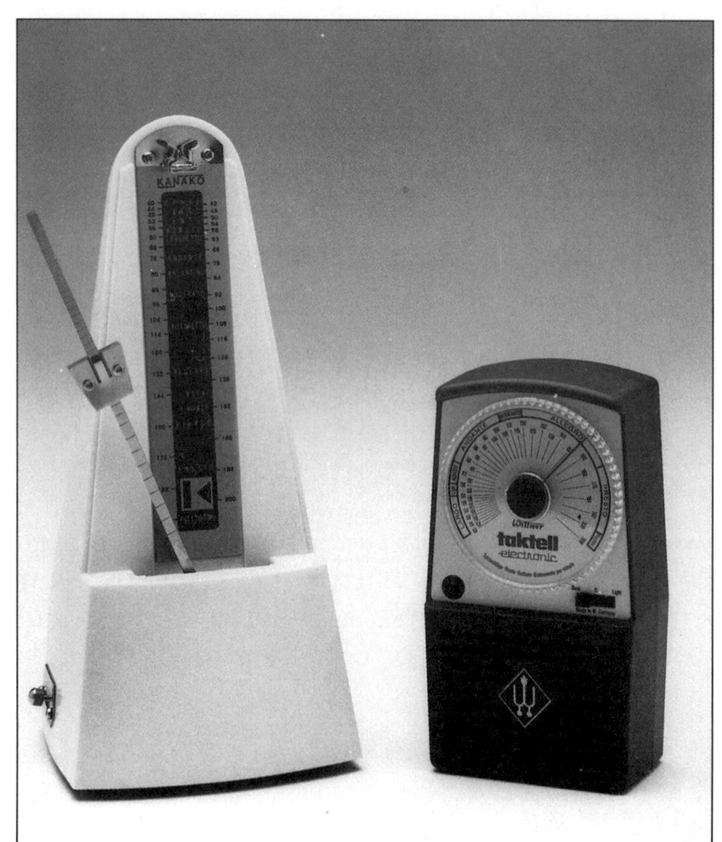

THE KEYBOARD

Throughout the book, the Piano keyboard is used as a reference for pitch. The keyboard is a good visual reference because the notes appear as black and white keys, making it easy to understand the distances between the notes. It is also a good aural reference because each note has an exact pitch, whereas a sung note has no fixed reference point. It is recommended that you work through the book using either keyboard or guitar as a reference to ensure you develop an accurate sense of pitch.

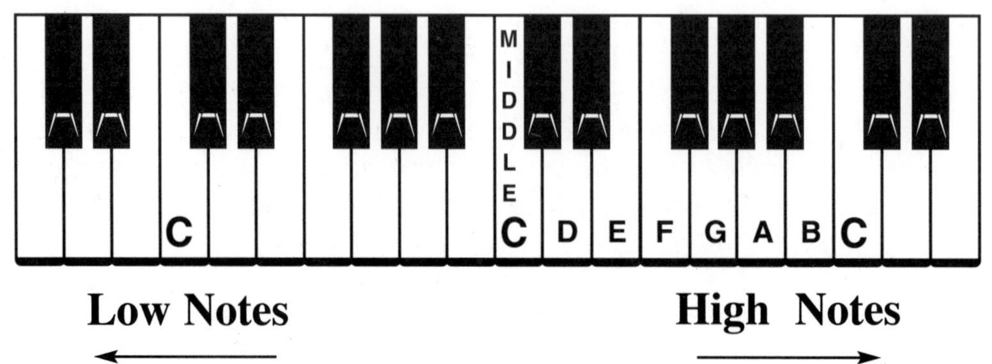

Section 1

BEFORE YOU BEGIN

EVERYONE CAN SING

Everyone has a natural desire to sing. It is a way of expressing feelings and emotions as well as a means of telling stories and reminding us of important events and times in our lives. For some the desire to sing is an instinctive personal thing and there is no wish to share the sound with others or perform. The classic example of this is singing in the shower. For others the feelings associated with singing are more significant and represent a desire to be involved in music, whether it is singing with friend, or in a choir, or with a band or even a whole orchestra.

Many people say they can't sing, but this is rarely true. It usually means the person is not confident about the sound of their singing voice. With a bit of knowledge of fundamentals such as learning to sing pitches and rhythms by ear and a little practice, it is the author's belief that everyone can sing well enough to gain a great deal of pleasure from the experience.

MATCHING PITCHES AND RHYTHMS

Probably the most important aspect of singing is to be able to sing a given pitch for a specific period of time. Many people have trouble with this at first, but it is really just a matter of **listening**, **practice** and **patience**. All notes used in music can be written down and therefore have a specific pitch and time value. Through the course of this book you will learn the fundamentals of all of the common time values for notes, as well as a method of identifying pitches and how they relate to other pitches in a song.

The best way to improve your ability to sing 'in time' and 'in tune' is to copy the sounds made by someone else. The easiest way to do this is to sing along with a recording of one of your favorite songs and try to copy the singer.

Listen to the following vocal phrase on the accompanying CD and try to copy it. Memorise the phrase and then sing along with the CD. Don't worry about the written music for now, just copy the sounds you hear on the recording. The more you do this with songs, the easier it will get.

CD 1 **1.**

VOCAL RANGE

The previous example was sung first by a female voice and then by a male voice. In general, female voices are higher in pitch than male voices, although everybody's voice range is individual and there are many variations.

The **range** of a person's voice is determined by the highest and lowest notes they can sing. Vocal ranges are discussed in detail in Lesson 3. When you are learning to copy recorded versions of songs by ear, you may feel that you have the correct notes but your version sounds higher or lower than the one you are copying.

For example, if you are a female singer learning from a version of a song sung by a male singer, your version may be higher. This is because you have a higher voice range than the male singer.

TIMBRE

If you are interested in singing, you probably have one or more favorite singers. A large part of what attracts us to a particular singer's voice is the way it sounds, rather than the notes used.

Every singer has an individual sound because everyone's anatomy is slightly different. Just as each person has a different height, weight, arm length, coarseness or fineness of hair, skin tone etc., we all have slightly different shapes, sizes and thicknesses of the parts of the body involved in singing. The lungs, windpipe, larynx, tongue, lips, and cavities in the mouth and behind the nose are all individual and combine to create a particular **timbre** (tonal quality or tone color).

All musical instruments have their own **timbre**, which makes them easy to distinguish from one another even when they are playing exactly the same notes. Listen to the following example which is played first on the guitar and then on the flute. Although they are both playing the same notes, they are easy to tell apart because each instrument has a different timbre.

CD 1 **2.**

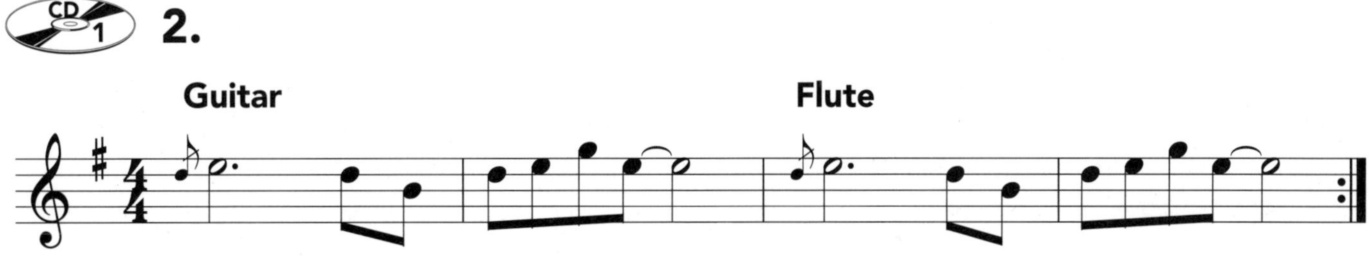

THE ULTIMATE MELODIC INSTRUMENT

The human voice can be thought of as the ultimate melodic instrument, because it is capable of instant expression with no other instrument required to translate thoughts and feelings into sound. The voice is capable of a huge variety and depth of expression. With the human voice, thought almost equals sound.

As a baby begins to communicate with parents and relatives, it instinctively learns how to reproduce all the sounds of language heard by the ears and processed by the brain. Later, when the child begins to learn about language at school, vowels, consonants, words, phrases, sentences, etc. are all analysed and classified and this natural learning expands into a whole world of communication. With singing it is largely the same process. There are many different sounds used in various styles of singing, including slides, dips, growls, pure bell-like tones, etc. These can all be learned simply by imitating the sounds you hear and then working at perfecting them.

Musical instruments often imitate the human voice because of its pure expression and feeling. A classic example of this is in African American music such as Blues or Gospel, where an instrument or group of instruments answers a vocalist in a 'call and response' style. This is demonstrated in the following example, where the voice is answered by the guitar. Because the human voice was used for expression before the invention of instruments and because all melodic instruments learn from the human voice, it can be said that **all music** is comes from vocal music.

CD 1 **3**

UNDERSTANDING MUSIC

Although singing is a natural process, it can be improved in quality, range and accuracy of pitch and rhythm just as an instrumentalist can improve their ability with practice. Since it is the brain which issues the information for singing, it is most important to train the brain to recognise sounds and to build up a bank of knowledge which makes it easier to understand the whole process of making music. This has the added benefit of helping you to relate to what other musicians are playing and understanding the way a song's melody and its accompaniment work together. It also enables you to understand the sheet music of songs you wish to learn.

HOW WE SING

The ability to sing is a by-product of the way nature has equipped the human body for speech. By simply imagining the pitch of a note, the body automatically knows how to achieve this note once the brain has issued the order to produce it. The sound which we know as singing is made primarily by air from an exhaled breath passing over the **vocal cords**, causing them to vibrate. The vocal cords are small muscular folds of skin located inside the **larynx** (commonly known as the voice box). The sound is then amplified (made louder) and modified by the **resonance spaces** in the mouth and throat and behind the nose. It may also be altered by the shape of the mouth, the lips and movements of the tongue as the sound leaves the mouth. Because everybody's anatomy is slightly different, each voice will have its own individual sound both when speaking and singing.

A singing breath usually starts with the **diaphragm** muscle and then travels upward from there. The air then flows over the vocal cords which are activated by a message from the brain. This produces the initial sound, just as in speech. The sound then travels up into the cavities in the throat and behind the nose. These cause the sound to **resonate**, which means they reinforce and prolong the sound by vibration. These resonance spaces affect the tone of the sound and contribute to the individual sound of each person's voice. The final aspect of singing is the **articulation** or shaping of the sound, which is done by the **tongue, throat and lips**. All these things combine to form the sounds we know as singing.

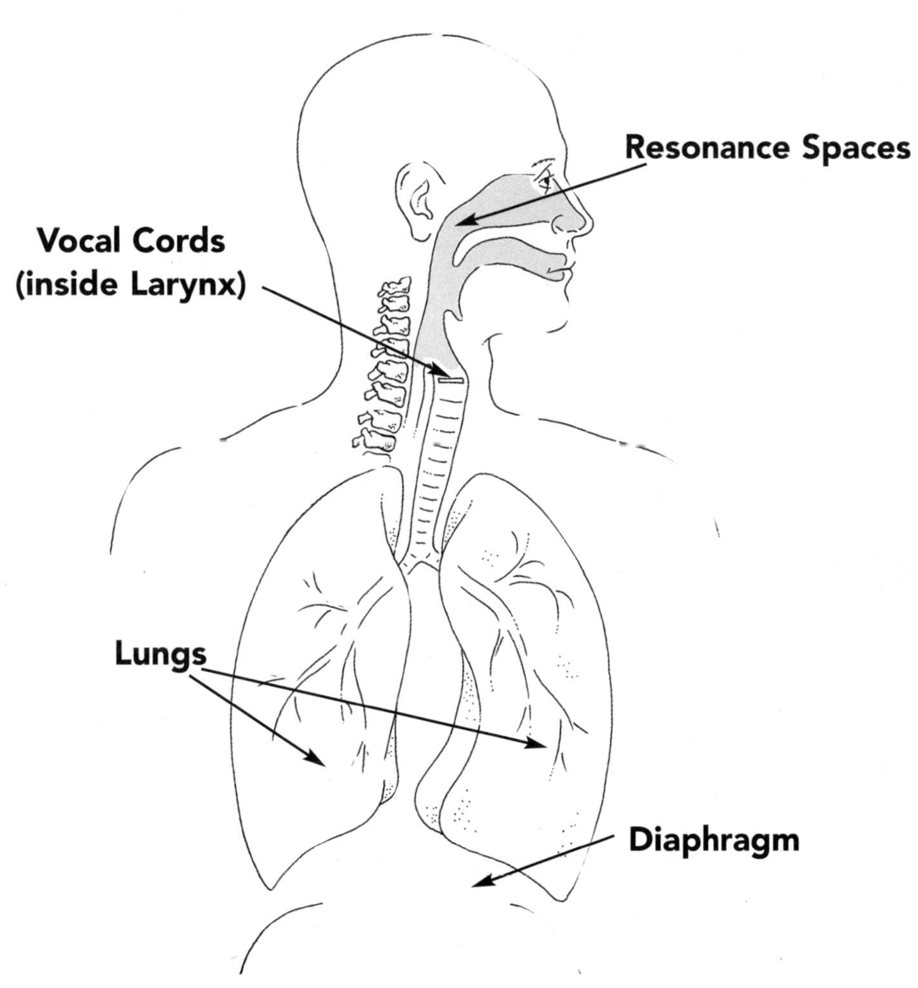

BREATHING

One of the most important elements of singing is a consistent and relaxed approach to breathing and breath control. A good singer always produces a strong, even tone and sounds relaxed regardless of how high or low the notes are. To achieve this, you need to develop a method of breathing which will help you gain more control over the way you breathe when singing. If you have a solid consistent approach to breathing correctly it will eventually become automatic, enabling you to forget about breathing and concentrate totally on the music you are making.

A good way to develop your breathing technique is through the use of visualisation. When you breathe **in**, think of an inflatable mattress which fills automatically when you pull out the plug. This will help you equate breathing in with relaxation. When you breathe **out**, think of a tube of toothpaste being slowly squeezed from the end (not the middle). This will help you use your breath economically in a controlled manner.

It is important to develop the habit of breathing from your diaphragm muscle. As you breathe **in**, let the diaphragm relax downwards and allow the lungs to fill with air right to the bottom. Then breathe **out slowly**, squeezing gently from the diaphragm (like the tube of toothpaste) and see how long you can sustain your outgoing breath. The more control you have of your diaphragm, the easier you will find breathing when you sing.

POSTURE

The term "posture" refers to the way the body is held (e.g. straight, slumped, etc) and its position when sitting or standing. For singing, it is best to stand rather than sit, as this allows the most open and unrestricted passage of air for both breathing and singing. Of course, if you are accompanying yourself on piano you will have to sit. In this situation, it is essential to sit up straight but relaxed for the best sound.

INCORRECT

The spine is not straight and the head and pelvis both tilt forward. In this position, it is not possible to move freely or produce the best sound.

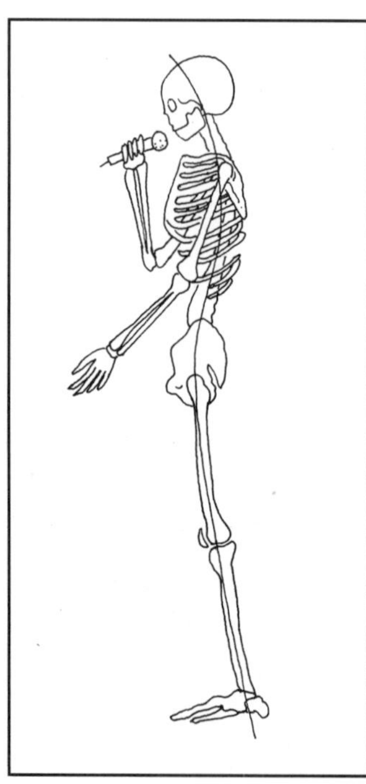

CORRECT

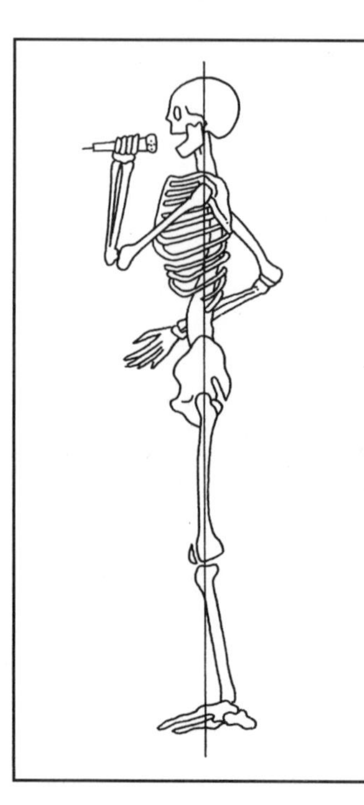

The spine is comfortably straight and in line with the head, legs and pelvis. This position keeps the airways open and makes movement easy and comfortable.

POSTURE AND MOVEMENT

If you think of a situation where a singer is performing with a band, it would look fairly dull if the singer stood straight in the one position all the time. Movement is a large part of any stage show. This means it is not always possible for the singer to maintain perfect posture. However, it is possible to keep the pathway from the diaphragm to the mouth open, flexible and relaxed most of the time, which means it is still possible to sing well while moving around. Relaxation and flexibility are keys to good posture, regardless of standing or sitting position.

LEARNING TO SING

The body instinctively knows how to sing. Becoming a better singer is simply a matter of training and improving a natural process. As with any activity, there will always be some people who seem able to do it well and sound great with very little work and others who have to spend much more time developing their voice and technique, but you can be sure that all the 'great' singers you can think of in any style of music have spent many years perfecting their craft. Everyone starts with a voice, only time will tell where it can go from there.

Although singing is a natural process, there are certain basic principles which can be applied to make the most of your particular voice. The most important of these is keeping the pathway of the voice as **open and relaxed** as possible. When you yawn, the pathway from your lungs to your lips is completely open. When singing, the mouth is not usually open as much as when yawning, but the general position and shape is the same.

When forming all the different words used in speech, the position of the lips, jaw, tongue and throat will all change, but if you keep in mind that the best sounds come from an open and relaxed approach, you will be able to achieve a better singing tone regardless of the words you are singing.

PRE-HEARING NOTES

Another principle of good singing is to avoid straining to reach high or low notes, particularly when your voice is getting tired. If you begin learning a musical instrument, it takes time to train the muscles involved in playing that particular instrument. It is the same with singing. The vocal cords are in effect muscles inside the larynx. With practice, your range will increase and you will find it easier to sing for longer periods. The secret of reaching high and low notes is to **imagine** them before you sing them. Try to develop the ability to hear the music in your mind before you sing it. This **visualizing** or **pre-hearing** will help you avoid reaching uncertainly for notes and will increase your general singing confidence as well as your ability.

COMMON PROBLEMS

When children learn to read, they usually begin by reading out loud before moving on to reading silently. In the transition period, they may read to themselves but their lips still form the words as they read. After a while they progress to reading without moving their lips.

This is a useful analogy for the process involved in learning to sing. Beginning singers instinctively move their larynx higher when singing high notes and lower when singing low notes. This creates tension in the throat and actually restricts the free flow of sound required for a good singing tone. When you move your larynx up or down, you are using the muscles outside the larynx instead of the vocal cords. You will achieve a better sound by keeping your larynx stable and relaxed as you sing. Let the air and the vocal cords make the sound. Imagine the sound of the note you wish to sing and trust your body to make that sound. If it can't, the answer is patience. A beginning pianist cannot be a virtuoso in three weeks and neither can a vocalist.

Another common problem is head movement when reaching for high or low notes. For the best sound, keep your head in the same position as you would when speaking to someone the same height as yourself. This allows the most open and relaxed pathway for your voice.

Incorrect
reaching for high notes

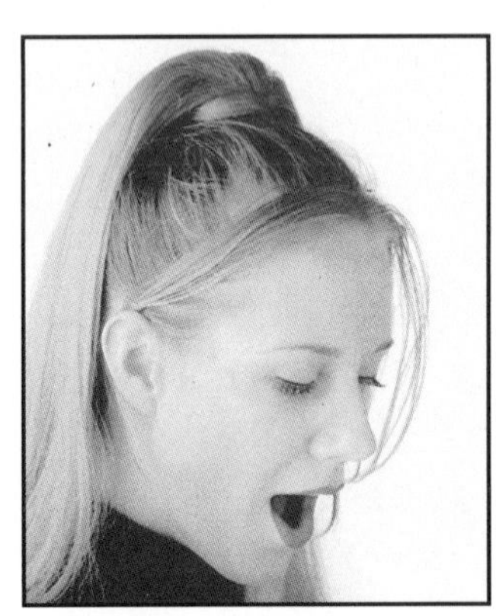

Incorrect
reaching for low notes

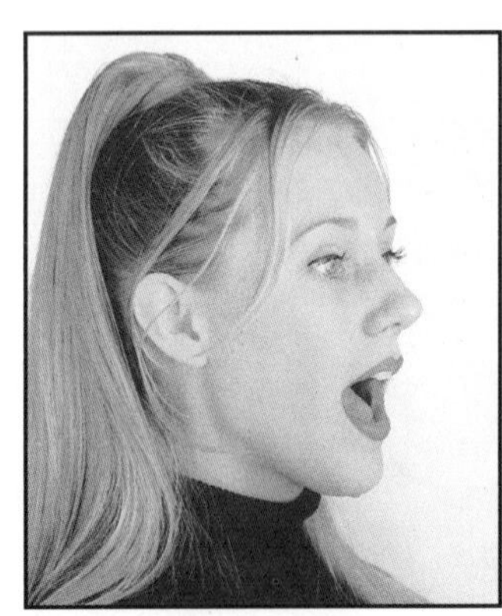

Correct
speech position

A third common problem which interferes with good tone is tension, particularly in the jaw. Before you sing, It is a good idea to tense your body and then let it relax. First try this with the whole body and then do it with specific areas like the shoulders, chest, throat, tongue, jaw, and face muscles.

REGISTERS

A **register** is a group of notes which have the same tonal characteristics. The singing voice is commonly divided into the **chest register** (or chest voice) and the **head register** (or head voice). When you sing a low note, you can feel the vibrations in your chest and throat. When you sing a high note, you feel the vibration in the roof of your mouth and nasal area, as well as your head. When singing notes in the middle of your range, you use a combination of chest voice and head voice. Some people call this another register, while others see it as a blend of the two basic registers. One of the most difficult aspects of training the voice is getting a smooth transition from one register to another. At some point there is what is commonly known as a **break**, where the voice cracks or partially seizes up before moving into a new register.

You can hear this if you sing a low note and gradually slide up to a high note while sustaining the sound. The eventual aim of all singers is to overcome this break and have one big register from the bottom to the top of their range. A break can be more noticeable if the sound is forced by too much air being used as the notes get higher or by straining the muscles around the larynx.

WORKING WITH A TEACHER

To work on this aspect of singing, it is best to work with a vocal teacher. In fact, if you are serious about singing, it is strongly recommended that you work with a teacher so as to learn the best technique right from the beginning. Find a teacher who is familiar with the style of music you are most interested in singing, but also keep your mind open to other styles of music. There is much to be learned from great singers in all styles of music. Listening to great singers and imitating them is another excellent way to develop your voice, particularly by being aware of the sounds and sensations involved in making good sounds.

BREATH CONTROL

It is common to use more air, movement and muscle activity than necessary when singing. There are two common exercises which are useful for learning to use less force and less air when singing.

The first of these is to slowly blow up a balloon, using slow sustained breaths controlled from the diaphragm. The idea is to take a comfortable breath using the technique described earlier, and then breathe into the balloon using an even sustained amount of air pressure. Repeat this until the balloon is full.

The second exercise is to sing in front of a lighted candle. This requires a more subtle release of air than blowing up a balloon, as the idea is to sing with as little effect on the flame as possible. Once you can sustain a note without moving the flame much, try beginning the note softly and gradually increasing the volume, then reverse the process. You could also try singing a whole verse from a song. As with all aspects of singing, be patient and you will see great improvement as long as you continue to practice.

HOW TO READ MUSIC

These five lines are called the **staff** or **stave.**

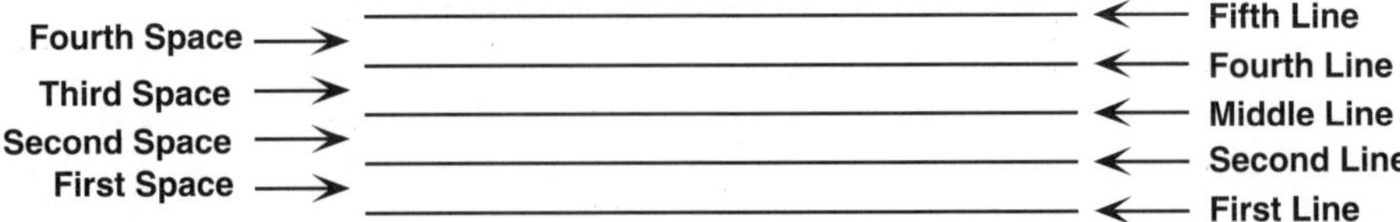

The Treble Clef

This symbol is called a **treble clef**. There is a treble clef at the beginning of every line of most vocal sheet music.

The Treble Staff

A staff with a treble clef written on it is called a **treble staff**.

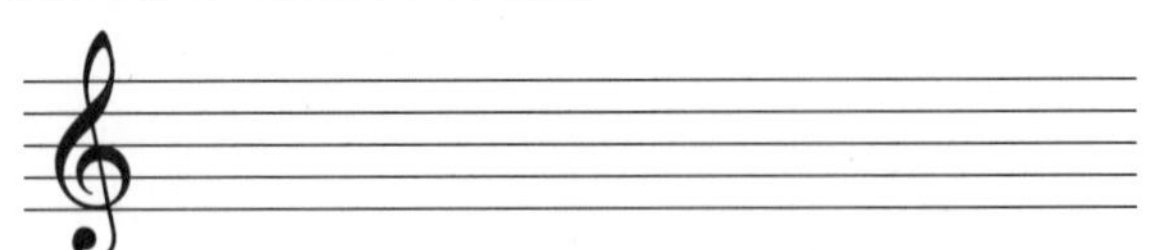

MUSIC NOTES

There are only seven letters used for notes in music:

A B C D E F G A B

These notes are known as the **musical alphabet.**
Music notes are written in the spaces and on the lines of the treble staff.

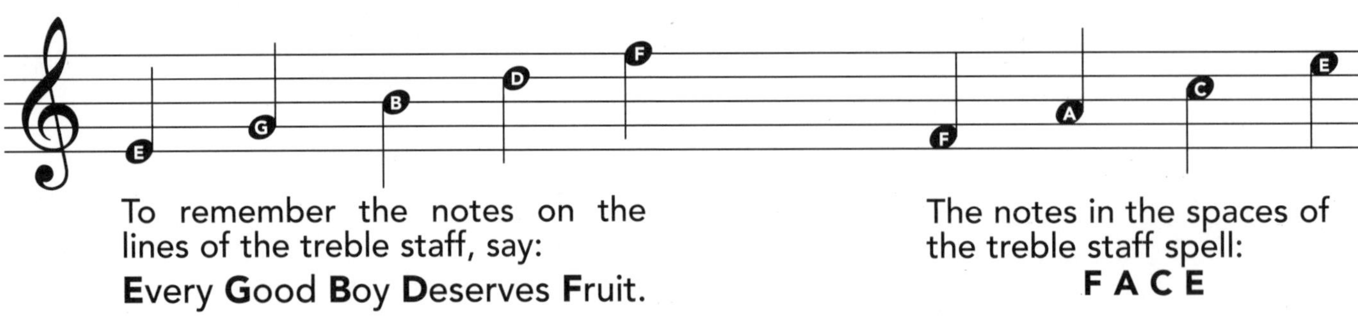

To remember the notes on the lines of the treble staff, say:
Every **G**ood **B**oy **D**eserves **F**ruit.

The notes in the spaces of the treble staff spell:
F A C E

THE QUARTER NOTE

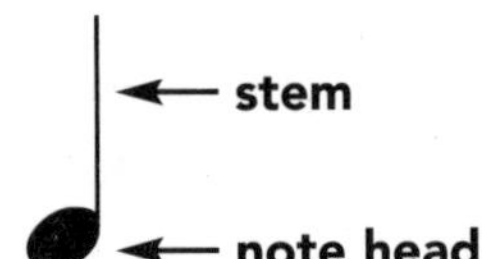

This music note is called a **quarter note**.
A quarter note lasts for **one beat**.

EXERCISES

✏ The staff below contains all the notes on the lines of the treble staff in random order. Write the name of each note in the box above the note.

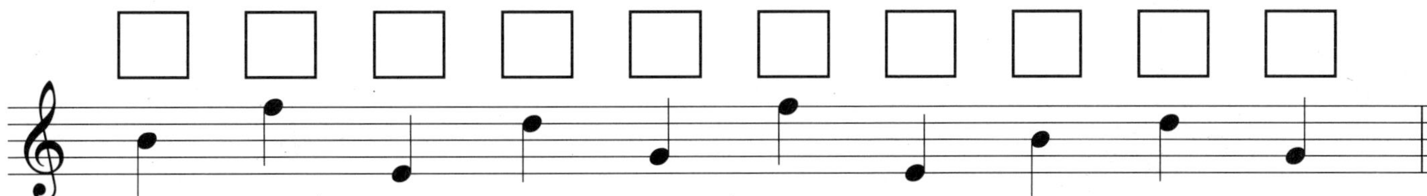

✏ This time the notes are in the spaces of the treble staff. Once again, write the name of each note in the box.

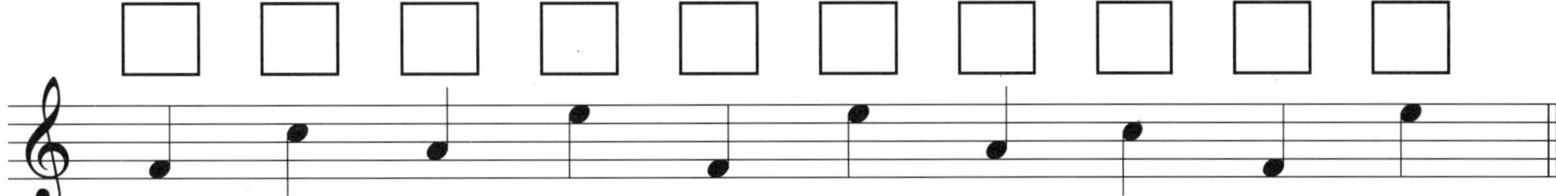

✏ Now the notes are both on the lines and in the spaces of the treble staff. As before, write the name of each note in the box.

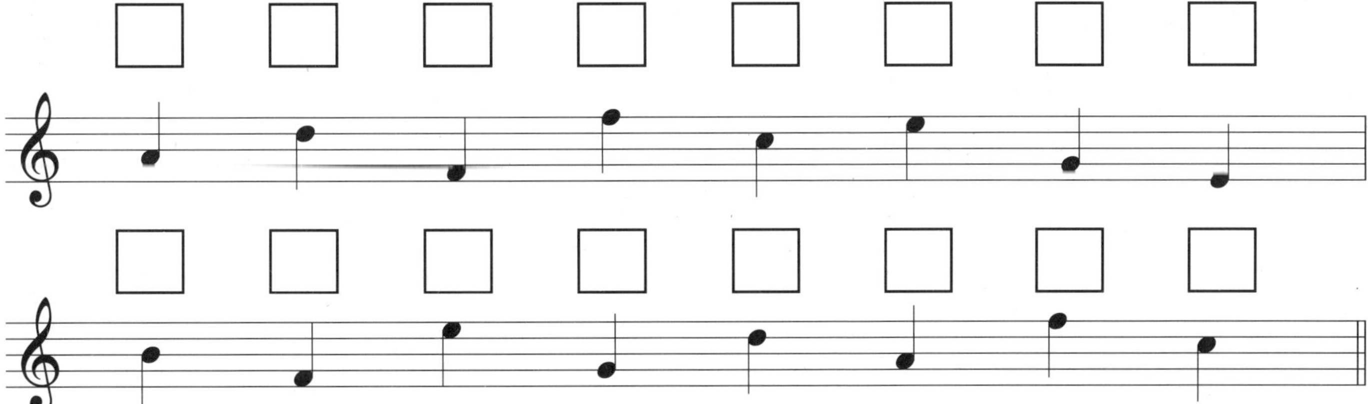

✏ Write the 7 letters of the musical alphabet:

____

✏ Write the treble clef at the beginning of this staff and then add all the notes that are written in the spaces, using quarter notes (♩).

✏ Write the treble clef at the beginning of this staff and add all the notes on the lines, using quarter notes.

✏ Once again, write the treble clef at the beginning and then add all the notes on the lines and spaces, using quarter notes.

LESSON ONE

NOTE AND REST VALUES

Here are the most common types of notes used in music, along with their respective time values (i.e. the length of time each note is held). You already know the quarter note. For each note value there is an equivalent rest, which indicates a period of silence.

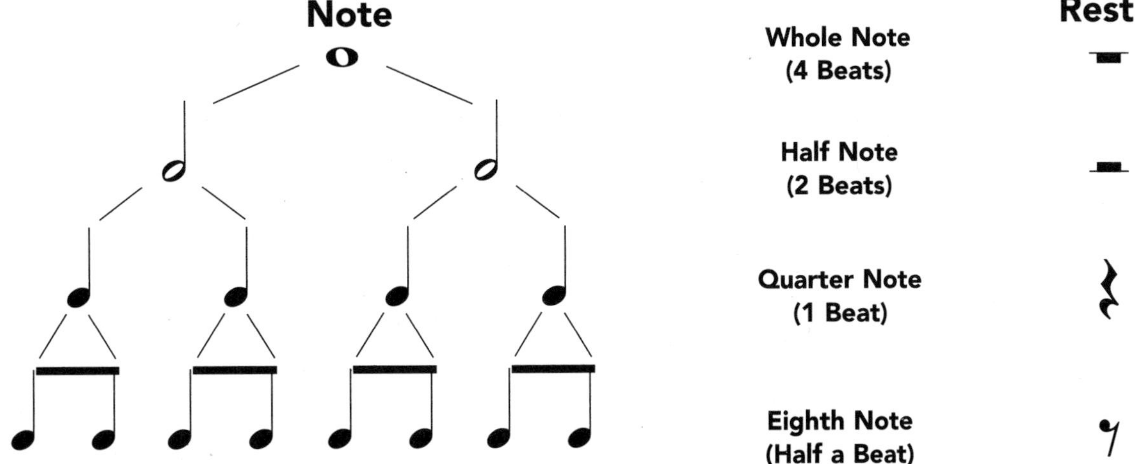

BAR LINES

In most music, **bar lines** or **measures** are drawn across the staff, dividing the music into sections. A **double bar line** indicates either the end of the music, or the end of an important section of it.

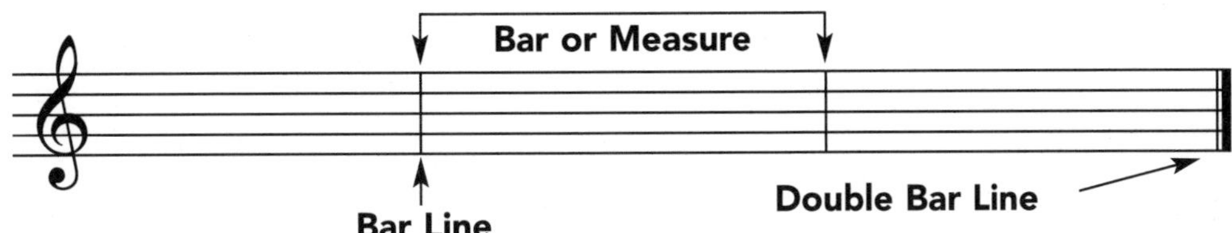

TIME SIGNATURES

At the beginning of each piece of music, after the clef, you will see a **time signature**. The top number indicates the number of beats per bar. The bottom number indicates the type of note receiving each beat. The $\frac{4}{4}$ time signature indicates that there are four quarter notes per bar.

4 – this indicates 4 beats per bar.
4 – each beat is worth a quarter note.

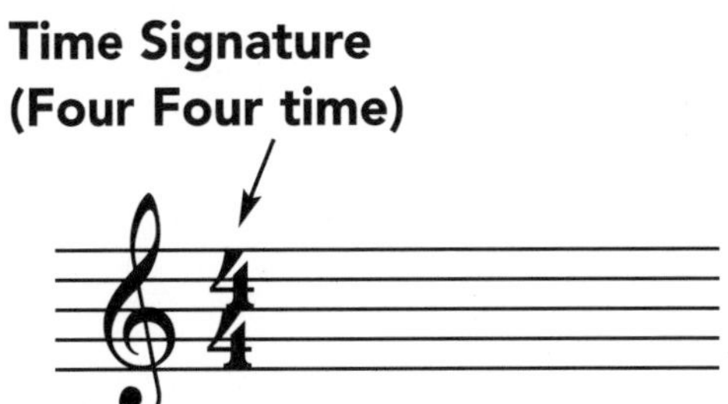

Here are two bars of quarter notes in 4/4 time. In the first bar, all four notes are on the same pitch (a middle C note) while the second bar contains four notes of varying pitches. The pitch of a note has no effect on how long the note should sound, i.e. a quarter note lasts for one beat regardless of whether it is a G, C, F, or any other pitch.

The most important thing here is the rhythm. Don't worry about the pitches too much at this stage. Listen to the example on the CD and then imitate the sounds you hear. Sing each note using the syllable **la**. Also practice reading the music and counting the rhythm out loud, then tap your foot and count on each beat while clapping the written rhythm.

4.

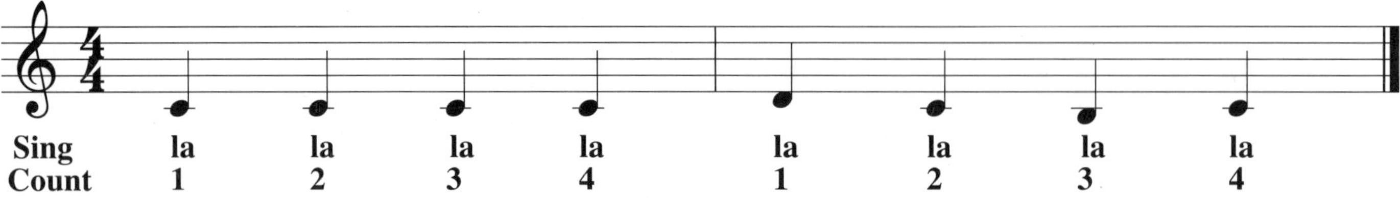

THE HALF NOTE

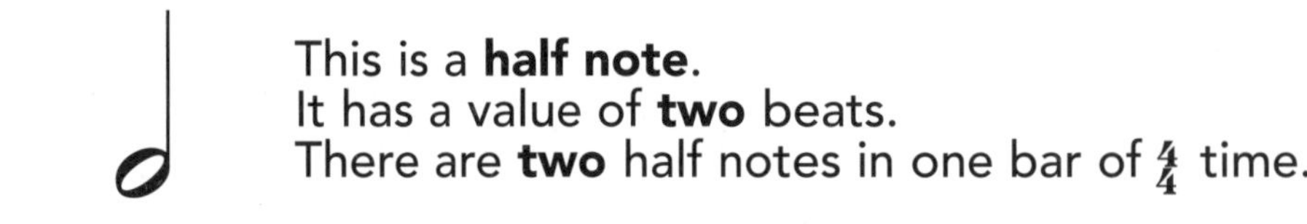

This is a **half note**.
It has a value of **two** beats.
There are **two** half notes in one bar of 4/4 time.

The next example contains two bars of half notes in 4/4 time. To make sure you start your first note in the right place, count 1, 2, 3, 4 before starting. This will help you get the feel of the rhythm. As you proceed through the example, think – **one two** – as you sing the first note in each bar and – **three four** – as you sing the second note in each bar. Tap your foot on each beat to help you keep time. On the recording there are **four** drumbeats to introduce examples in 4/4 time. Count along with the beats to help you establish the correct tempo (speed).

5.

The **big** numbers **1** and **3** tell you to sing the note. The **small** numbers 2 and 4 tell you to sustain that note until the next one. Remember that there are four beats in each bar. Once again, use the syllable **la** to sing this example.

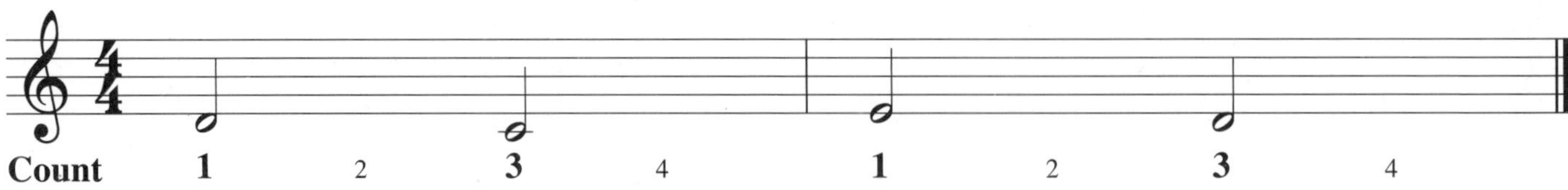

A WORD ABOUT PITCH

Although there are only seven alphabetical letters used in music – **A B C D E F G** – these are repeated at higher and lower pitches over a large range of notes. Because everybody has a different voice range, not all singers will be comfortable with the same pitches. The actual pitch of the notes given in the examples in this book are just a guide, so if you feel comfortable singing the examples higher or lower than indicated, that is fine. The important thing at the moment is to get the correct **timing**. Try this example which combines half notes and quarter notes.

6.

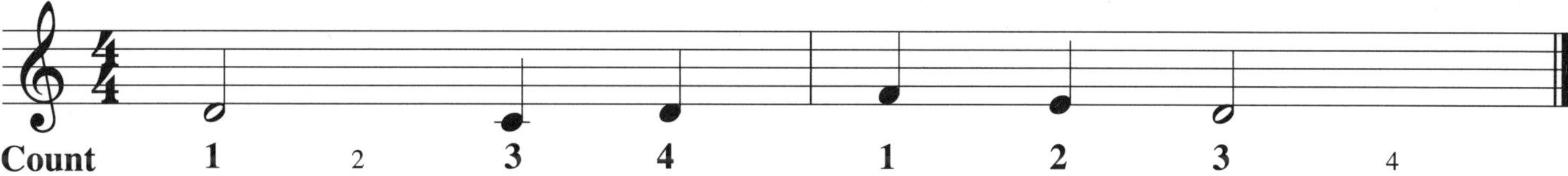

WHEN TO BREATHE

When you are singing a song, you will have to find places in the music where you can take a breath. A good place to breathe is at the end of a phrase (group of notes), at the end of a bar or at the end of a long note. Breathing takes up some of the time value of the note, but sometimes this is inevitable. In time you will instinctively find places to breathe which cause the least disruption to the flow of the music. Remember to breathe from the diaphragm and be careful not to lose your timing when you breathe. Counting mentally and tapping your foot on the beat as you sing will help you become more confident with this.

THE WHOLE NOTE

This is a **whole note**.
It lasts for **four** beats.
There is **one** whole note in one bar of $\frac{4}{4}$ time.

Count: 1 2 3 4

7.

This example is four bars long and contains whole notes in bars 2 and 4. A good place to breathe here would be at the end of each whole note.

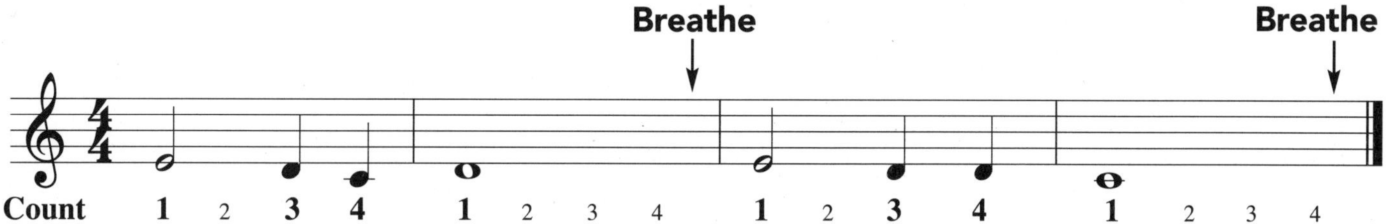

Music in $\frac{4}{4}$ time can use any combination of note values which add up to the equivalent of four quarter notes per bar. Notice the two dots before the double bar at the end of the following example. This **repeat sign** indicates that the piece of music is to be played again from the beginning. On the recording, this melody is played on guitar. It is important to be able to learn melodies played by instruments, particularly if you wish to improvise. You will learn more about this in Lesson 21.

8.

$\frac{4}{4}$ is the most common time signature and is sometimes represented by the **common time** symbol.

RHYTHM TRAINING

One of the most important elements of singing is a strong sense of rhythm and the ability to place notes anywhere in the bar effortlessly. Regardless of whether you read music well, or learn primarily by ear, it is essential to develop this ability. This is best done by doing exercises which concentrate purely on rhythm rather than pitch and rhythm.

This example uses only one pitch but contains quarter, half and whole notes. First clap the rhythm while counting and tapping your foot on each beat. Once you can do this, sing the notes using the syllable **da** while tapping your foot on each beat. Make sure your foot stays independent of your voice. If you do this for a short time each day, you will soon feel more confident with rhythms using these note values.

9.

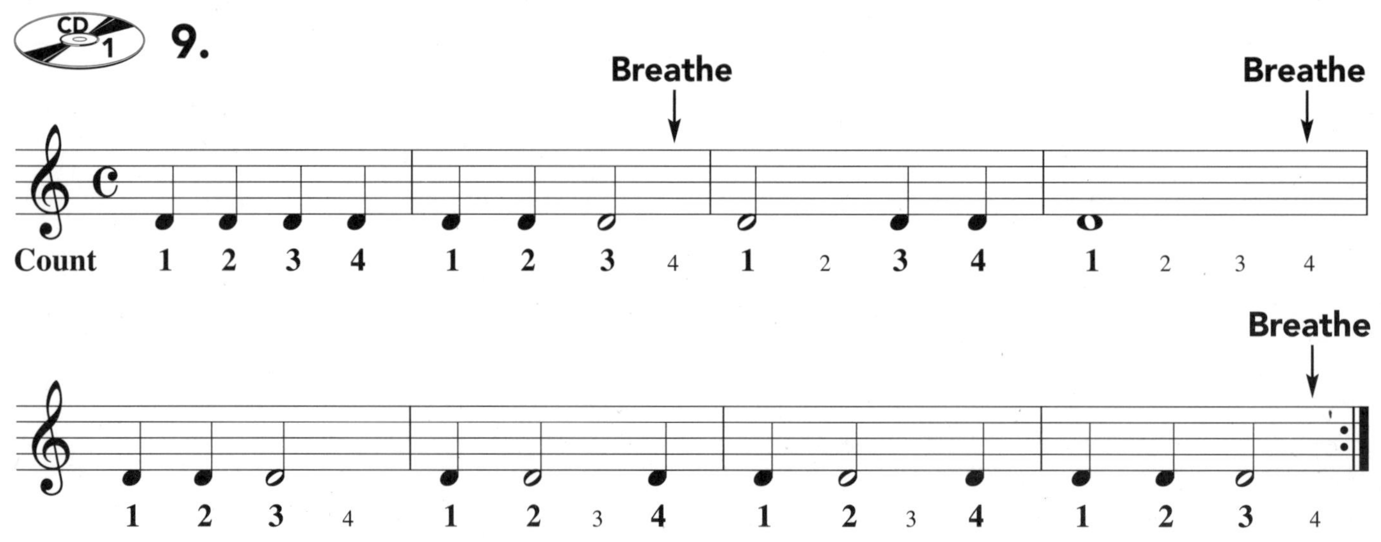

LESSON TWO

RESTS

Rests are used in music notation to indicate a period of silence. For every note value, there is an equivalent rest. Rests provide a natural space to take a breath, as well as helping to group notes into phrases. Just as speech is organised into words, phrases and sentences, a song melody is made up of notes grouped into phrases with spaces between them. These spaces are usually indicated by rests.

THE HALF REST

This symbol is a **half rest**.
It indicates **two** beats of silence.
A half rest sits on **top** of the **third line** of the staff.
When you see this rest, count for **two beats** without singing.

Count: 1 2

10.

In this book, **small** counting numbers are used under rests. Use the syllable **ah** to sing this example. Use a metronome and and tap your foot on each beat.

THE WHOLE REST

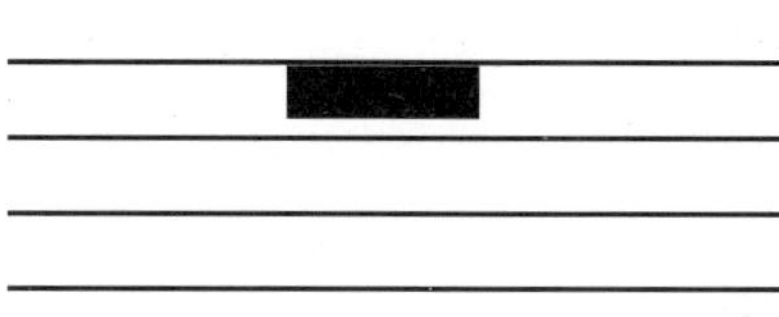

This symbol is a **whole rest**.
It indicates either **four** beats of silence.
The whole rest hangs **below** the **fourth** line of the staff.
When you see this rest, count for **four beats** without singing.

11.

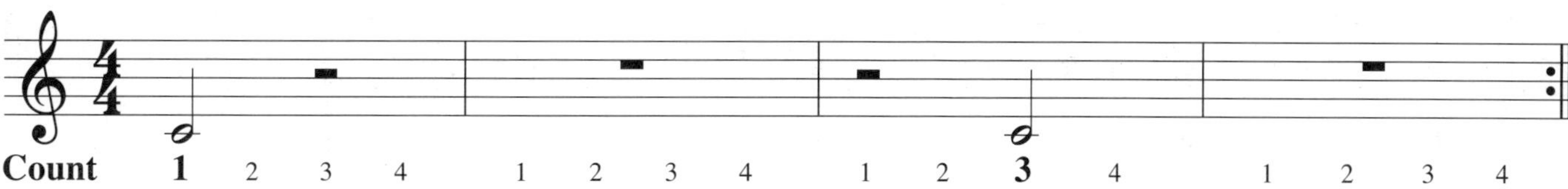

THE QUARTER REST

This symbol is a **quarter rest.**
It indicates **one beat of silence**.
Do not sing any note.

Count: 1

12.

Remember to **count** silently to keep time regardless of whether you see notes or rests in the music. This example is sung using the syllable **ba**.

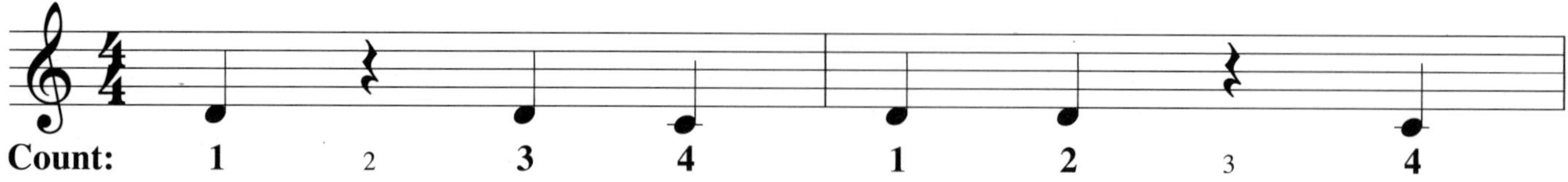

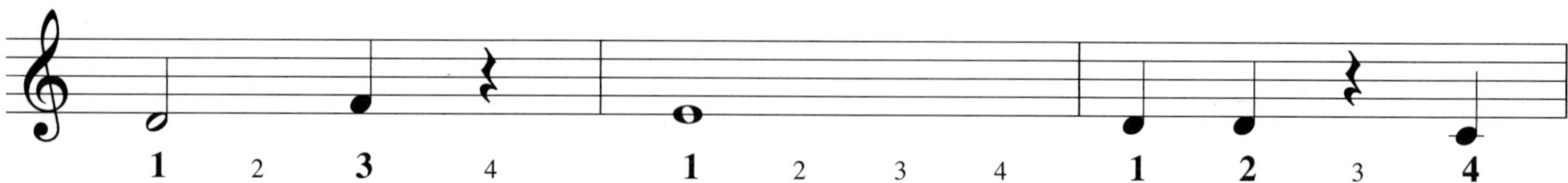

13.

Here is one which features whole, half and quarter rests. Count out loud and clap the rhythms along with the CD. On the recording, this example is played on an electric bass.

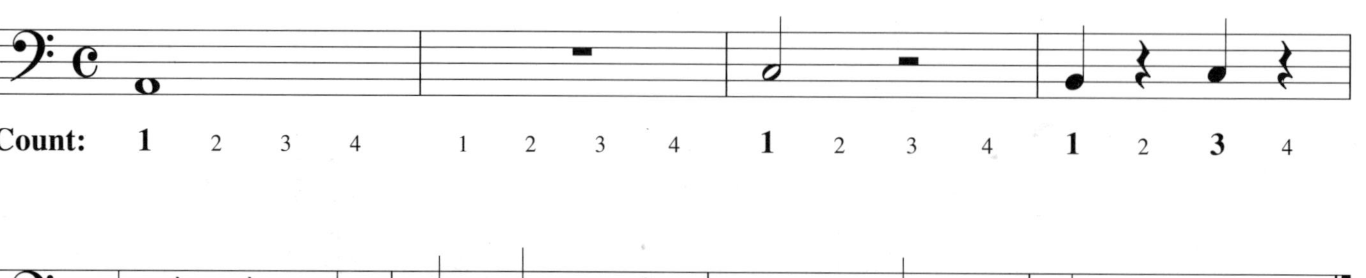

THE IMPORTANCE OF TIMING

Great singers always have great **timing**. This means they have developed the ability to begin and end a note or phrase at precisely the right moment. They are able to make their singing fit in with the accompaniment for maximum musical and dramatic effect. There are two good ways to develop your timing: one is to read rhythms from written music in time with a metronome or drum machine; the other is to have someone else play or sing rhythms and then copy those rhythms by ear.

Rap singers are able to improvise incredibly complex and dramatic rhythms on the spot. This is called **freestyling**. Even though these singers use complex rhythms, they all had to start with the same simple note values (lengths) that you are learning here. The distinctive rap sound is created by the way those notes are put together. It is important to remember that all music regardless of style uses the same note values. The notes are just put together in different ways to create different sounds.

Listen to the following examples on the CD to hear first the guitar and then the voice produce each short phrase. Each example is then repeated with the guitar playing the phrase, followed by a space left for you to reproduce the sound with your voice. All these examples are in $\frac{4}{4}$ time. Tap your foot in $\frac{4}{4}$ to help you keep time and remember to keep track of the beginning of each bar.

14. Listen to CD

LESSON THREE

VOICE TYPES AND RANGES

The **range** of your voice is determined by the highest and lowest notes you can sing. Although everybody has a different voice range, there are some general categories used to describe typical ranges. In traditional four part vocal arrangements, voices are broken up into four categories: **soprano** (highest female voice), **alto** (lower female voice), **tenor** (higher male voice) and **bass** (lowest male voice). In other arrangements there may be six categories. The female voices are then categorized as **soprano** (highest), **mezzo soprano** (a little lower) and **alto** or **contralto** (lowest). The three male voice types are **tenor**, **baritone** and **bass**. The middle voices (mezzo soprano and baritone) are the most common voices. Another unusual voice type is the male alto. All of these voice types are descriptions of adult voices. Children and teenagers have voices which are not fully developed, so they cannot be classified as a final voice type.

It is a good idea to determine your range as soon as you understand how to find the notes on a keyboard. However, it is unwise to classify yourself immediately as any particular voice type. It is always best to consult a singing teacher and work with them for a while before classifying a voice. Young students may not be able to classify their voice type until they are adults. The most important thing is to know your individual note range and work with it, rather than straining against it to sing higher or lower than is practical for you.

HOW TO FIND YOUR VOICE RANGE

The easiest way to find the highest and lowest notes in your range is to test them against a piano or keyboard. Even if you don't intend to play any instrument, it is important to understand the layout of a keyboard in order to identify notes and understand the relationship between them. A keyboard is tuned to concert pitch, which is an international standard for identifying notes. This enables musicians in bands and orchestras to play in tune with each other. When you sing, your perception of pitch may change depending on your state of mind or how tired you are. For this reason, it is important to have a reference from an instrument tuned to concert pitch.

REFERRING TO THE KEYBOARD

The black keys always appear in groups of two or three. The note **C** is often the starting note for relating all other notes to. The **C note** is a **white key**. It is occurs on the left hand side of every group of two black keys. The C note in the middle of the keyboard is **Middle C**. This note is in the range of all of the voice types, although it will be towards the top of some male voice ranges and towards the bottom of some female ranges.

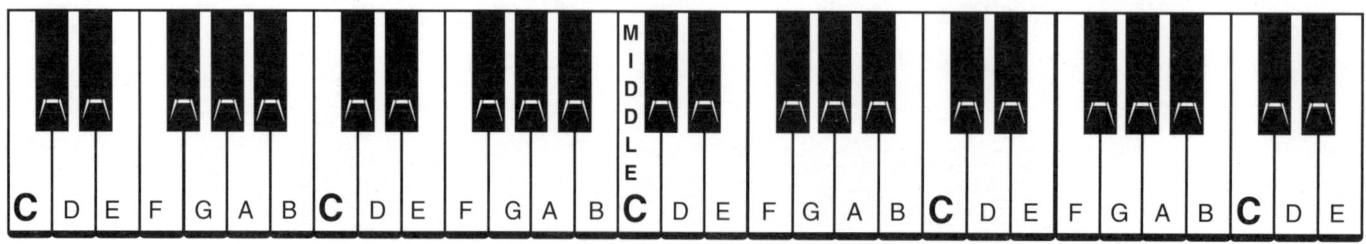

THE BASS STAFF

Male voice ranges are commonly written on a **bass staff**. Notes on the bass staff have different positions to those on the treble staff.

THE BASS CLEF

This symbol is a **bass clef**. The bass clef is placed at the beginning of a music staff for lower (bass) notes.

THE BASS STAFF

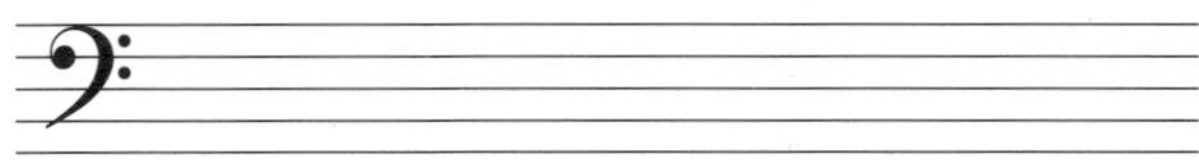

The lines and spaces on the bass staff are named as follows:

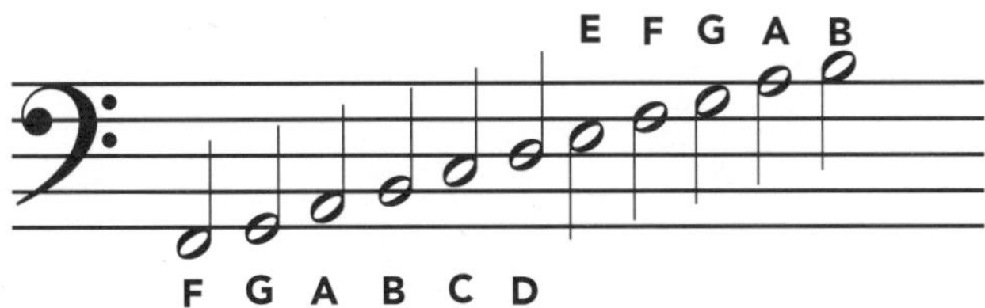

Extra notes can be added by the use of short **leger lines**.

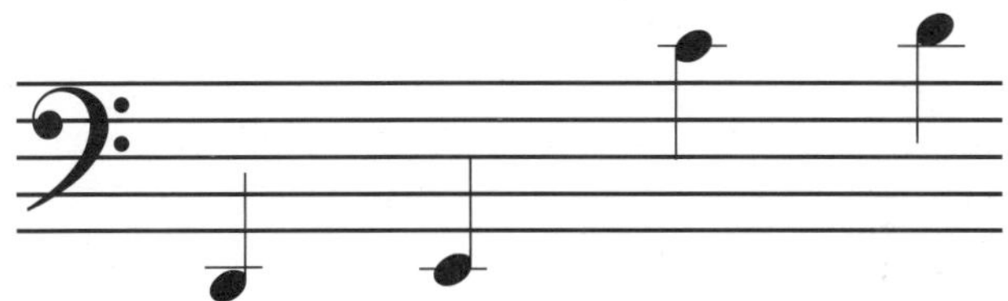

As with the treble staff, when the note head is below the middle staff line the stem points upward and when the head is above the middle line the stem points downward. A note placed on the middle line (**D**) can have its stem pointing either up or down.

NOTES ON THE BASS STAFF

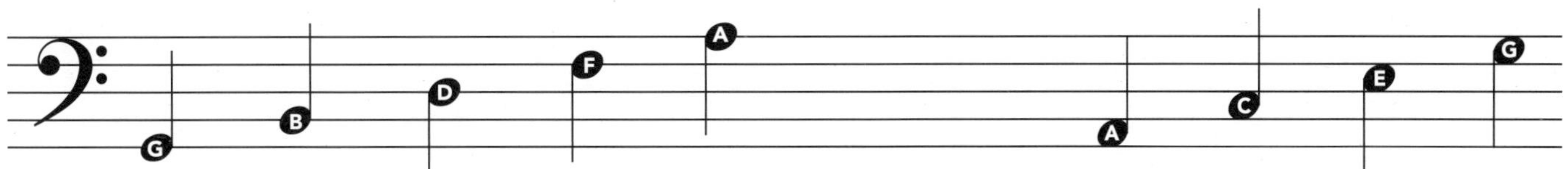

To remember the notes on the lines of the bass staff, say:
Good **B**oys **D**eserve **F**ruit **A**lways.

To remember the notes in the spaces of the bass staff, say:
All **C**ows **E**at **G**rass.

The staff below has notes written on the lines and in the spaces of the bass staff in random order. Add note names below each note.

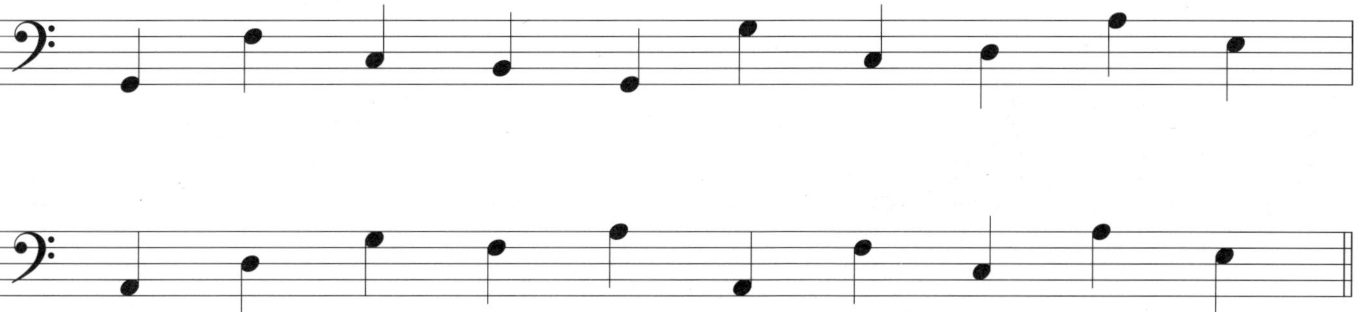

EXERCISES

Write the bass clef at the beginning of the staff below and then add in all the notes that are written on the lines and spaces, using quarter notes

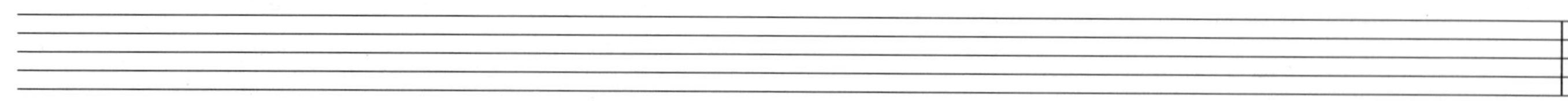

Write the correct clef at the start of each staff.

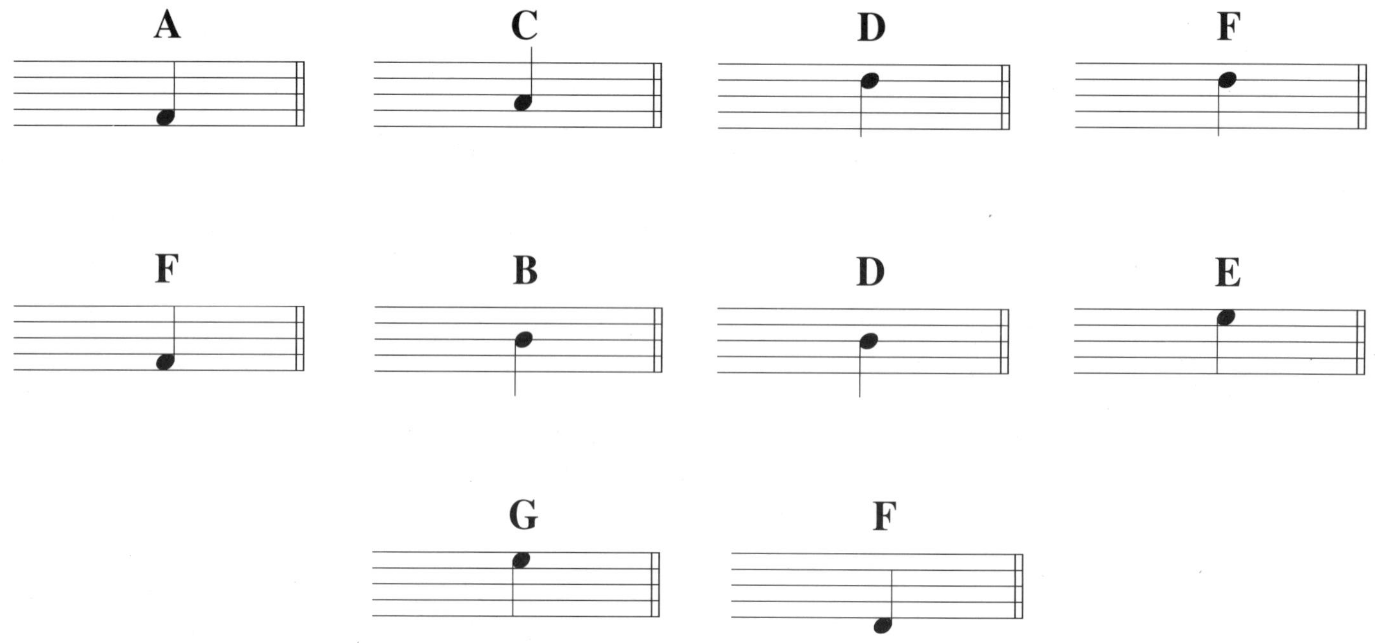

Write a C note above the bass staff on a leger line:

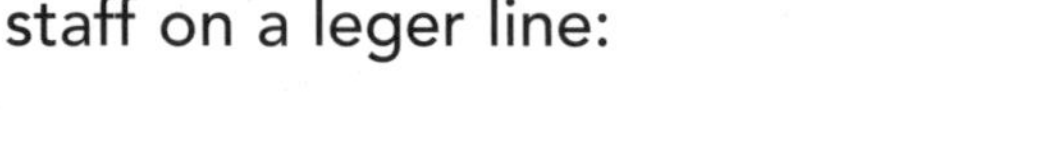

Write an E note above the bass staff on a leger line:

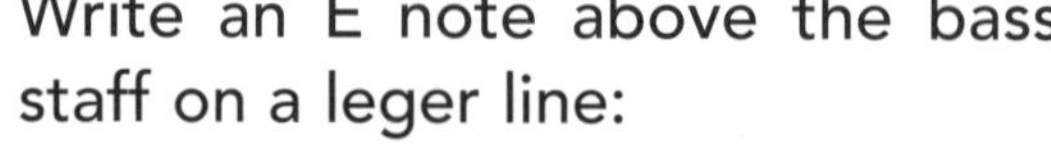

Write a B note below the treble staff by using a leger line.

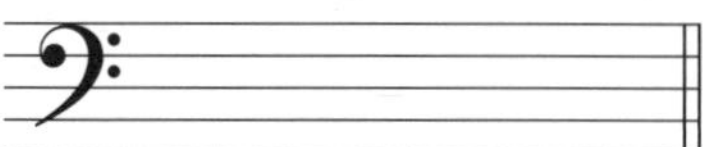

Write a C note below the treble staff on a leger line.

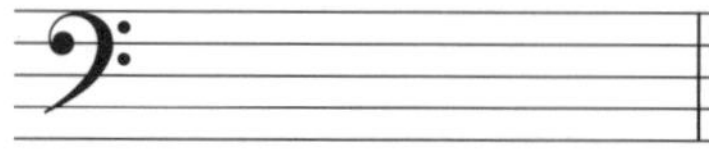

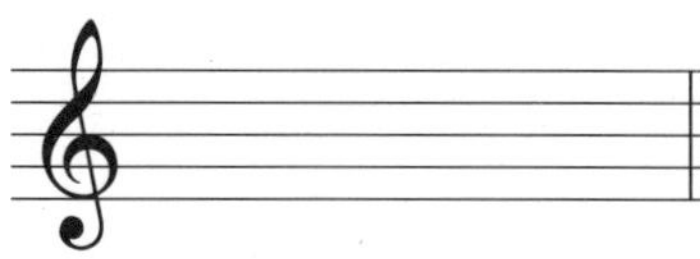

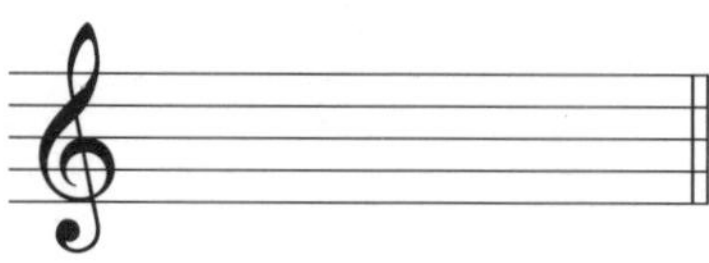

THE GRAND STAFF

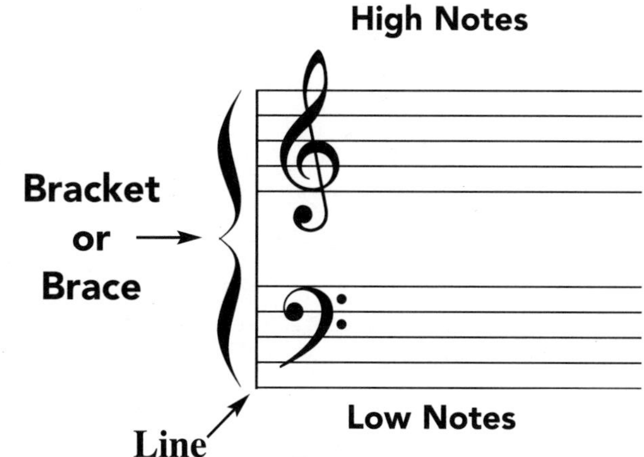

When the treble and bass **staves** are joined together by a line and a bracket, they are called a **grand staff**.

Piano music is written on the grand staff.

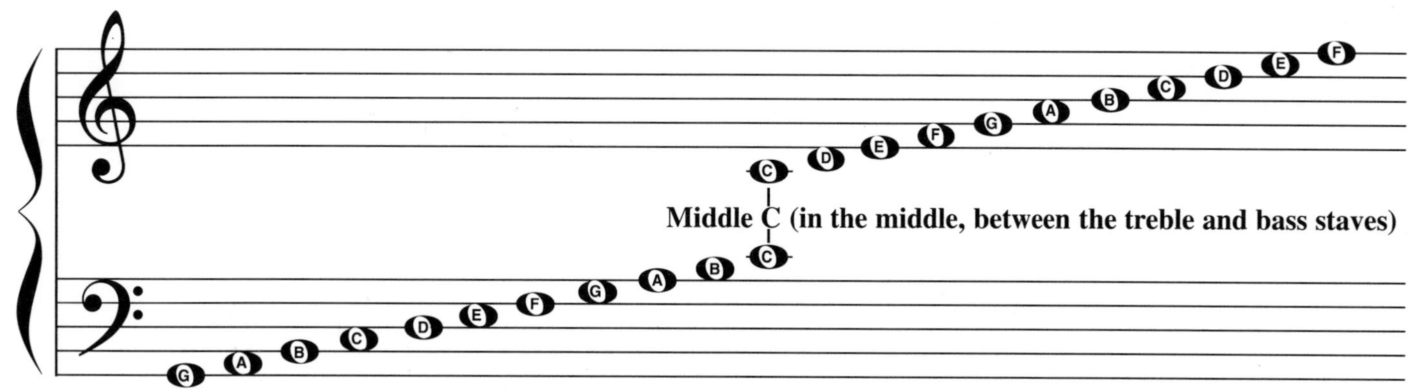

✏ Here are some random notes on the grand staff. Write the name of each note in the appropriate box.

Continue to write the names of the notes above examples in this book until you can 'read' them at a glance. Use a pencil so that you can erase the note names and test your memory as it improves.

These keyboard diagrams show typical ranges of the six basic voice types. Remember that voice range are individual and that your own may fall between any of the traditional categories. Another important thing to keep in mind is that these are voice ranges of fully developed singing voices. When you start learning to sing you may have a smaller range than those shown here. Many tenors have larger ranges than the one shown here. Listen to the CD to hear the highest and lowest notes of each range.

15.0 Soprano

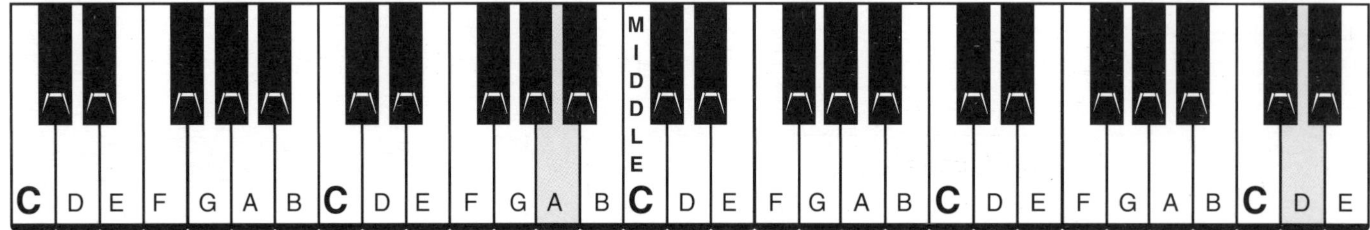

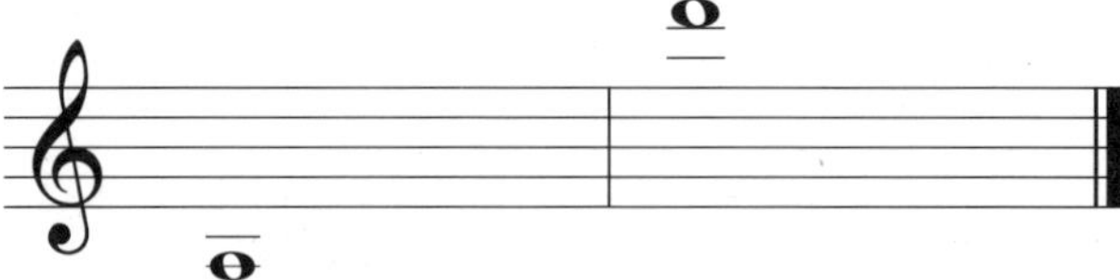

15.1 Mezzo Soprano

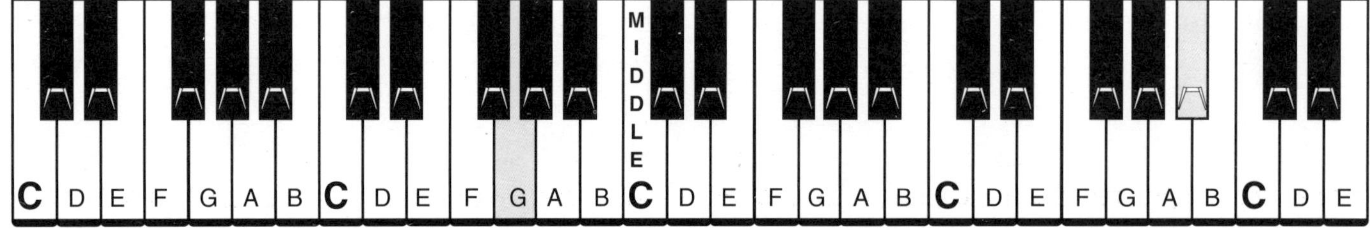

15.2 Alto

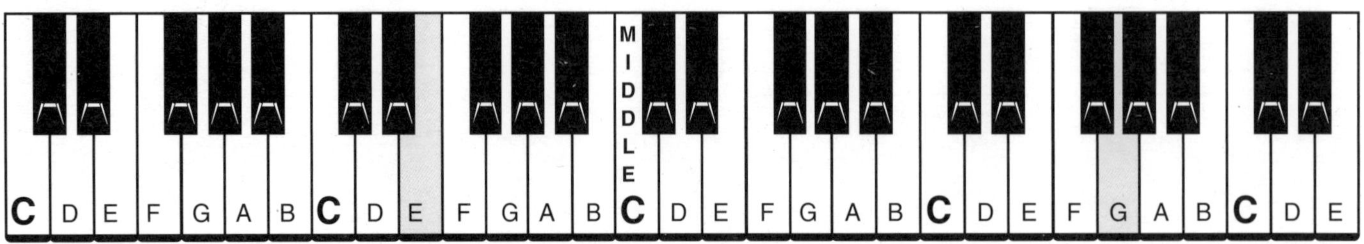

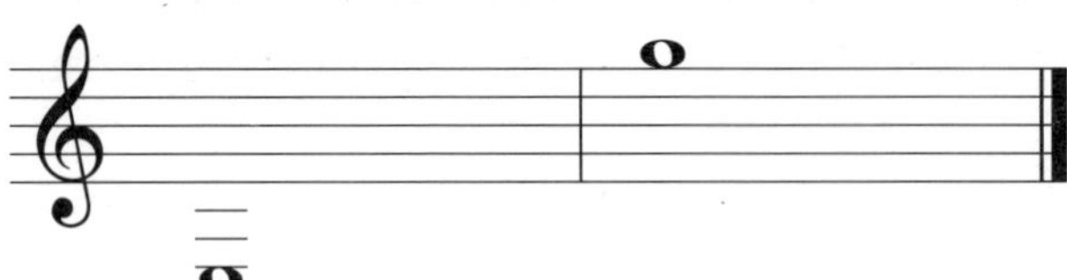

15.3 Tenor

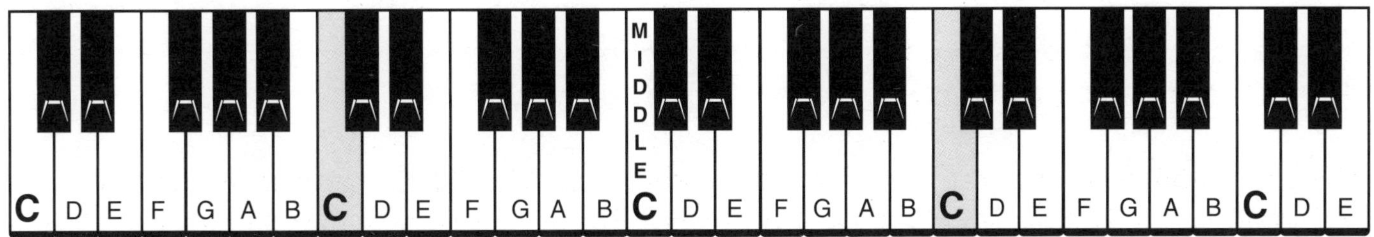

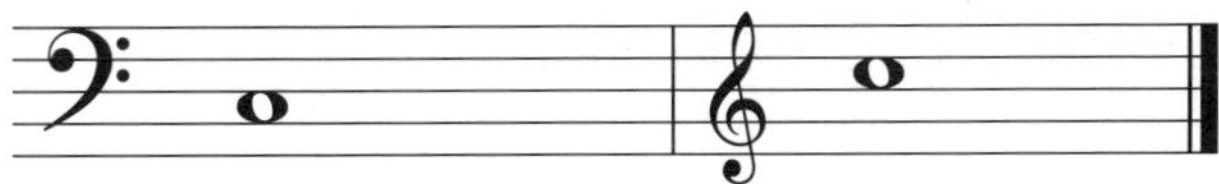

15.4 Baritone

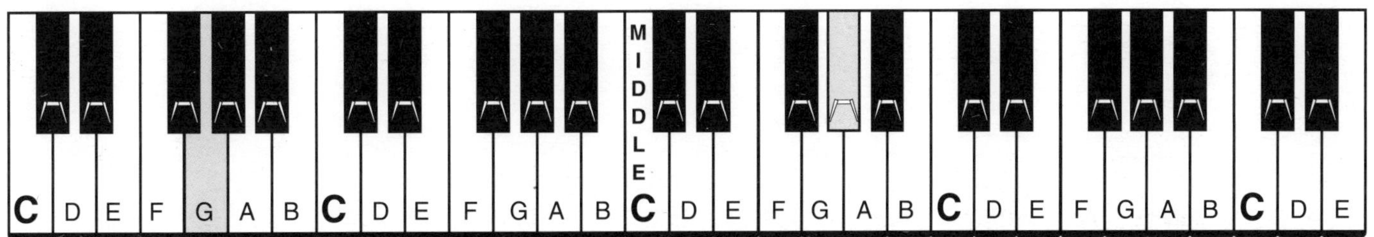

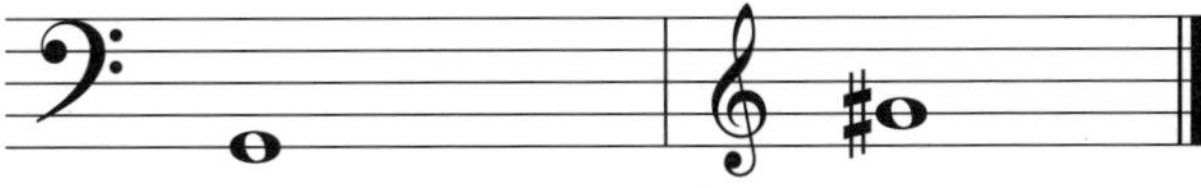

15.5 Bass

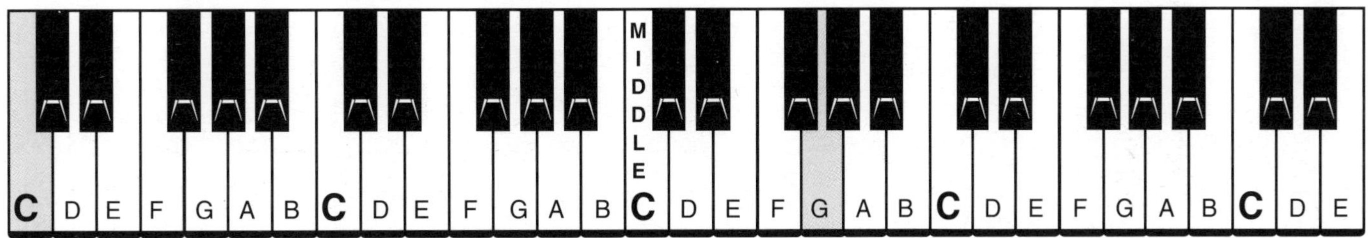

LEGER LINES

Because there are many higher and lower versions of notes in music, it is sometimes necessary to write notes above or below a staff. This is done using short **leger lines** above or below either a treble or bass staff. There is no restriction in the number of leger lines that can be used; the note sequence simply continues from the highest or lowest note on the staff, depending on whether the music goes up or down.

The most common use of a leger line is for the note **Middle C**, which falls between the treble and bass staves. Middle C is also at the note at centre of a piano keyboard. It is a reference note against which higher and lower notes can be measured. This note is shown below, along with other notes using leger lines.

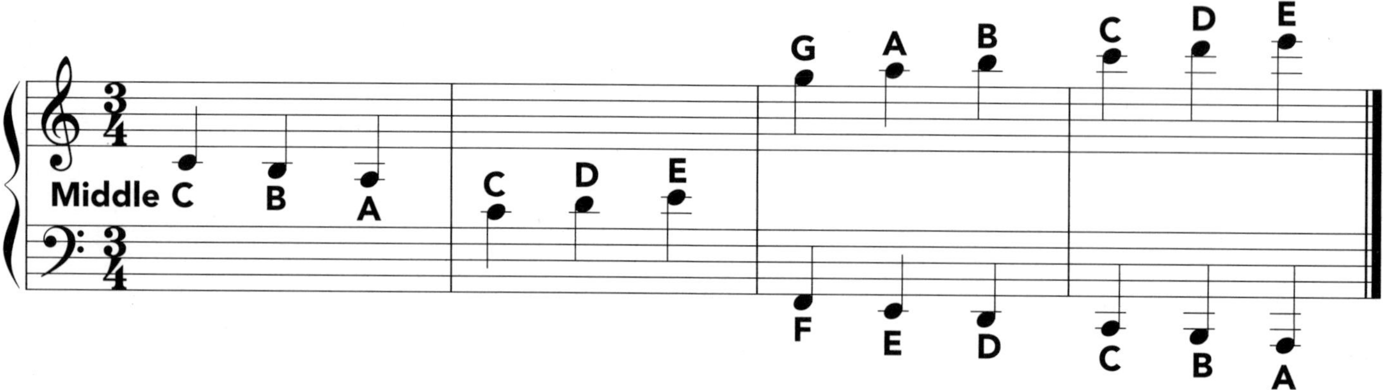

EXERCISE

✏ Write the name of these notes in the boxes.

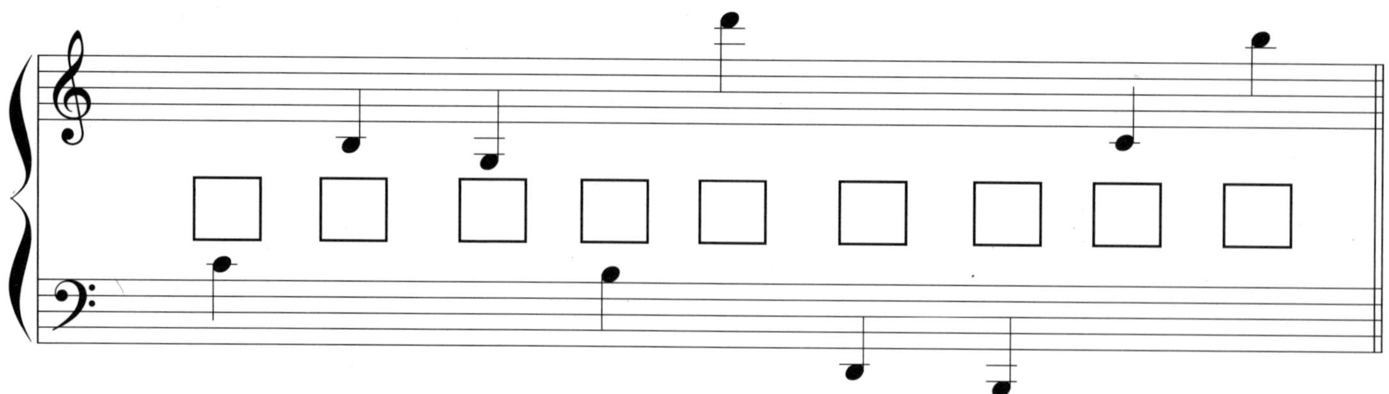

MATCHING PITCHES

It is important to be able to sing any desired pitch accurately. A good way to develop your pitching ability (**intonation**) is to play,, or have someone else play notes on an instrument (e.g. keyboard) and copy the pitches with your voice. Some people find this easy immediately while others have to work at it for a while before they can do it. Listen carefully to the pitch being played and trust your body to be able to produce that pitch. Relax and let the sound come out naturally. The following examples demonstrate this exercise. Listen to the CD to hear first the keyboard and then the voice produce each pitch. Each example is then repeated with the keyboard playing the pitch, followed by a space left for you to reproduce the pitch with your voice. Each pitch is a half note (two beats) and is followed by a half note rest. Sing the pitches with the syllable **la**.

16. Female

17. Female Practice

18. Male

19. Male Practice

THE OCTAVE

If you listen to both the male and female versions of the previous examples, you will notice that the sequence of notes is relatively the same. The male voice example is simply a lower version of the female voice example. These male and female versions are one **octave** apart. The following example demonstrates all the natural notes from **A** in the bottom space of the bass staff to **A** on the first leger line above the treble staff. This covers a range of **three octaves**. An octave is the range of eight notes between and including any two notes of the same name. Every time you come to a new A note a new octave begins. The same applies to all the other notes. For example, Middle **C** is one octave above the **C** in the second bottom space of the bass staff; the **F** in the bottom space of the treble staff is one octave below the **F** on the top line of the treble staff, etc.

20.

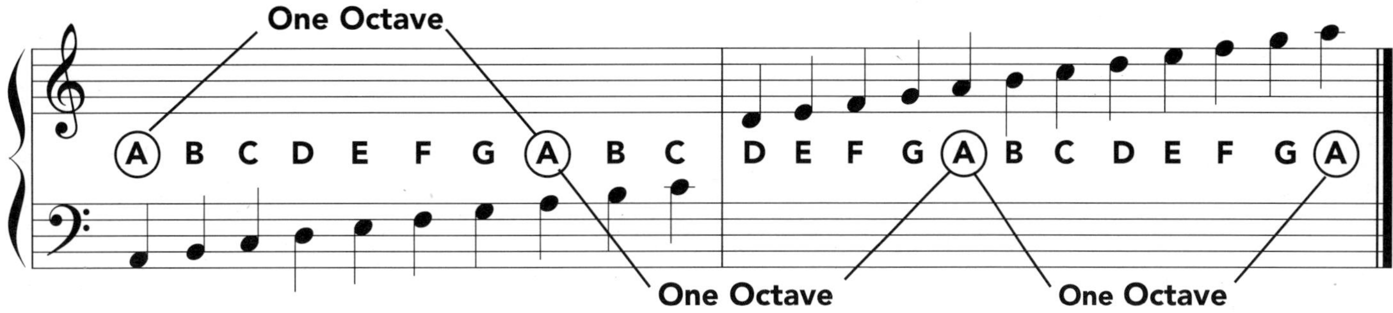

LESSON FOUR

THE MAJOR SCALE

The most common building block for melodies is the **major scale**. The simplest of these is the **C major scale**, which starts and ends on the note **C** and contains all of the natural notes used in music.

A major scale is a group of eight notes that produces the familiar sound:

Do Re Mi Fa So La Ti Do

In the **C major scale**, these sounds are represented by the notes:

C D E F G A B C

On the keyboard, the C major scale represents all the **natural** (white) notes, beginning and ending on C in any octave.

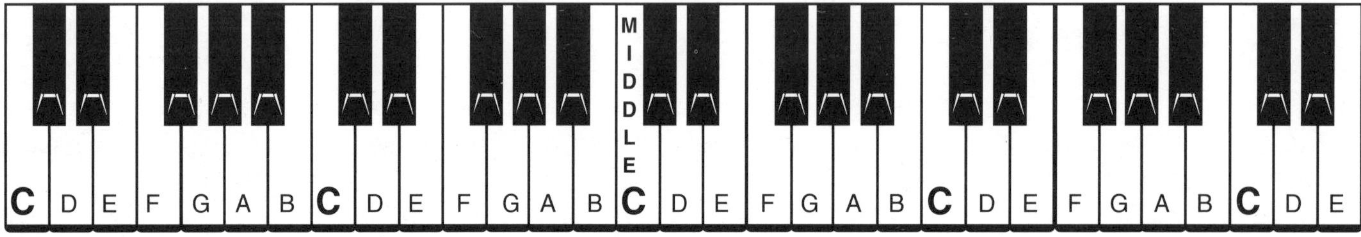

The first note and last note of a major scale always have the same name. In the **C major** scale the distance from the lowest C to the C note above it is one octave.

Here is one octave of the C major scale, sung by both female (treble staff) and male (bass staff) voices. Sing along with the one that best suits your voice range. This example is one octave of the C major scale. Each of the voices is also one octave apart.

21. C Major Scale

The major scale is built up from a pattern of tones (indicated by **T**) and semitones (indicated by **ST**). A semitone is the smallest **interval** (distance between two notes) used in western music. Notes which are a tone apart leave room for other notes between them. These in between notes are the **sharps** and **flats**, represented by the black notes on a piano.

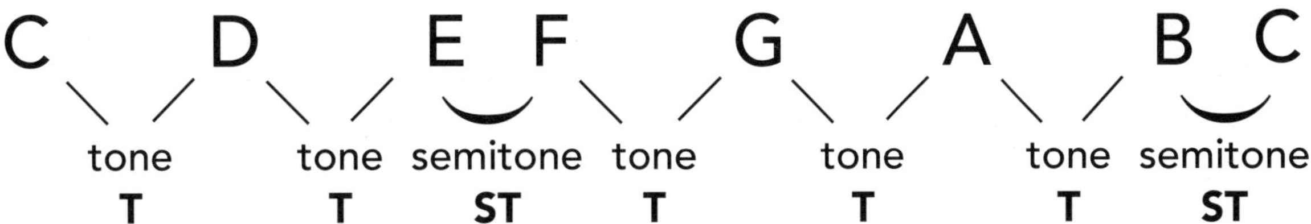

On the keyboard, the distance between one key and the key directly next to it on either side is a semitone. Semitones involve one black and one white key, except for E to F and B to C which are semitones involving two white keys. As you can see from the scale and the keyboard, all notes apart from E to F and B to C are a whole tone (two semitones) apart.

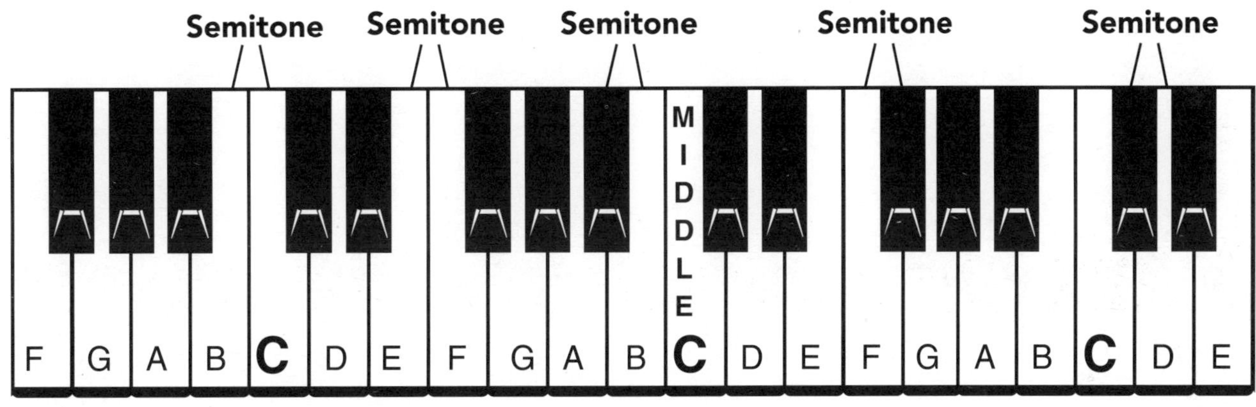

OCTAVE DISPLACEMENT

Many of the melodies you already know will use notes derived from the major scale. This example created from the C major scale is written on the treble staff only. Male singers can sing the same melody one octave lower, at the same pitch as the male singer on the CD (second time through). This **octave displacement** and is indicated in written music by the symbol *8vb* which tells you that the part is to be sung or played an octave lower than written, or *8va* which tells you to sing or play the part an octave higher than written.

CD 1 **22. (Male Voice 8vb)**

SOL-FA SYLLABLES

These short exercises will help you become more familiar with the sounds which can be derived from the major scale. Each of them uses the syllables **do**, **re**, **mi**, **fa**, **so**, **la**, **ti**, **do**. These are called **sol-fa syllables**. They are useful for practicing many of the basic sounds used in singing. As you sing each of these exercises, remain as relaxed as possible and sing with an open flowing sound. Keep your posture straight and focus your voice straight ahead as if you were singing into a microphone at a comfortable height. Do not 'reach' for any of the notes as they get higher or lower, but simply allow the sounds to come out naturally. You may not be able to sing these exercises easily to begin with. Be patient and practice them regularly, but only for short periods of time at each session.

Learn and practice these exercises using all three of the following methods:

1 Sing from the written music. This is called **sight singing** and takes quite a while to develop. To learn to sight sing well, it is best to work with a teacher.

2 Sing from the sol-fa syllables. You have probably heard them before and may find them a useful guide to the pitch of each note relative to **do**.

3 Listen to the recording and imitate the pitches until you have them all memorized.

LESSON FIVE

THE THREE FOUR TIME SIGNATURE

$\frac{3}{4}$

This is the **three four** time signature.
It tells you that there are **three** beats in each bar.
There are **three** quarter notes in one bar of $\frac{3}{4}$ time.
Three four time is also known as waltz time.

27.

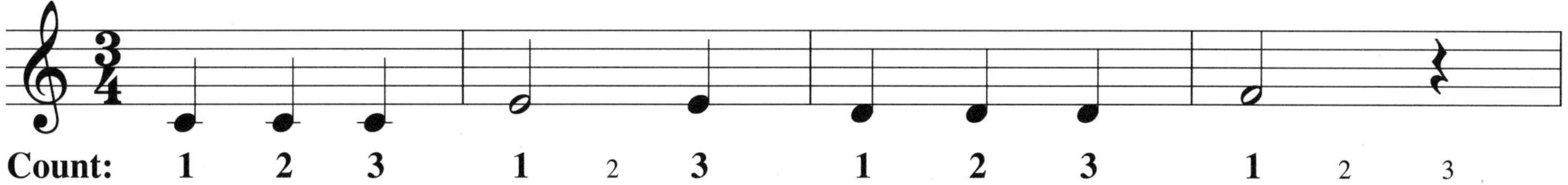

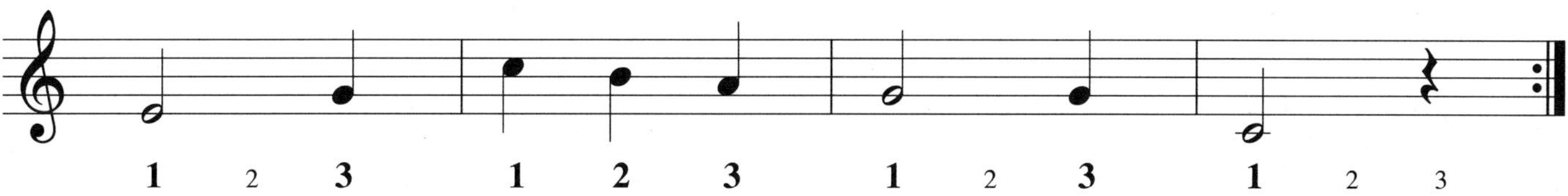

THE DOTTED HALF NOTE

A **dot** after a note extends its value by **half**.
A dot after a half note means that you hold it for **three** beats.
One dotted half note makes one bar of music in $\frac{3}{4}$ time.

A good way to become familiar with any new note or rest value is to combine it with other note values and clap the rhythms. Here is an example using dotted half notes in $\frac{3}{4}$ time along with quarter notes and half notes. Clap the rhythm and count out loud.

28.

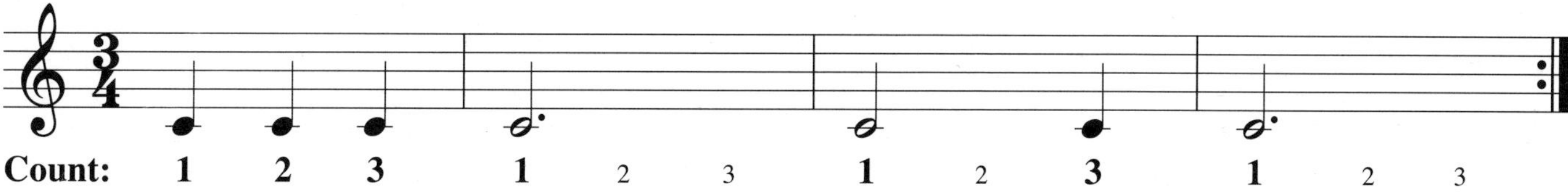

CHORD SYMBOLS

The **chord symbols** above the notation of the following example (**C**, **Em** ,etc.) are for the accompanying instruments. Chords will be discussed in Lesson 24.

 29. Slow Waltz

Peter Gelling

This melody uses dotted half notes are used in $\frac{3}{4}$ time. Once you can sing it using the syllable **la**, work out the sol-fa syllable for each note and then sing it using these syllables. If you have trouble keeping accurate time while you are singing, try clapping the rhythms while counting the beats out loud and tapping your foot.

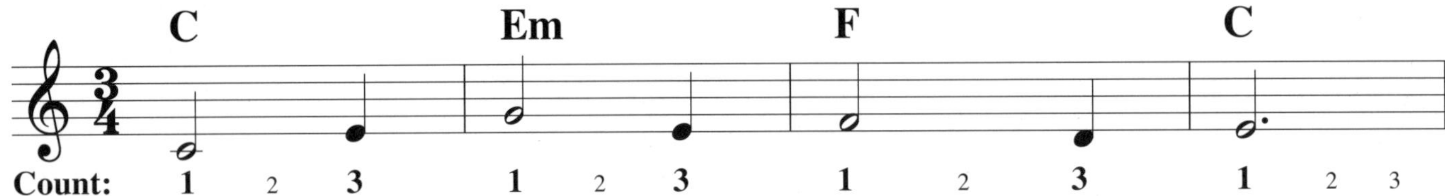

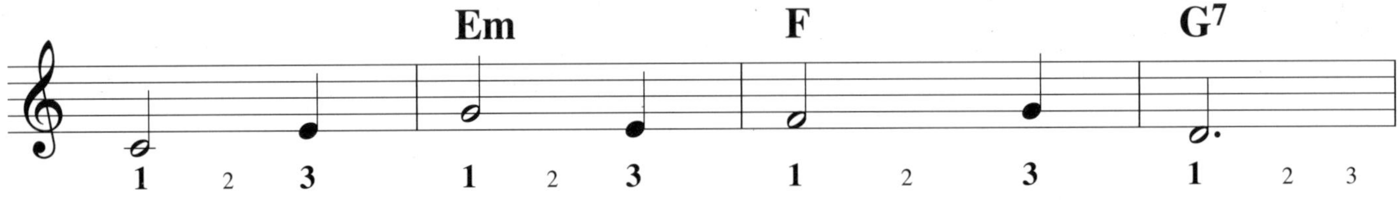

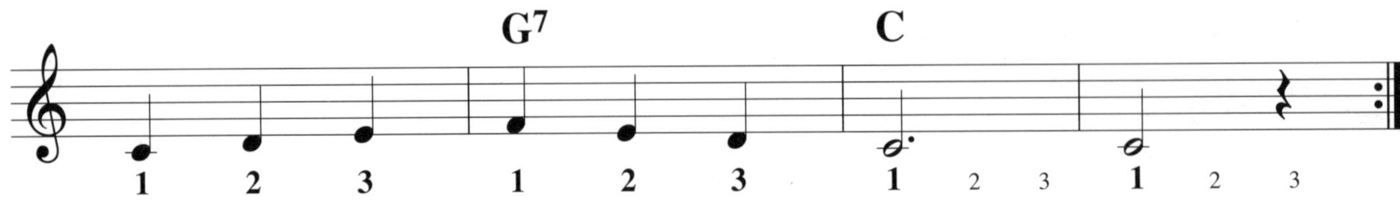

LESSON SIX

THE EIGHTH NOTE

An **eighth note** lasts for half a count. There are eight eighth notes in one bar of $\frac{4}{4}$ time. When eighth notes are joined together the tails are replaced by a beam.

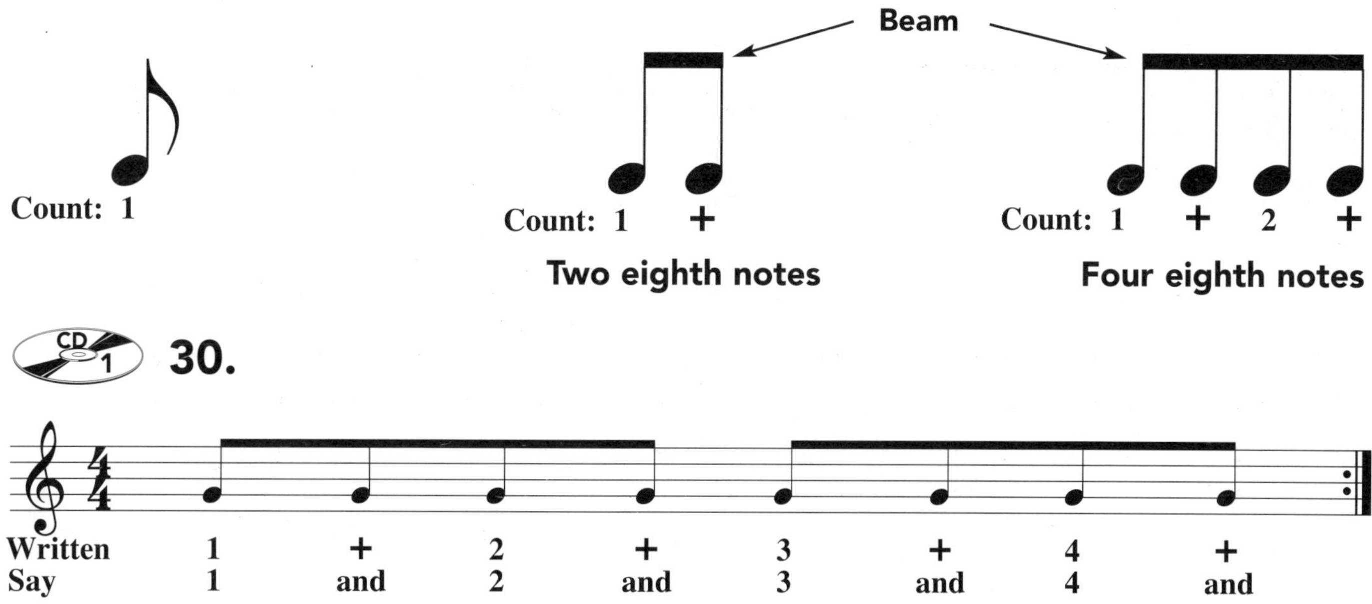

Here is a sol-fa exercise using eighth notes. Take them slowly and evenly until you can do them easily, then sing them along with the CD backing. On the recording, the example is sung the first time and then a space has been left for you to sing on the repeat. Breathe at the end of each half note.

31.

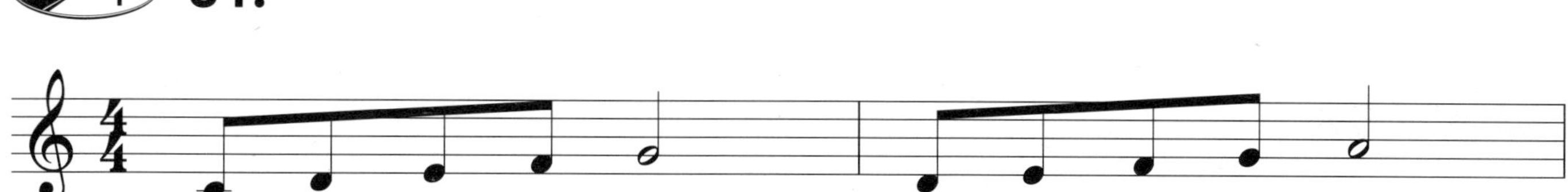

EIGHTH NOTE RHYTHMS

This example contains some common groupings of eighth notes, along with all the other note values you have learnt. Clap the rhythms with your hands before singing this example and remember to count and tap your foot. Sing through the example using the syllable **la**.

32.

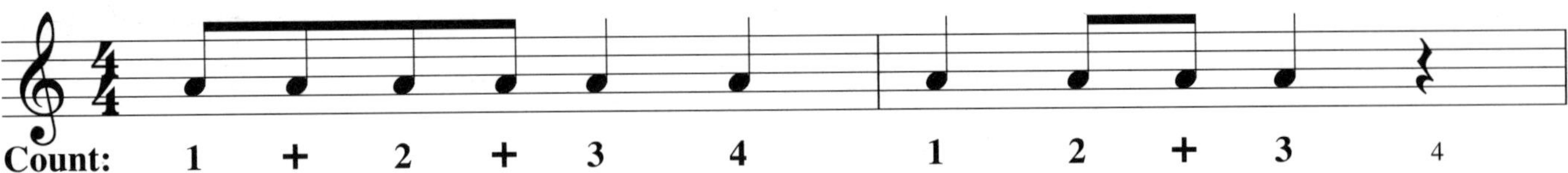

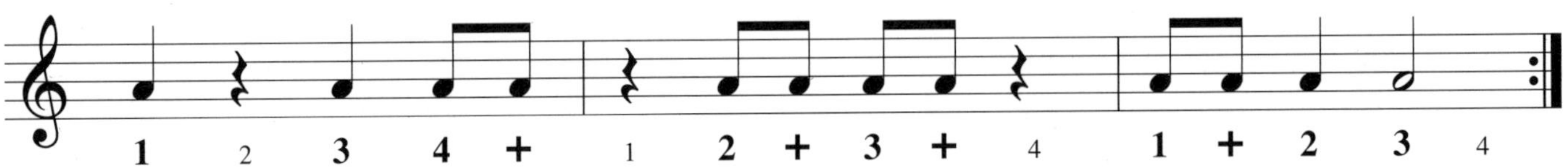

33.

These phrases contain eighth notes along with quarter notes. Breathe wherever a rest occurs. Keep the rhythm strong and steady as you sing and tap your foot on each beat.

THE DOTTED QUARTER NOTE

A dot after a quarter note means that you hold the note for **one and a half beats**.

Count 1 2 +

A dotted quarter note is often followed by an eighth note.

34.

Sing this example using the syllable **ka** or **ba**. In a Rock band these rhythms are often used in the drummer's bass drum patterns (played with the right foot).

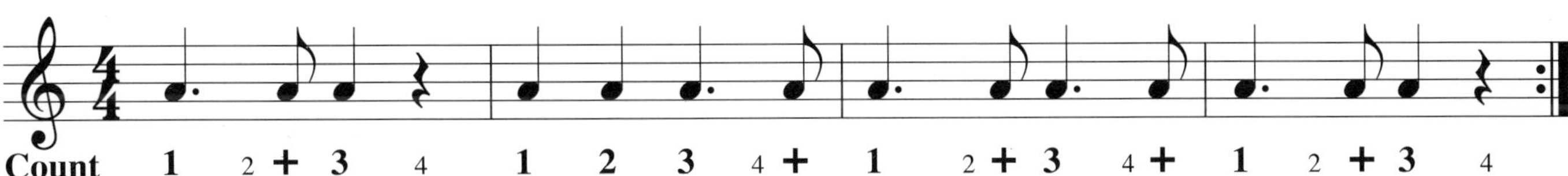

35.

Here is the rhythm from the previous example applied to a melody. As always, keep the rhythm strong and even, and tap your foot on each beat as you sing.

36.

This melody in $\frac{3}{4}$ time makes use of dotted half notes and dotted quarter notes. Write sol-fa syllables under the notes, and practice it slowly with your metronome until you are comfortable. Then gradually increase the tempo until you can sing along with the guitar on the CD. Use whichever octave is comfortable for your voice.

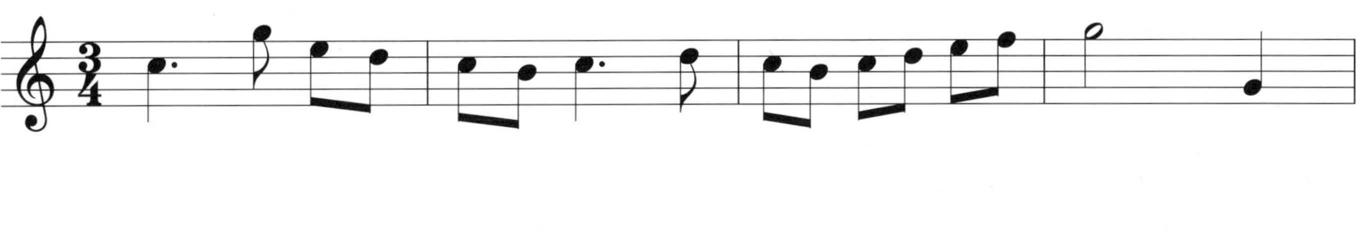

SINGING SONGS

Singing is all about communication and story telling through **songs**. It is easy to get bogged down with specifics of pitch, rhythm, theory, etc and lose sight of the most important elements which are **communication and enjoyment**. When most people listen to a singer, they feel good because they are moved by the lyrics and the emotion, combined with the music. As a singer, all your study should be directed towards improving your performance of songs and communication with your audience.

Having said that, if you know nothing about music, your communication skills will be limited. Once you understand some of the basic concepts of how music is written, it becomes a lot easier to understand sheet music. Once you understand sheet music, a whole repertoire of songs becomes available to you.

On the facing page is the song **Silent Night**, which contains many of the things you have learnt up to this point. It is in $\frac{3}{4}$ time and the melody is made up of half notes, quarter notes and eighth notes, as well as dotted half notes and dotted quarter notes. The final bar contains a whole rest, which represents a full bar rest when used in $\frac{3}{4}$ time.

This song is made up entirely of notes from the C major scale. At this stage, you may not be able to read all the individual pitches of the notes from the written music, so sing the melody by ear but pay close attention to the timing of the notes. If you have trouble, listen to the CD and watch the written music as you listen. Count along with the music as you hear it. On the recording you will hear a second voice in the background singing **harmony** – i.e. a different line to the melody.

CUE NOTES

On the recording you will also hear a piano playing a chord and then a note before the count-in to the song begins. This is to establish the sound of the key in your mind and give you the starting pitch before you begin singing. In this case the chord is a **C chord**, which establishes the sound for the **key of C major**. The note following the chord is a **G note**, which is the **starting note** of the song. As you hear the **C** chord, think **do** in your mind, then as you hear the **G** note, think **so**. This process is used with all the songs on the recording.

When you sing with other musicians, ask one of them to play both the chord which establishes the key and the starting note before you count the song in. If you ask for a **cue note** they will know what you mean. This way you will always be confident of starting on the correct pitch and will easily hear its relationship to the key note (**do**).

37. Silent Night

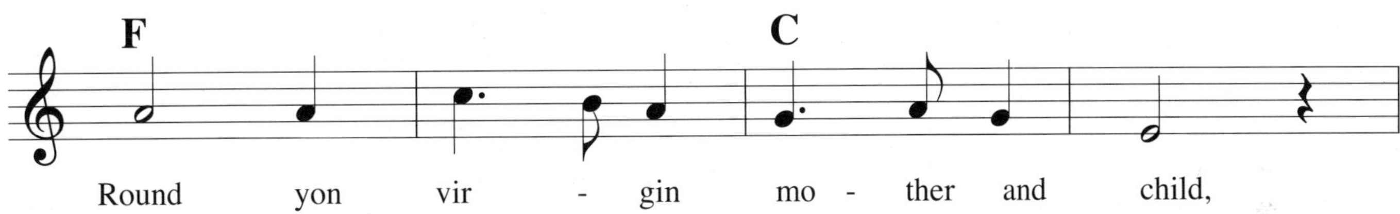

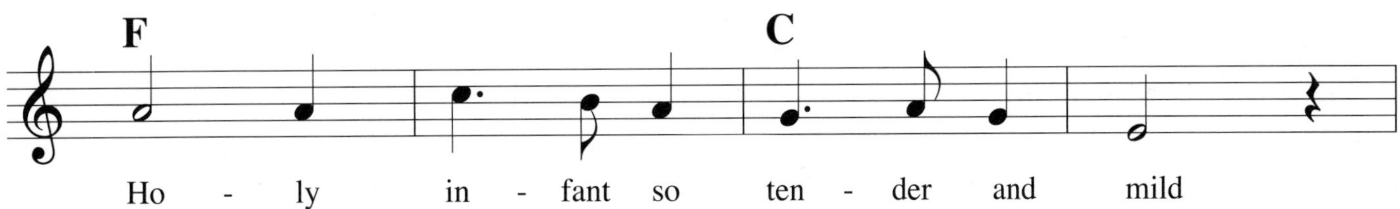

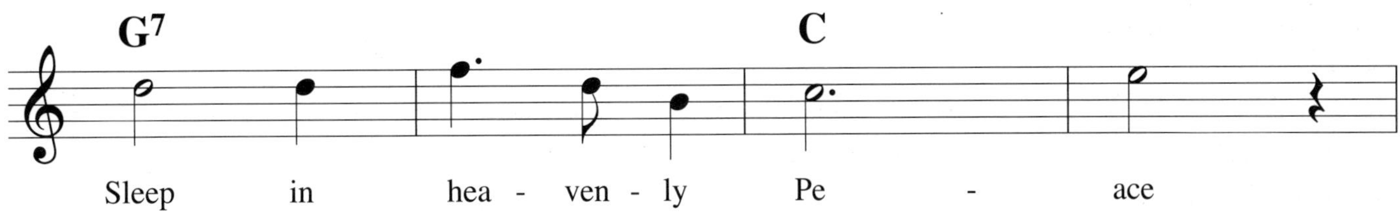

2. Silent night, holy night,
   Shepherds quake at the sight;
   Glories stream from heaven afar,
   Heavenly hosts sing Alleluia:
   Christ the Saviour is born!
   Christ the Saviour is born!

3. Silent night, holy night,
   Son of God, love's pure light;
   Radiance beams from Thy holy face,
   With the dawn of redeeming grace,
   Jesus, Lord, at Thy birth.
   Jesus, Lord, at Thy birth.

LESSON SEVEN

SOUNDS USED IN SINGING

As in speech, the basic sounds used in singing fall into two categories – vowels and consonants. The vowels are all open sounds which flow uninterrupted from the vocal cords out through the mouth. Each vowel is given its particular sound by the shape of the mouth. Consonants, on the other hand, are sounds which interrupt the flow of air produced by a vowel sound. Consonants are articulated by the lips, front, middle or back of the tongue, and even the throat. In general, the vowels are the long or sustained sounds in singing and the consonants are kept as short as possible.

VOWELS

In spoken language, the five basic vowels are **E**, **A**, **I**, **O** and **U**. In singing these are modified to the sounds **EE**, **AY**, **AH**, **OH** and **OO**. Run through these sounds several times on one pitch and become aware of the way the shape of your mouth and position of your lips changes as you move from one sound to the next. As you sing these sounds, your tongue should remain relaxed in the bottom of your mouth and your jaw should also remain relaxed. Aim for an 'open' sound and feeling as you sing each vowel. Once you are comfortable with all the sounds on a single pitch, try the following exercise, which descends through the major scale. It is important to do this exercise slowly at first.

CD 1 **38.**

DIPTHONGS

Some words consist of two successive vowel sounds within one syllable. These vowels are called **diphthongs**. With all dipthongs, the vowel starts with one sound and ends with another.

Examples of Diphthongs:

"AH" + **"EE"** as in Might

"OH" + **"EE"** as in Noise

"EH" + **"EE"** as in Pain and Weight

Try to keep the vowel as natural-sounding as possible, letting the second sound flow out of the first. Do not over emphasise the second sound of the vowel; allow it to disappear naturally.

THE SHAPING OF VOWELS

Try practicing your vowels in front of a mirror to ensure that you develop the habit of using the correct mouth shapes.

EE

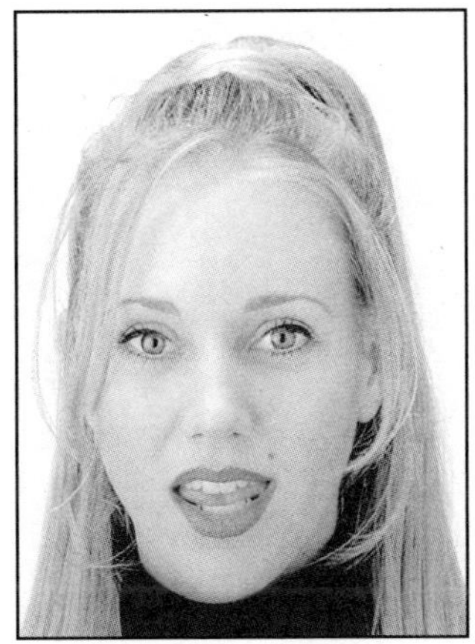

As in 'Meet': Do not allow your mouth to spread sideways, as this will produce extra tension. Your tongue should be resting comfortably on the back of your bottom teeth, but will arch slightly forward.

AY

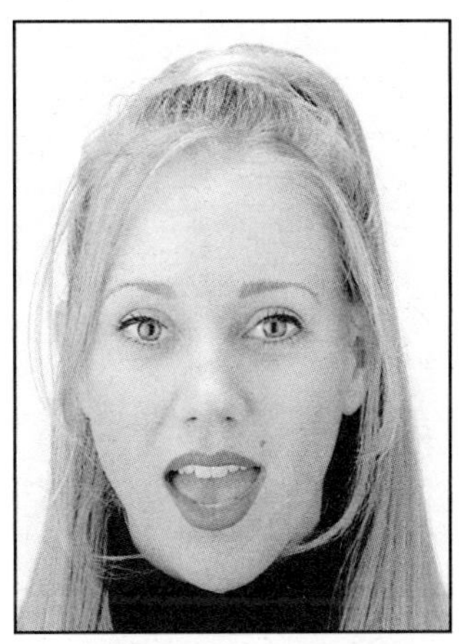

As in 'Say': This vowel is sometimes pronounced as a diphthong, because the vowel starts with one sound and ends with another (**EH-EE**). Keep the tongue resting on the bottom of the mouth and the jaw relaxed.

AH

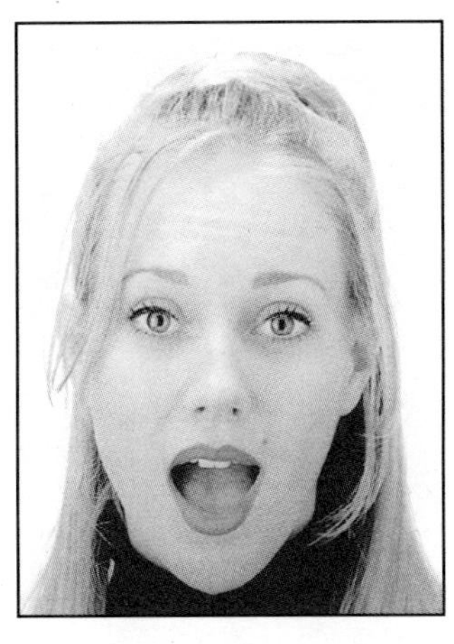

As in the expression 'Ah': Try not to force this vowel. The sound should come from low in your throat. This is an excellent vowel to use when practicing scales and exercises, as it allows for a very open relaxed pathway and doesn't put tension on the larynx.

OH

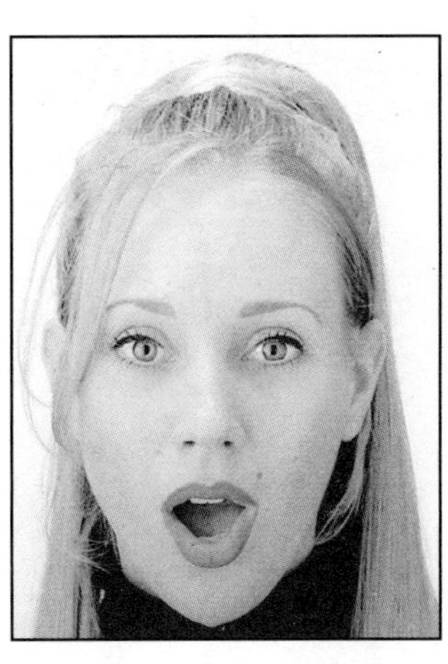

As in 'Coat': Allow the jaw to drop naturally and keep the mouth relaxed and in a similar position to the **AH** vowel. The lips should move forward and the inside of the mouth should feel open.

OO

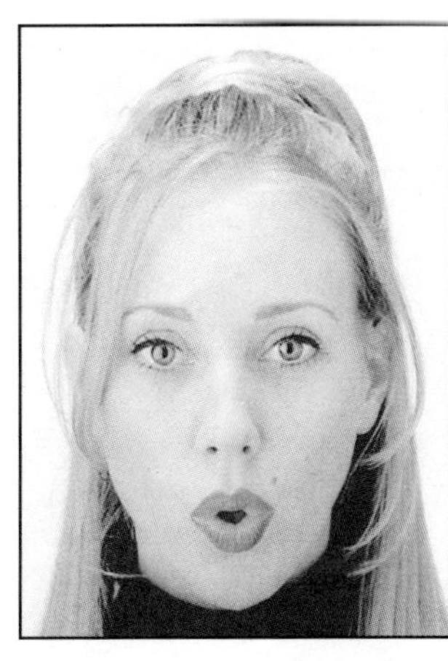

As in 'Room': The lips should form an oval shape. Once again, the jaw should be relaxed and the tongue should sit comfortably on the bottom of the mouth.

CONSONANTS

Consonants are letters other than vowels. They are the sounds that define words and are articulated by the **lips**, **teeth**, **tongue**, **soft palette** and occasionally the **throat**. Consonants actually interrupt the smooth, natural flow of the vowels but are very important to a singer's craft as they provide the focus for words and shape them so that they are understandable to an audience.

As a general rule, consonants should not be over-emphasised. Whereas vowels will open the vocal passages, consonants will restrict the free flow of air. Therefore, when singing a verse or phrase, concentrate on reproducing full, open vowel sounds while only lightly articulating the consonants.

A good way to work on consonants is to take a particular consonant and follow it with each of the vowel sounds, as shown in the example below. Gradually work your way through all the consonants in the alphabet using this technique. Be aware of whether it is the lips, teeth, tongue, throat or soft palate (or combination of these) that articulates each consonant. For example, **B** and **M** involve the lips, **K** involves the soft palette, **S** and **T** involve both the tongue and teeth, and **G** involves the throat and soft palette. Once again, remember that when singing the main emphasis is usually on the vowel sound. Consonants are only lightly articulated so as to express the words without sounding harsh or restricting the air flow more than necessary.

39.

There are occasions in both speech and singing where a sound is made up of two consonants in a row, e.g. sh (as in 'shot'), ng (as in 'song'), or ch (as in 'chew'). As with single consonants, it is worth practicing these sounds along with vowels in the manner shown above, always remembering to keep the emphasis on the vowels.

LANGUAGE AND STYLE

The grammar used in the lyrics of a song may be quite different from that used in written language. For example, perfectly correct grammar can sound out of place in a Rock or Blues song, as these styles are based on a language tradition that has always included slang. This is demonstrated in the following song, where "comin'" is used instead of "coming". You could also change the word "been" to "bin". Being aware of the language commonly used in a particular style of music can help you sound more authentic in any genre. Listening to a wide variety of music will help you with this regardless of the style you like to sing.

40. Comin' Home to Me

Peter Gelling

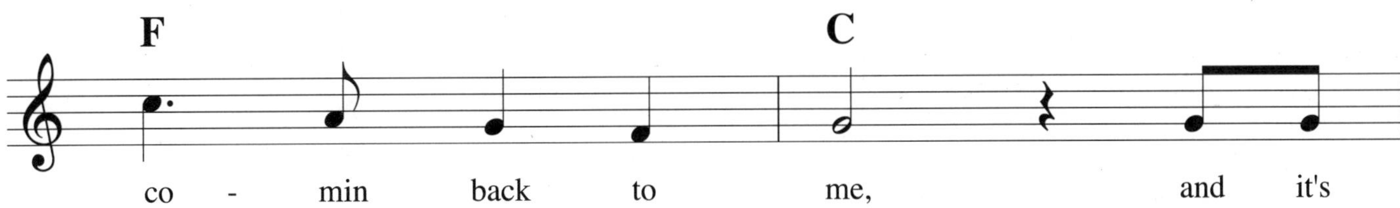

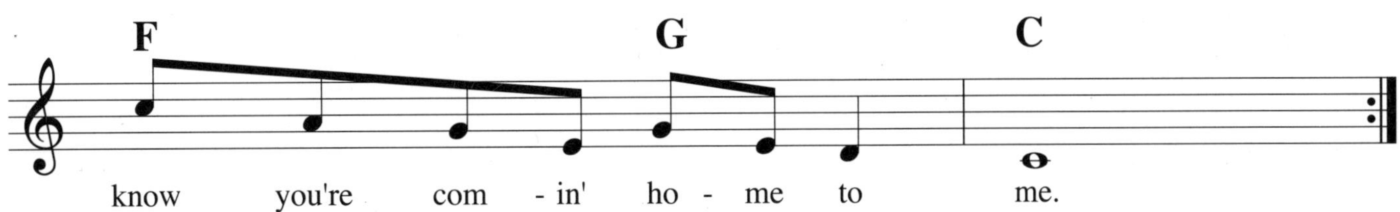

LESSON EIGHT

DYNAMICS

The term **dynamics** refers to the volume at which music is played or sung. If all music were played at the same volume it would lack expression and become boring. Therefore it is essential to be able to sing at a variety of dynamic levels, ranging from very soft to very loud. Here are some of the most commonly used markings for dynamics:

pp	very quiet	***p***	quiet	***mp***	moderately quiet
mf	moderately loud	***f***	loud	***ff***	very loud

Two other symbols used to indicate dynamics are the **crescendo** (meaning a gradual increase in volume) and the **diminuendo** (a gradual decrease in volume).

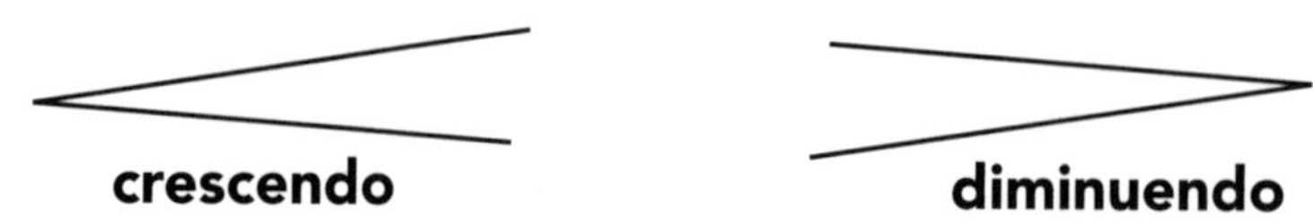

This exercise will help you gain control over dynamics in your singing. The aim is to apply the crescendo and diminuendo to a single note while maintaining an even tone. Listen to the CD if you are not sure how this should sound.

41.

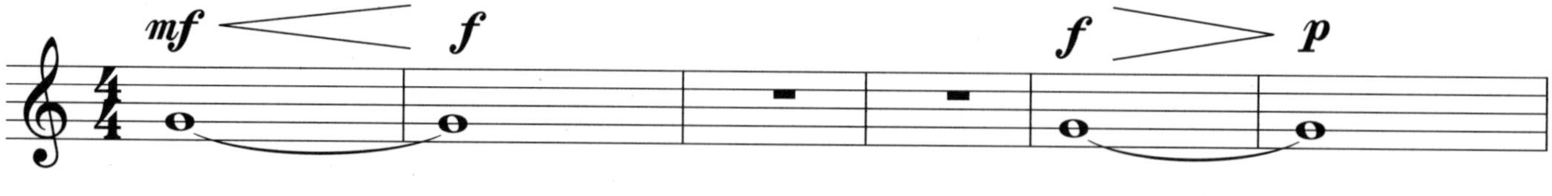

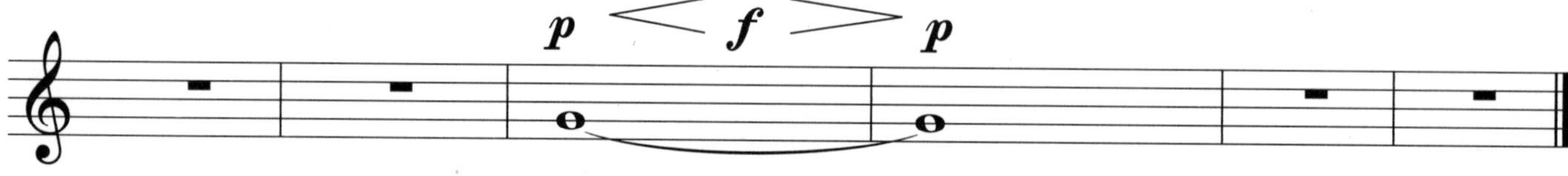

MUSICAL USE OF DYNAMICS

Remember that the aim is always to work new knowledge into your singing until you can use it naturally. This is usually achieved in several steps. When working on dynamics, another useful exercise is to apply dynamics to a major scale, i.e. sing **do** softly and gradually increase the volume as you ascend through the scale, until you are singing loudly by the time you reach the **do** an octave above. Then do the same thing as you descend the scale. Next try starting loudly and get softer with each syllable until you reach the end of the scale.

The final step in adding dynamics to your singing is to apply them to a song. This is a much more personal thing and also depends on the emotional content of the lyrics. Obviously some lyrics call for a quiet, subtle approach while others need strength and volume.

Listen to recordings of your favorite singers and pay particular attention to the way they use dynamics. If you are singing with an accompanist or a band, you will need to rehearse your dynamics with them so that the music can 'rise and fall as one'. When this happens, it feels great as well as giving the ensemble the ability to move an audience more intensely.

TEMPO MARKINGS

The term **tempo** refers to the **speed** at which music is played. As with dynamic markings, tempo markings come from Italian words. Some of them are listed below, along with their English translations. It is important to be able to recognize these markings and to be able to sing melodies comfortably at each tempo.

largo (very slowly)

adagio (slowly)

andante (an easy walking pace)

moderato (a moderate speed)

allegro (fast)

presto (very fast)

TEMPO CHANGES

There are also markings for changes in tempo.

accelerando (gradually faster)

ritenuto (***rit***) (immediately slower)

rallentando or ***ritardando*** (gradually slower)

a tempo (return to original tempo)

EXERCISES

✏ Connect the correct definitions with the correct terms by drawing a line from one to the other. Be aware that there are more definitions than terms, so there will be some left over.

adagio	very fast
p	slowly
presto	an easy walking pace
andante	pianissimo
ff	a moderate speed
pp	fortissimo
mf	piano
	fast
	mezzo forte

✏ Draw the following signs:

crescendo

accent

diminuendo

LESSON NINE

SLURS

A curved line joining two or more notes of **different** pitches indicates a **slur**. Only the first note has a definite beginning. This is common in singing where two or more notes may occur while singing a single syllable.

In the first bar of the example below, the syllable **ah** is occurs on two consecutive notes and is **articulated** on each note. In the next bar the same two notes are connected by a slur, so **ah** is sung again but then 'slides' or 'glides' down to the second note. In the third bar, the syllable **ah** occurs for the last time, this time covering three notes connected by a slur. Once again, **ah** is only articulated on the first note, and then glides or slides to the other notes.

42.

A good example of the way this occurs in a song is the opening phrase of **Silent Night**, which you learned in the previous lesson. It is shown below with slur markings.

To keep the notation uncluttered, slur markings are often left out of sheet music. You can usually tell where they occur because a syllable will stretch over two or more notes, and this will be indicated in the lyrics by a hyphen (e.g. **Si - lent night**).

43.

THE TIE

A **tie** is a curved line joining two or more notes of the **same** pitch. The first note is sung, and is then held for the value of the extra note (or notes). The initial note is sung for the value of all the tied notes.

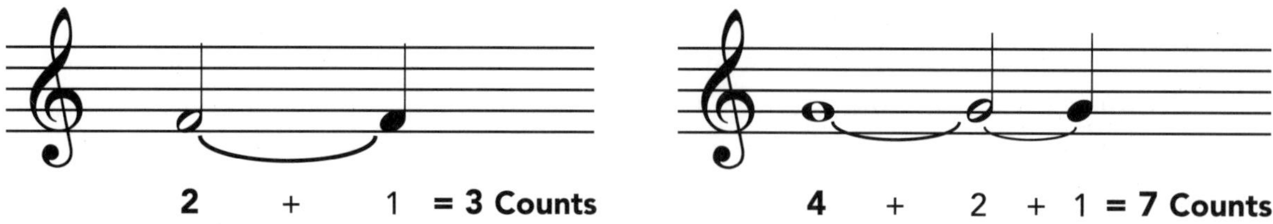

Sing the note G in this example and sustain it for six beats.

44.

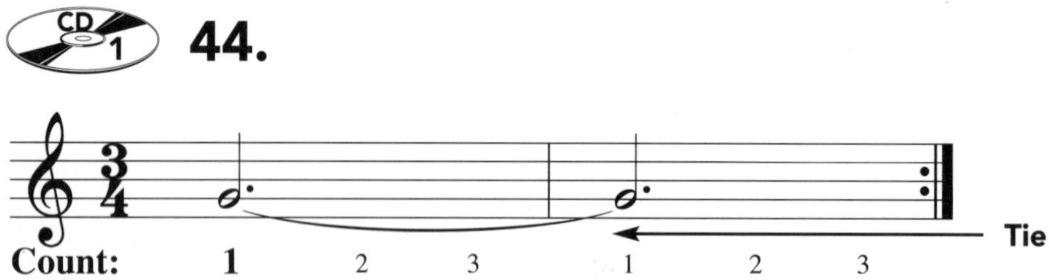

A tie is the only way of indicating that a note is to be held across a bar line (as shown above). It is also way of increasing the length of a note within a bar.

Do not confuse the tie with the slur, which connects two notes of different pitches.

IMITATING INSTRUMENTS

As mentioned earlier, you can learn a lot by copying melodies played by instruments. Jazz singers often improvise in a style known as 'scat' where they use syllables instead of lyrics and sing lines inspired by horn players. Soul singer Johnny Adams sometimes imitates a trombone with his voice. Try copying the sound of the trombone in the following example.

45.

This exercise will help you become more familiar with the use of ties. First clap the rhythms while counting the beats out loud. Then try singing the rhythms while tapping your foot on the beat. Make sure you don't start tapping your foot on the rhythm of the notes instead of evenly on each beat.

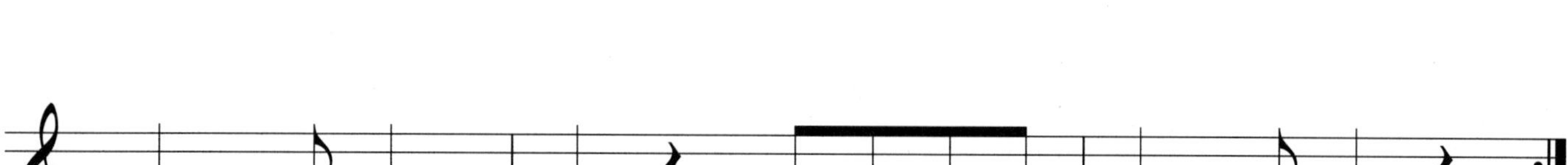

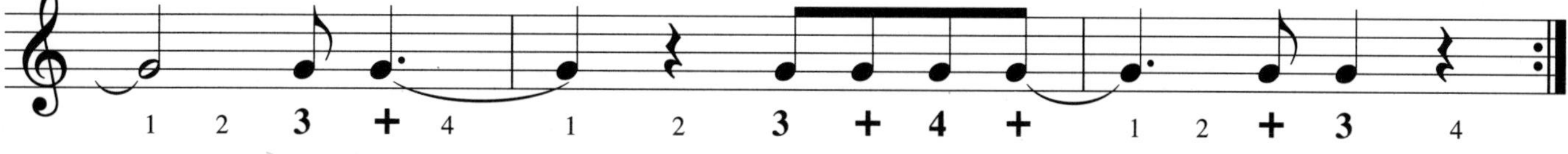

EXERCISE

Write the letter 't' near each tie and the letter 's' near each slur in the following exercise.

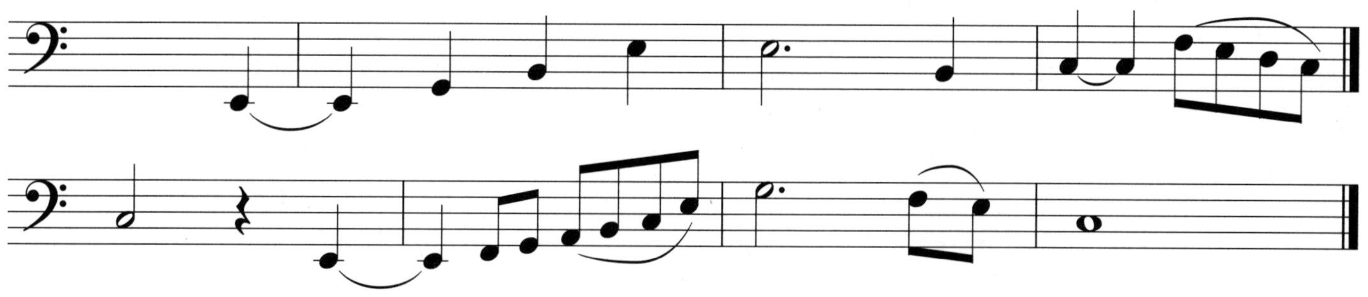

PHRASING AND EXPRESSION

Apart from the actual notes and words used, a large part of the feeling and meaning of a song is conveyed by the expressions, inflections and phrasing that individual singers use. This is a very personal thing, partly determined by the way the singer thinks about the song and how it relates to their own musical taste and experience of life. This is why two singers can sing the same song and produce dramatically different versions.

The term **phrasing** refers to the individual grouping of notes and/or lyrics and the placing of punctuation and emphasis. As in speech, this can alter both meaning of the words and the feeling they convey to a listener. Here are two different ways of delivering the same set of words.

1. (angrily) "**<u>You</u> did it, you <u>know</u> you did**."

2. (enthusiastic and complimentary) "**You <u>did</u> it you know, you <u>did</u>**."

When singing any song, it is important to think about phrasing so as to be able to communicate fully with the listener. This because phrasing is a vital part of your interpretation of the song. Instrumental musicians are also aware of the power of lyrics and vocal phrasing. Many improvising musicians strive to achieve a 'vocal' style of phrasing when they play. The great Jazz saxophonist Lester Young once said that he would never improvise on a song he didn't know the words to.

MOVING BETWEEN REGISTERS

One of the most difficult aspects of singing is achieving an even tone when moving between low and high registers. Most mature voices have a vocal range of about 2 octaves (approximately 13 or 14 white notes on the keyboard). When moving from high notes to low notes and back again, many singers have one or more notes near the middle of their range that require(s) practice to develop an even tone. As mentioned earlier, this is called the **break**. The eventual aim of a singer should be to have the all the notes in their range, from the lowest notes of the chest voice up to the highest notes of the head voice, connected in a smooth, even manner.

A good way to work at reducing the effect and severity of a break is to practice slurring from one octave of a note up to the next octave of that note, and then back down again to the original note. This is demonstrated in the following example, which begins on a C note and glides up to another C note an octave above, before falling back to the first C note. This pattern then continues up a semitone on a C♯ note, then a D note, and so on up to a G note. This example is not notated, so you will need to listen carefully to the CD. If some notes feel too high or too low for your voice, start and finish on whatever notes feel most appropriate for you. As you move through the different pitches, try to keep each note at the same volume and tone as the preceding ones. Work on this exercise for short periods and remember to stop if you feel you are straining your voice.

47. Female

48. Female Practice

49. Male

50. Male Practice

VIBRATO

Another expressive technique common to both singers and instrumentalists is **vibrato**. This is a method of altering the quality of a note once it has been sounded. It generally occurs on longer sustained notes and can be heard as a slight wavering of the pitch and volume of a note; this may be fast, slow or anywhere in between. The speed and width of vibrato are a matter of personal taste and often depend on the musical situation.

There are several methods of producing vibrato with the voice. These involve movement of the diaphragm, the throat and the larynx in various combinations. The easiest way to is to imagine you are your favorite singer and to imitate the sound of their vibrato. It is a good idea to exaggerate at first, but once you have control of it, don't forget to ease off, as singers who over-use vibrato can be very irritating.

Vibrato can add a lot of character and warmth to your voice but it may take some time to develop. It is probably a good idea to work on it with a teacher, as it can be difficult to obtain a good sound at first.

One of the most important aspects of learning is **listening**. By this stage in your development, you should be listening to albums featuring great singing every day.

51.

Listen to the CD to hear the effect of vibrato and then try it yourself. The note begins without vibrato and the vibrato is added while the note sustains.

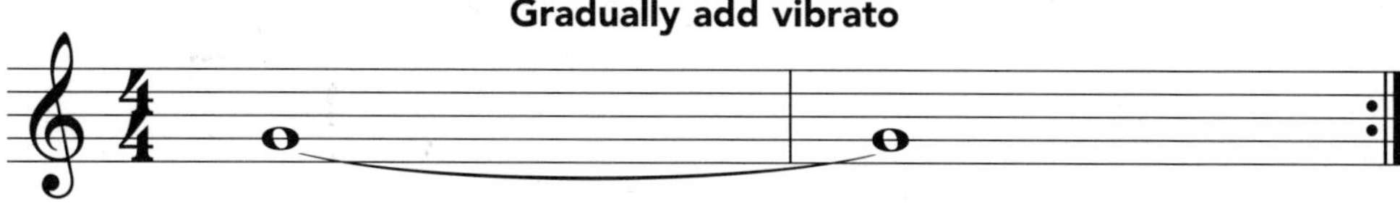

Once you have some control of vibrato, try using it on a long note at the end of a phrase. Try singing this example along with the backing on the CD.

CD 1 **52.**

LESSON TEN

TONES AND SEMITONES

As you already know, a **semitone** is the smallest distance between two notes used in western music. The **natural** (unmodified) notes **B and C** are a semitone apart, as are the notes **E and F**. All the other **natural** notes are a **tone** (two semitones) apart, which means that another note (a **sharp** or **flat**) can occur between them. On a piano keyboard, the black keys are sharps and flats, while the white notes are all natural notes.

SHARPS

A sharp sign(♯) placed **before** a note raises the pitch of that note by **one semitone**.

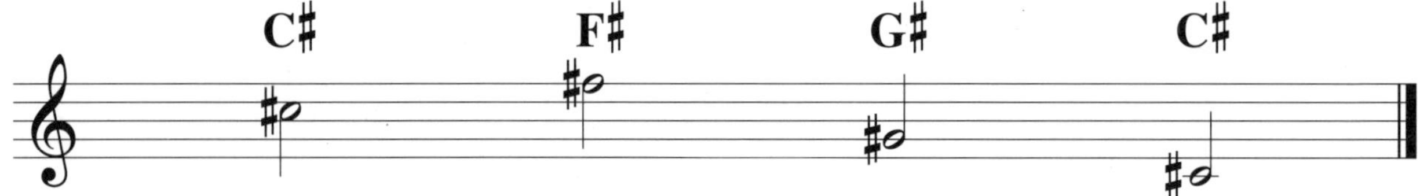

THE CHROMATIC SCALE

Using sharps you can create five new notes, which occur between the seven natural notes you already know. The following example demonstrates all twelve notes which occur within one octave of music. It is an example of a **chromatic scale**. Chromatic scales consist entirely of **semitones** (i.e. they move up or down one semitone at a time) and the start and finish notes are always the same (called the **keynote** or **tonic**), although they are an octave apart. The chromatic scale uses **all twelve notes** used in western music and can be built on **any** note. In this example there are no sharps between **B** and **C**, or **E** and **F**. These are the ones that are a semitone apart so there is no room for an extra note between them. Try singing this scale, naming each note as you go.

53. The A Chromatic Scale

The chromatic scale can be built on **any** note. Here is the **D** chromatic scale:

54.

THE NATURAL SIGN

This is a **natural** sign.

A natural sign cancels the effect of a sharp or flat for the rest of that bar, or until another sharp or flat sign occurs within that bar.

A sharpened note stays sharp until either a **bar line** or a **natural sign** (♮) cancels it:

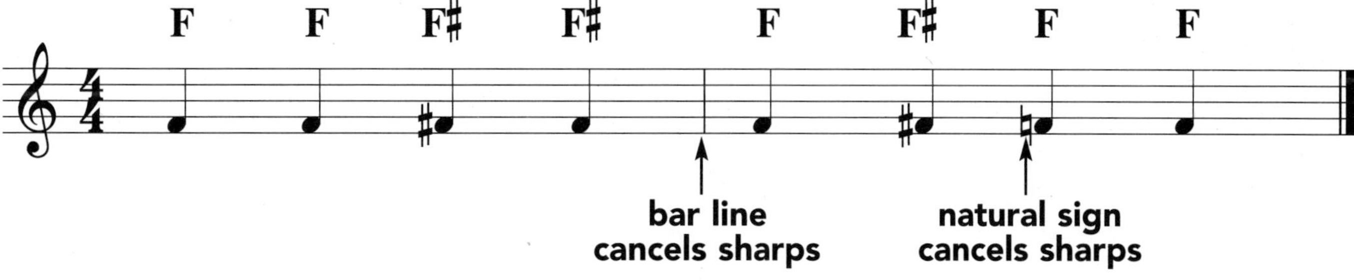

55.

This example contains both sharps and natural signs. Write the names below the notation. Singing music which contains many semitones is difficult at first. Listen to the CD while watching the music and imitate the guitar melody with your voice. The most important thing for now is to become familiar with the symbols and know what they mean.

✏ To improve your knowledge of sharps and natural signs, write the names of these notes below the notation.

FLATS

A **flat** (♭) does the opposite of a sharp. Placed immediately **before** a note, it **lowers** the pitch of that note by one semitone.

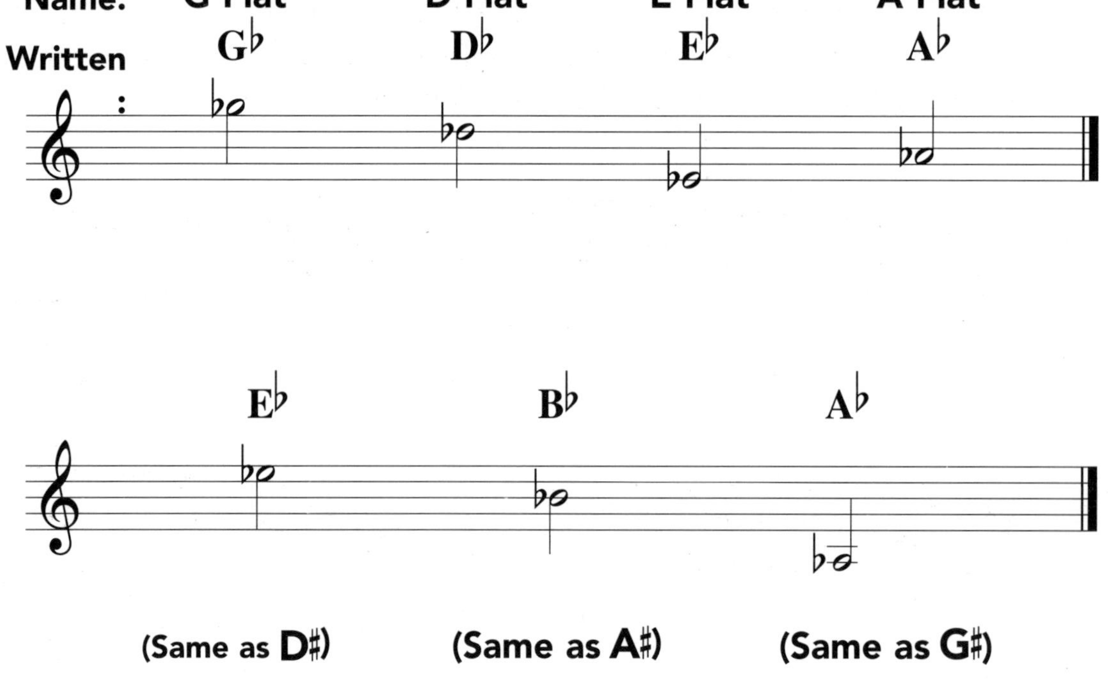

The use of sharps and flats means that the same note can have two different names. For example, F♯ = G♭ and G♯ = A♭. These are referred to as **enharmonic** notes.

Here are two octaves of the **E chromatic scale written on the bass staff**. Notice that sharps are used when the scale ascends and flats are used as it descends. This is common practice when writing chromatic passages in music.

56.

As with sharps, flats are cancelled by a bar line or by a natural sign.

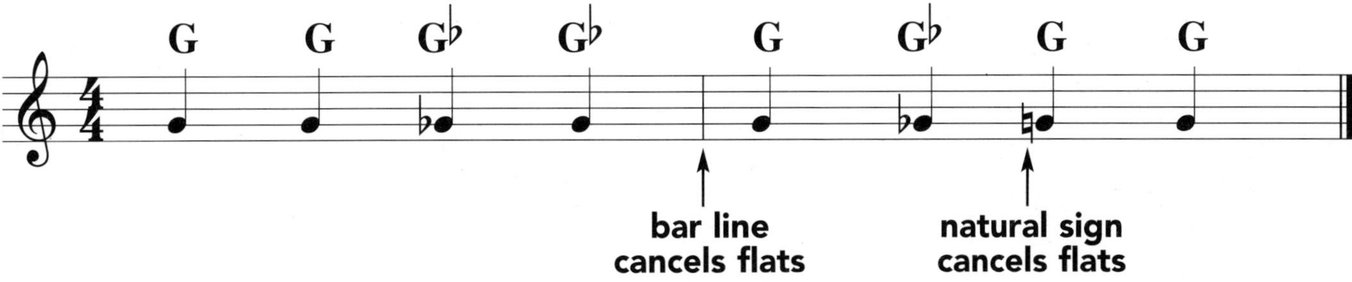

✏ To improve your knowledge of flats, write the names of these notes below the notation.

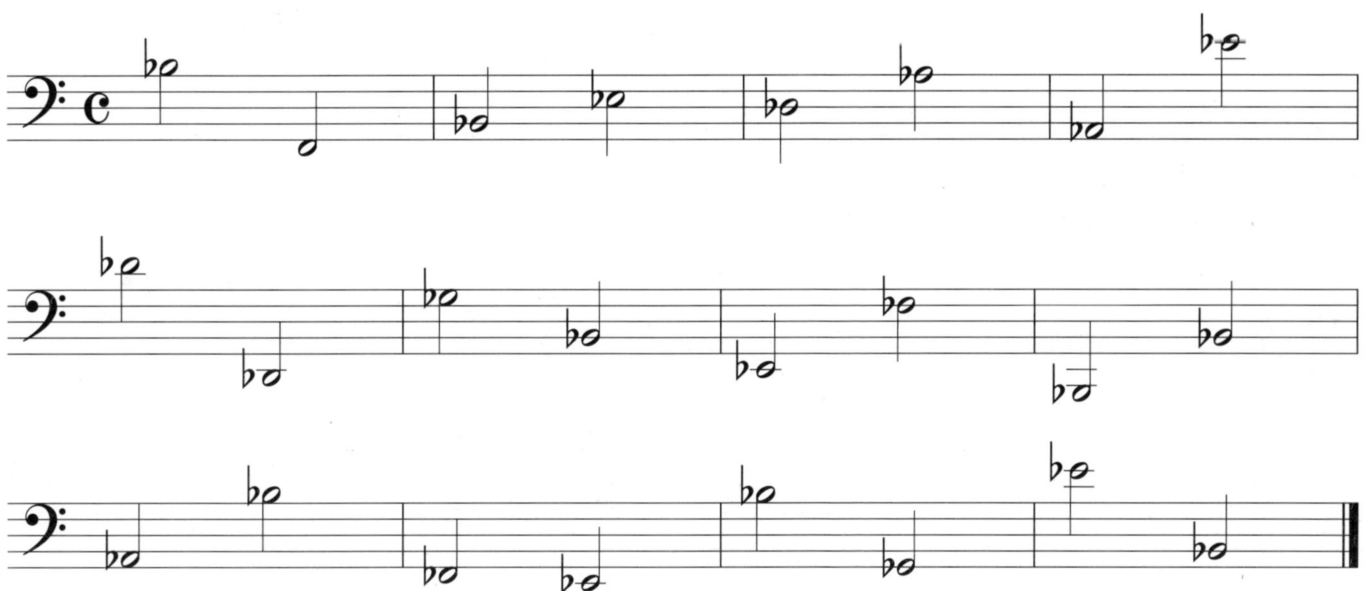

EXERCISES

✏ On the staves below, write the ascending chromatic scales of **G** and **E**.

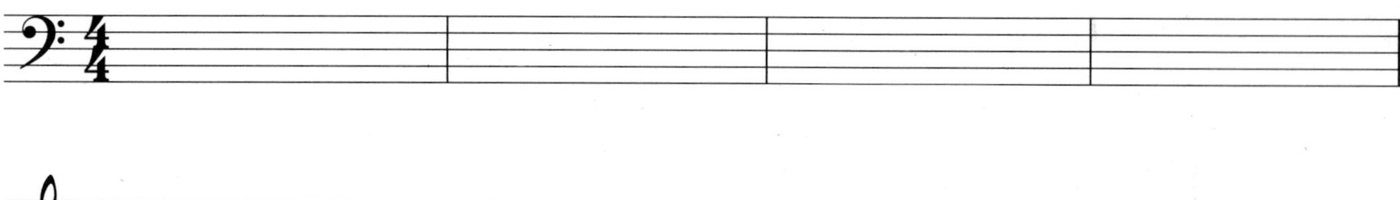

✏ Next to each note, add another quarter note a tone lower.

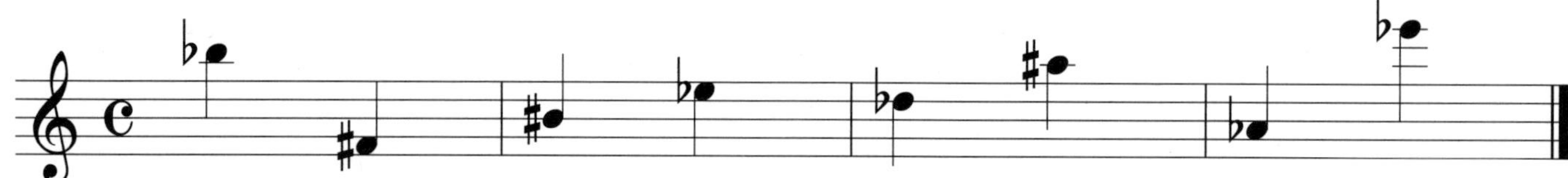

✏ Next to each note, add another quarter note a semitone higher.

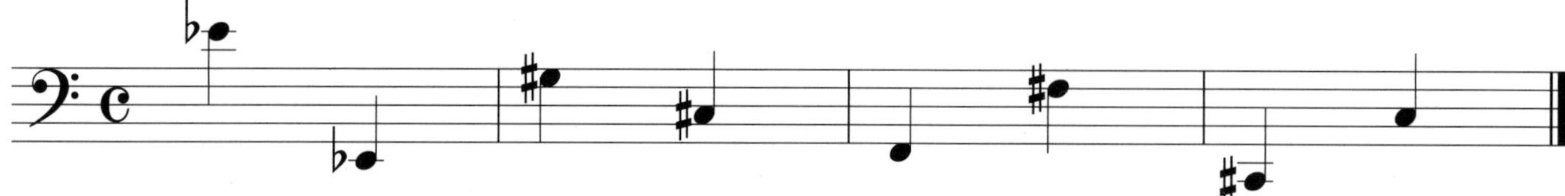

✏ Under each note, write the sign that will lower it by a semitone.

✏ Finish adding the (T) and semitones (ST) above the first line and below the second line of this notation.

LESSON ELEVEN

MORE ABOUT MAJOR SCALES

You already know that the major scale has the familiar sound:

Do Re Mi Fa So La Ti Do

And that the **C major scale** contains the following notes:

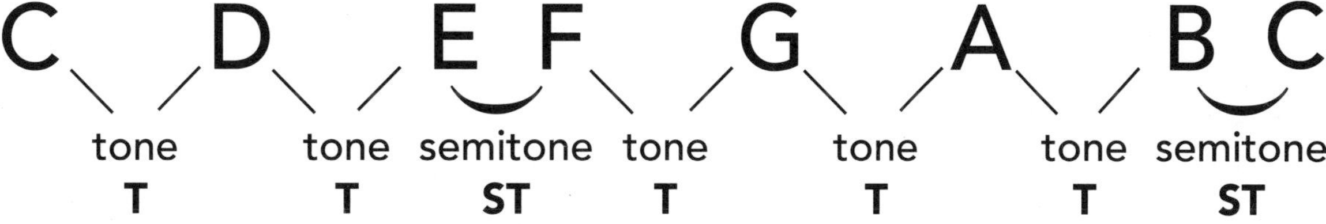

SCALE DEGREES

Each of the 8 notes in the major scale is given a **scale degree** (or scale **number**). So the C major scale could now be represented as:

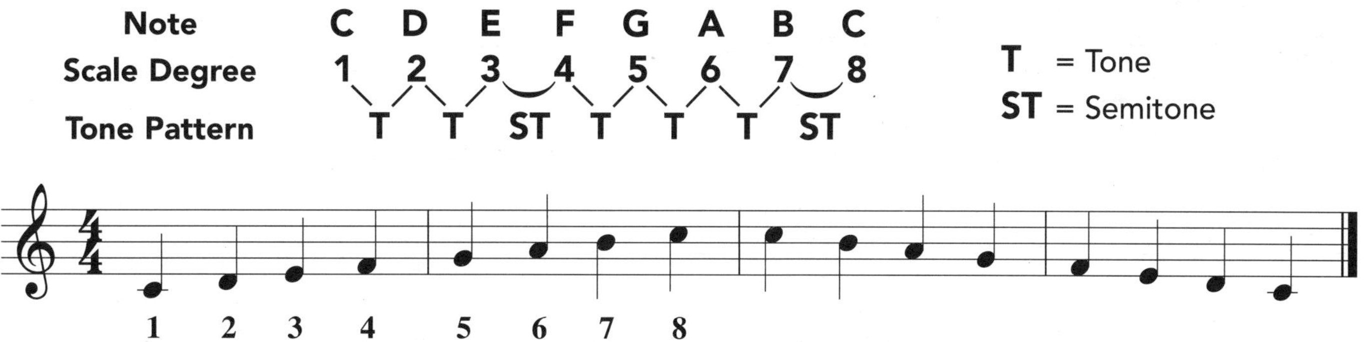

MAJOR SCALE PATTERN

Once you know the pattern of tones and semitones used to create the C major scale, you can build a major scale on any of the twelve notes used in music. It is important to memorize this pattern.

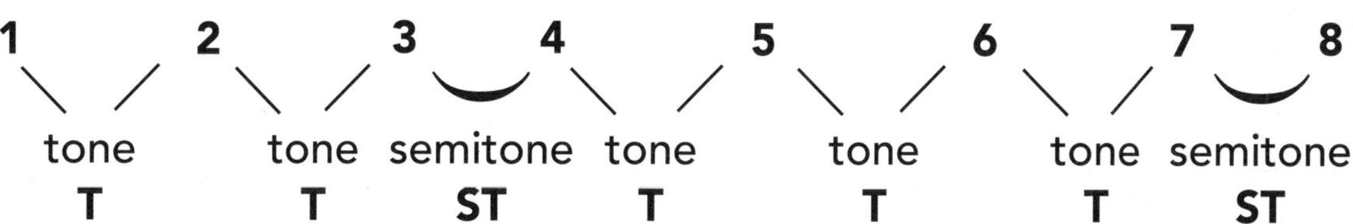

Remember that the tones and semitones represent the distances **between** the notes, not the notes (or scale degrees) themselves. The **semitones** are always found between the **3rd and 4th**, and **7th and 8th** degrees of the scale. All the other notes are a tone apart.

THE G MAJOR SCALE

To demonstrate how the major scale pattern works starting on any note, here is the **G major scale**, with the tone/semitone pattern below it and the degrees above. Notice that the 7th degree is F sharp (**F♯**) instead of F. This is done to maintain the correct pattern of tones and semitones and thus retain the typical sound of the major scale (**do re mi fa so la ti do**).

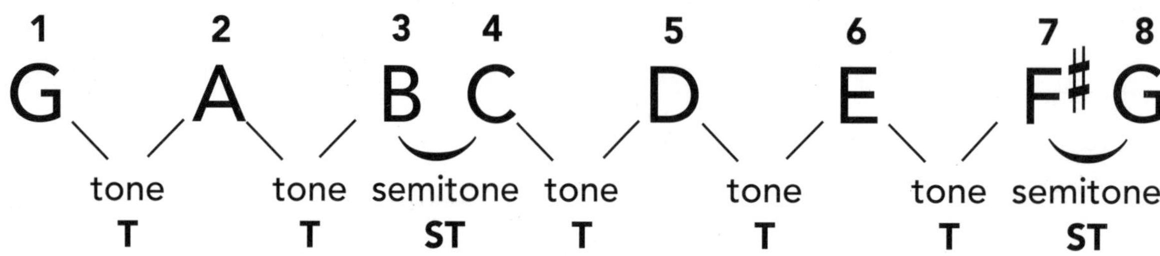

57. G Major Scale

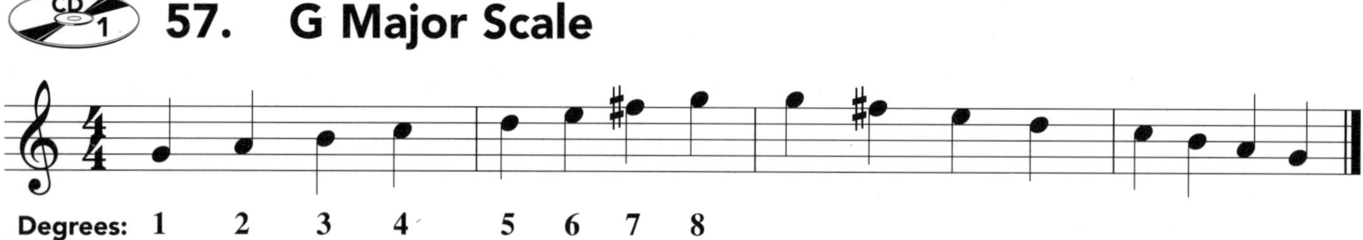

THE F MAJOR SCALE

By starting the major scale pattern on the note F, it is possible to create an **F major scale**. In this scale, it is necessary to **flatten** the 4th degree from B to **B♭** to maintain the correct pattern of tones and semitones.

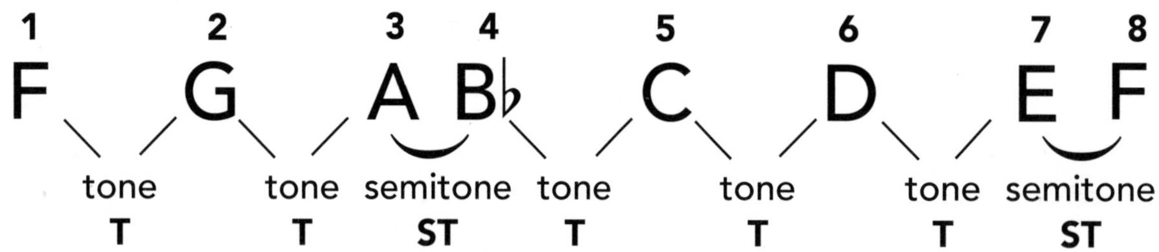

58. F Major Scale

Here is the F major scale written in standard notation.

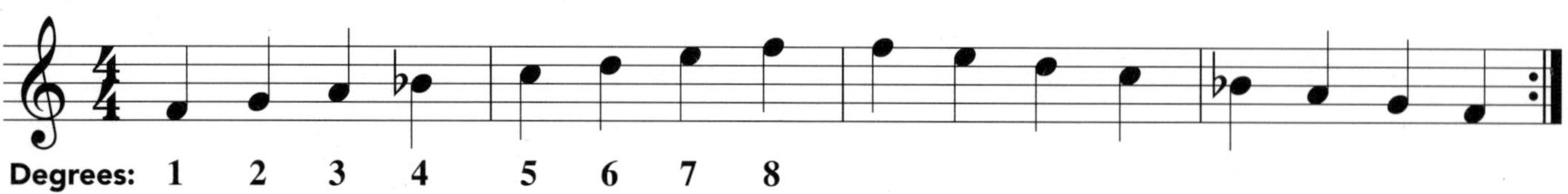

OTHER MAJOR SCALES

By simply following the same pattern of tones and semitones, it is possible to construct a major scale starting on any of the twelve notes of the chromatic scale. The scale will be named by the note it starts on. Here are several more major scales. If they do not suit your voice range, try them in a higher octave.

CD 1 **59.**

D major scale

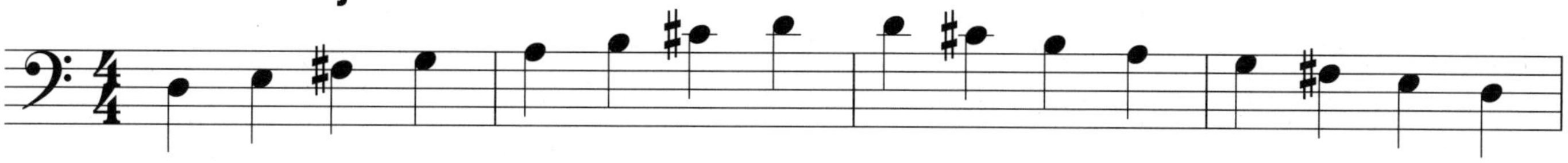

E major scale

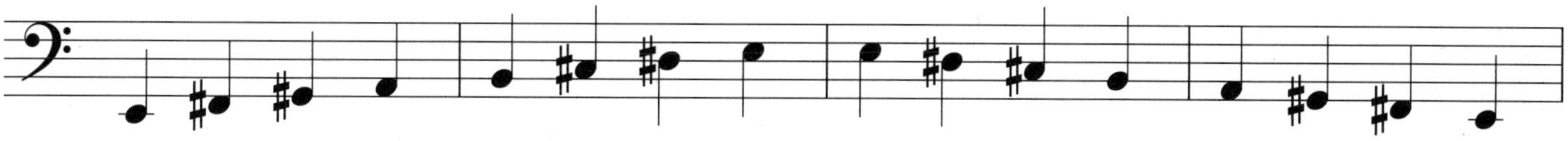

B♭ major scale

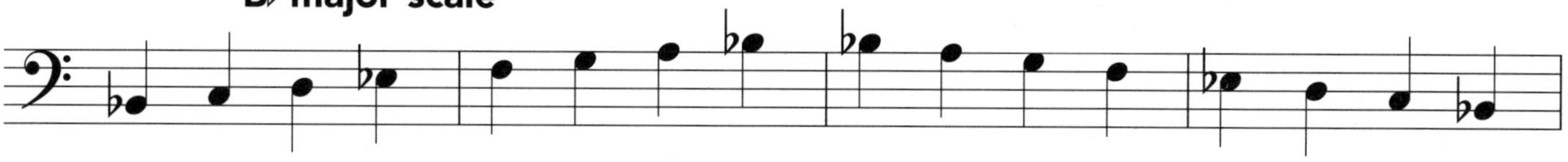

A♭ major scale

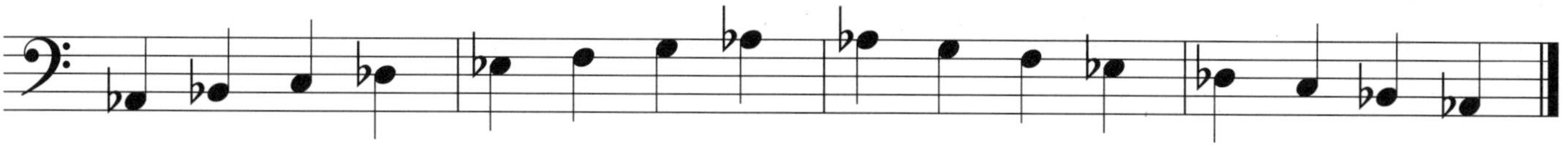

MOVEABLE SOL-FA SYLLABLES

Sol fa syllables can be applied to any major scale. Once you have the correct notes, you simply call the first degree **Do**, the second degree **Re**, the third degree **Mi**, etc. This is known as a **moveable sol-fa system** (sometimes called **moveable Do**). Here are the sol-fa syllables applied to the G major scale.

CD 1 **60.**

Do	Re	Mi	Fa	So	La	Ti	Do
G	**A**	**B**	**C**	**D**	**E**	**F♯**	**G**

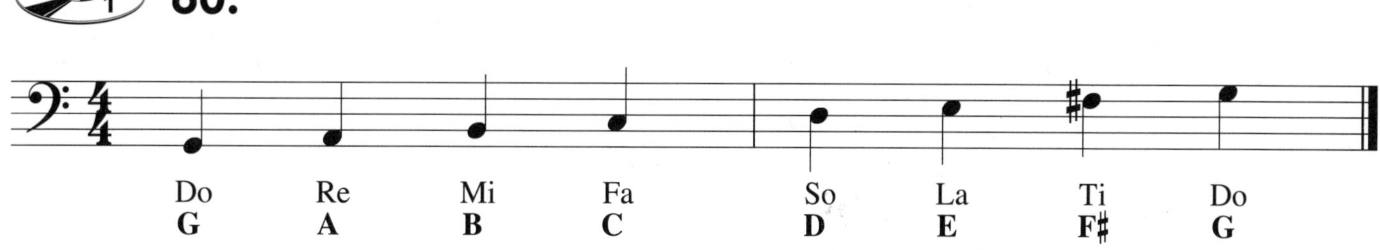

KEY OF C MAJOR

When a song consists of notes from a particular scale, it is said to be written in the **key** which has the same name as that scale. This song contains notes from the **C major scale**, so it is said to be in the **key of C major**.

 61. Lavender's Blue

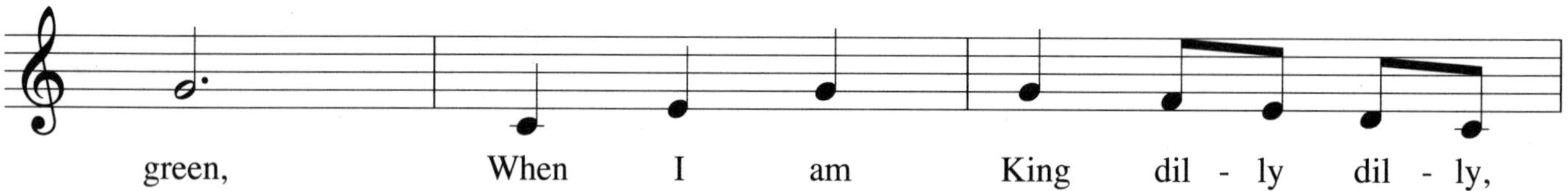

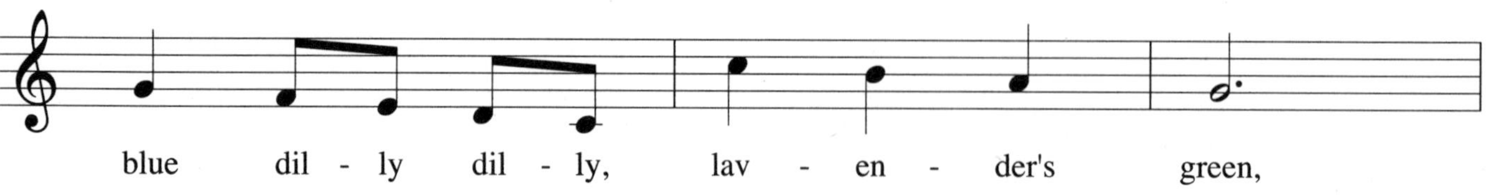

KEY SIGNATURES

A **key signature** consists of one or more **sharps or flats** written after the treble clef, or in the case of the key of C major, **no** sharps or flats. Because the **G major scale** contains the note **F♯**, the key signature for the **key of G major** will consist of an **F♯** note written after the clef.

This is the key signature for the key of **G major**. It has **one** sharp sign after the treble clef.

The C major scale contains no sharps or flats, therefore the key of **C major** contains **no** sharps or flats.

When a key signature contains sharps or flats, there is no need to place sharp or flat signs before individual notes. All the notes indicated by the key signature are sung as sharps or flats throughout the song.

It is possible to sing or play any melody in more than one key. You have just learned this song in the key of C major. Here it is again in the key of **G major**, which means that all F notes are now **F♯**. Changing the key of a piece of music is called **transposing**. This process will be discussed in detail in Lesson 14.

LESSON TWELVE

KEYS AND KEY SIGNATURES

The **key** describes the note around which a piece of music is built. When a song consists of notes from a particular scale, it is said to be written in the **key** which has the same notes as that scale. For example, if a song contains mostly notes from the **C major scale**, it is said to be in the **key of C major**. If a song contains mostly notes from the **F major scale**, it is said to be in the **key of F major**. If a song contains mostly notes from the **G major scale**, it is said to be in the **key of G major**. In any major key other than C, the key will contain at least one sharp or flat, and possibly as many as six. The sharps or flats in the key signature are the same as the sharps or flats in the corresponding major scale. The major scales and key signatures for the keys of **F** and **G** are shown below. Without sharps and flats, these scales would not contain the correct pattern of tones and semitones and would therefore not sound like a major scale.

G MAJOR SCALE

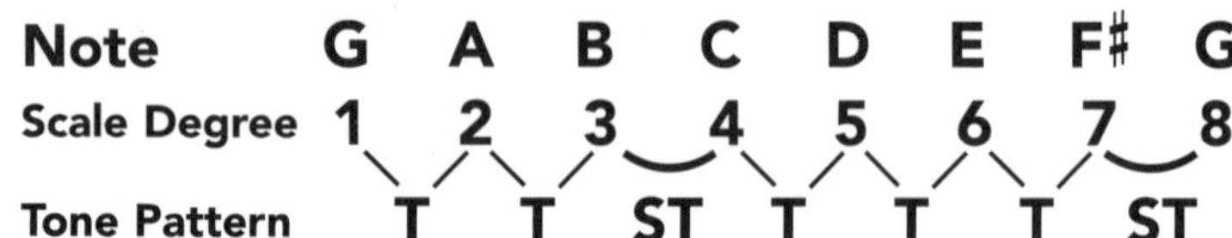

KEY SIGNATURE OF G MAJOR

F MAJOR SCALE

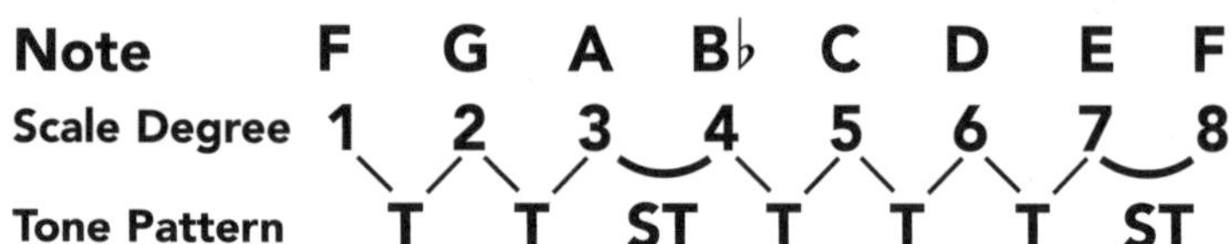

KEY SIGNATURE OF F MAJOR

Some scales contain sharps while others contain flats because there must be a separate letter name for each note in the scale. For example, the G major scale contains F♯ instead of G♭ even though these two notes are identical in sound. If G♭ was used, the scale would contain two notes with the letter name G and no note with the letter name F. In the key of F major, the note B♭ is chosen instead of A♯ for the same reason. If A♯ was used, the scale would contain two notes with the letter name A and no note with the letter name B. The note each major scale starts on will determine how many sharps or flats are found in each key signature because of the necessity for the scale to have the correct pattern of tones and semitones in order to sound right.

The charts on the facing page show the key signatures of all major scales that contain sharps or flats. The C major scale is not represented because it contains no sharps or flats. As there are twelve notes used in music, including sharps and flats, there are twelve possible starting notes for major scales. However, you can see from the charts that since F♯ and G♭ are enharmonic notes (i.e. the same notes), the scales F♯ major and G♭ major are actually the same. Note too that only some of the keys that contain sharps or flats have sharps or flats in their name.

SHARP KEY SIGNATURES

The new sharp **key** is a fifth interval * higher

Key	Number of Sharps	Sharp Notes
G	1	F♯
D	2	F♯, C♯
A	3	F♯, C♯, G♯
E	4	F♯, C♯, G♯, D♯
B	5	F♯, C♯, G♯, D♯, A♯,
F♯	6	F♯, C♯, G♯, D♯, A♯, E♯

The new sharp **note** is a fifth interval * higher

FLAT KEY SIGNATURES

The new flat **key** is a fourth interval * higher

Key	Number of Flats	Flat Notes
F	1	B♭
B♭	2	B♭, E♭
E♭	3	B♭, E♭, A♭
A♭	4	B♭, E♭, A♭, D♭
D♭	5	B♭, E♭, A♭, D♭, G♭,
G♭	6	B♭, E♭, A♭, D♭, G♭, C♭

The new flat **note** is a fourth interval * higher

* An **interval** is the distance between two notes. Intervals are named according to the number of letters they are apart, plus the notes themselves, e.g. C to G is a fifth.

THE KEY CYCLE

There are many reasons why you need to be able to play equally well in every key. Bands often have to play in keys that suit their singer. That could be **F♯** or **D♭** for example. Keyboard players tend to like the keys of **C**, **F** and **G**, while **E** and **A** are fairly common keys for guitar. Horn players like flat keys such as **F**, **B♭** and **E♭**. Apart from this, Jazz tunes often contain many key changes in themselves. For these reasons, you need to learn how keys relate to each other so you can move quickly between them.

One way to do this is to use the **key cycle** (also called the **cycle of 5ths** or **cycle of 4ths**).

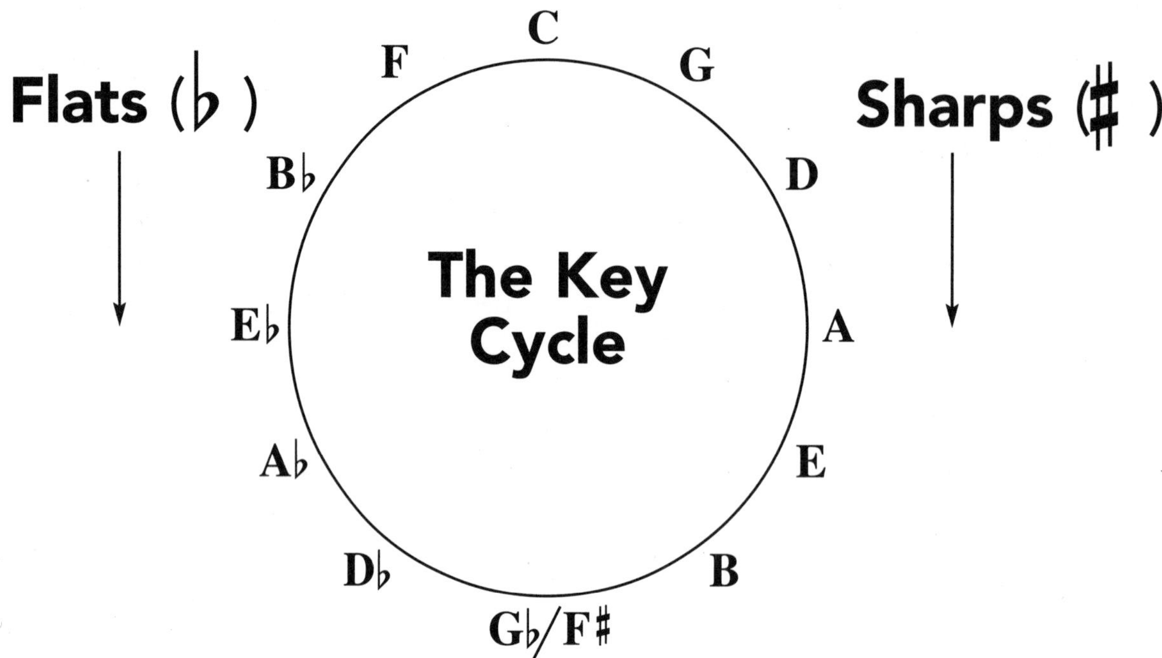

Think of the key cycle like a clock. Just as there are 12 points on the clock, there are also 12 keys. **C** is at the top and contains no sharps or flats. Moving around **clockwise** you will find the next key is **G**, which contains one sharp (**F♯**). The next key is **D**, which contains two sharps (**F♯** and **C♯**). Progressing further through the sharp keys each key contains an **extra sharp**, with the new sharp being the **7th note (degree) of the new key**. Therefore the key of **A** would automatically contain **F♯** and **C♯** which were in the key of D, plus **G♯** which is the 7th note of the A major scale. When you get to **F♯** (at 6 o'clock), the new sharp is called **E♯** which is enharmonically the same as **F**. Remember that **enharmonic** means two different ways of writing the same note. Another example of enharmonic spelling would be **F♯** and **G♭**. This means that **G♭** could become the name of the key of **F♯**. The key of **F♯** contains six sharps, while the key of **G♭** contains six flats – all of which are exactly the same notes.

If you start at **C** again at the top of the cycle and go **anti-clockwise** you will progress through the flat keys. The key of **F** contains one flat (**B♭**), which then becomes the name of the next key around the cycle. In flat keys, the **new flat** is always the **4th degree of the new key**. Continuing around the cycle, the key of **B♭** contains two flats (**B♭** and **E♭**) and so on. **Practice singing all the notes around the cycle, both clockwise and anticlockwise.** Test the pitches on a keyboard or guitar as you go, until you are confident you can get around the cycle accurately without a reference for each note.

MAJOR SCALES IN ALL KEYS

✏ Learning scales may not seem as interesting as singing melodies, but a little effort at this stage will pay off later, regardless of which style of music you are learning. Write out the remaining major scales with the appropriate key signatures, using eighth notes as demonstrated below. Memorize the notes of each scale and then try playing it on the keyboard and singing it. Once you know all the scales, you will be able to read music and learn songs in any key more easily, as well as being able to write your own melodies in any key. All twelve major scales are shown on pages 194-195, along with their key signatures. You should eventually learn all these from memory.

LESSON THIRTEEN

THE EIGHTH REST

This is an **eighth rest**.
It indicates **half a beat of silence**.

62.

There are two common positions for eighth note rests – off the beat and on the beat. Sing this example with the syllable **ba**.

63.

Now try these rhythms which contain eighth rests. Count and clap them first, then sing them using the syllable **da**. Try singing the whole example with the CD backing.

SYNCOPATION

When you count along with music, there is often a natural pattern of accents on each beat. However, when eighth rests are used on the beat, this displaces some of the natural accents from on the beat to off the beat (in between the beats). This effect is known as syncopation. A good way to become comfortable with syncopation is to practice singing a scale using the following rhythm. On the recording it is sung using the syllable **da**.

64.

The use of eighth rests on the beat is a common way of achieving syncopated rhythms. This **12 Bar Blues progression** is written in the style of Jazz singer Bobby McFerrin, who often mimics instrumental solos with his voice. This progression. is dealt with in detail in Lesson 20 on Blues singing. The 12 Bar Blues progression is the basis of thousands of popular songs. Sing this example using the syllable **ba**, then try it with some other syllables. If you're feeling adventurous, try some scat singing with the CD.

CD 1 65. In Sync

Peter Gelling

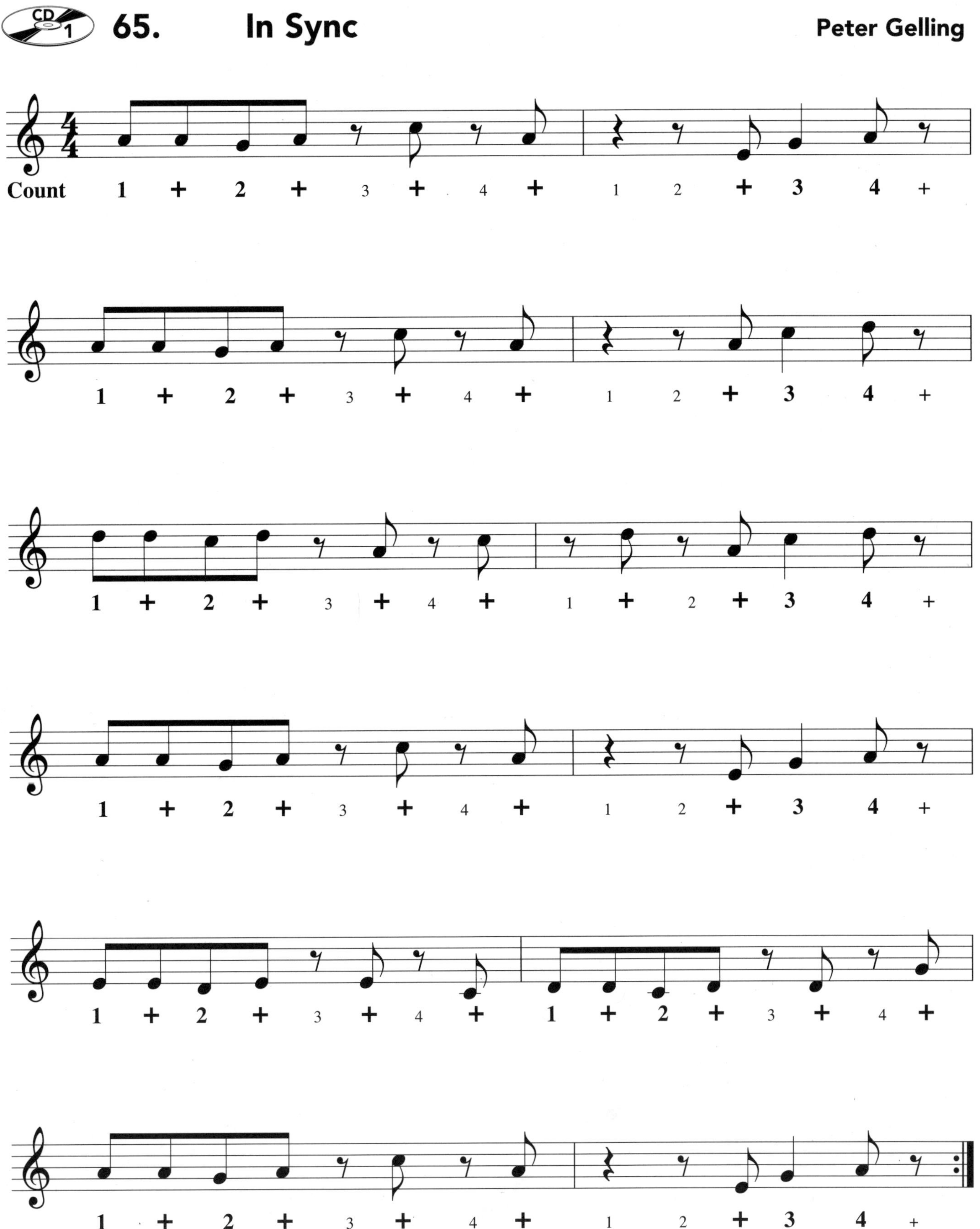

SYNCOPATION USING TIES

Another common way of creating syncopated rhythms is by using ties with eighth notes. Listen to the way the accent is thrown to the **+** (**and**) part of the count by the use of ties.

66.

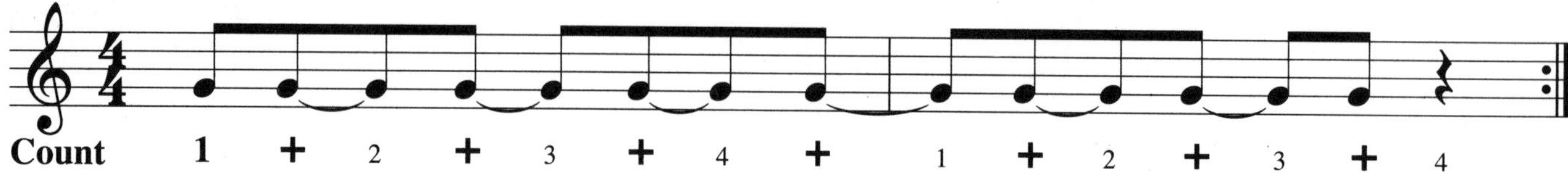

Syncopation is common in melodies. It is often used to make rhythms more dramatic and to propel the music forward. Here are some phrases to practice which contain syncopated rhythms created by the use of ties. Listen to the vocalist on the CD and then sing the example with the backing when the music repeats.

67.

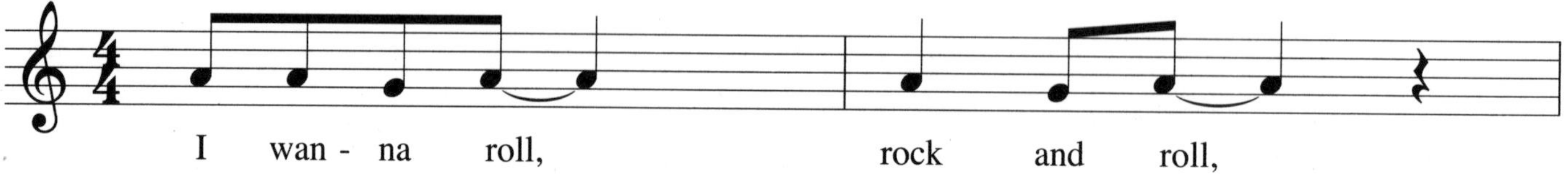

Syncopation using ties can be practiced with a scale in a similar manner to that of eighth rests, as demonstrated in this example.

68.

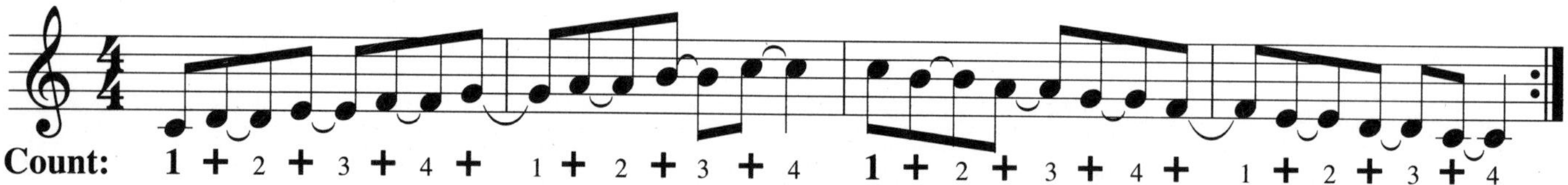

IDENTIFYING EIGHTH NOTE RHYTHMS

It is important to be able to identify the position of each note in the bar. The notes **off** the beat are named according to the beats they follow. Within a bar of continuous eighth notes in $\frac{4}{4}$ time, there are **eight** possible places where notes could occur. The first beat is called **one** (1), the next eighth note is called the "**and of one**", then comes beat **two**, the next eighth note is called the "**and of two**", then beat **three**, followed by the "**and of three**", then beat **four**, followed by the "**and of four**" which is the final eighth note in the bar. These positions are shown in the notation below.

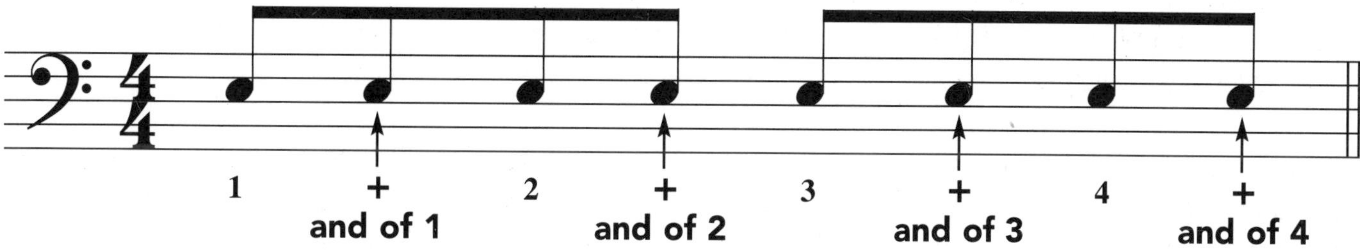

If you are having trouble with the timing of a rhythm, use this method to identify where the notes occur in relation to each beat, and then count them slowly until you have memorized the rhythm. Try it out on the rhythms in the following song and then sing along with the CD. Minor keys are discussed in Lesson 15.

69. Minor Melody

Peter Gelling

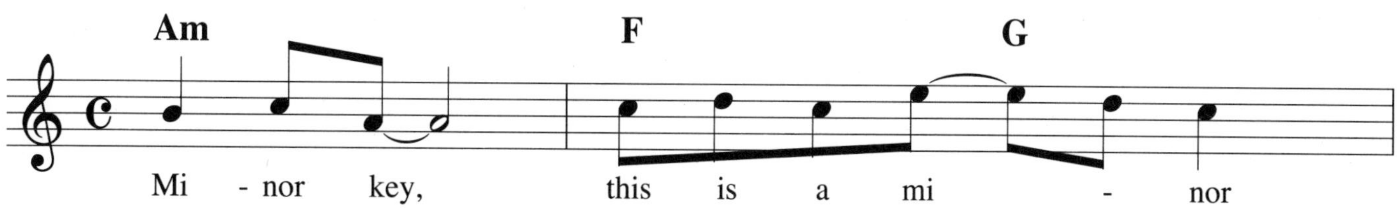

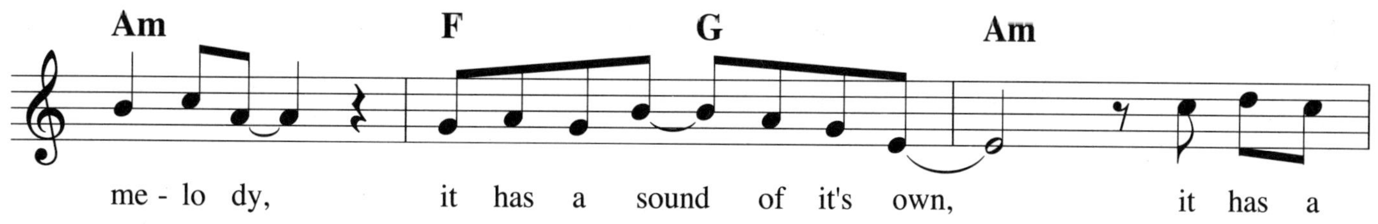

The following traditional Caribbean song makes much use of syncopated rhythms. It is written here in the key of D major, which suited both our female and male vocalists. The difference is that they are singing it in different octaves. You will also notice slight differences in timing and phrasing between the two versions. This is a natural part of each singer's personal expression. Phrasing, interpretation and improvisation are dealt with in Lesson 21.

Once you have learned the song, you could try singing it in several other keys until you find the most comfortable key for your voice. The key note (**do**) in this case is the final note of the song (a **D** note). To sing this in another key (e.g. key of F) play and sustain an **F** note on a keyboard or guitar while you sing the final phrase of the song. Check to see that your voice is finishing on the note F along with the instrument. Then sing the whole song in that key. Try keys which are both higher and lower than D by a small distance at first.

It is a good idea to try every song you know in several keys until you find the most comfortable key for your voice. Then you can instantly tell the musicians who accompany you which key you prefer to sing the song in. This will always be appreciated and can save a lot of time at rehearsals.

70. Jamaica Farewell

Traditional

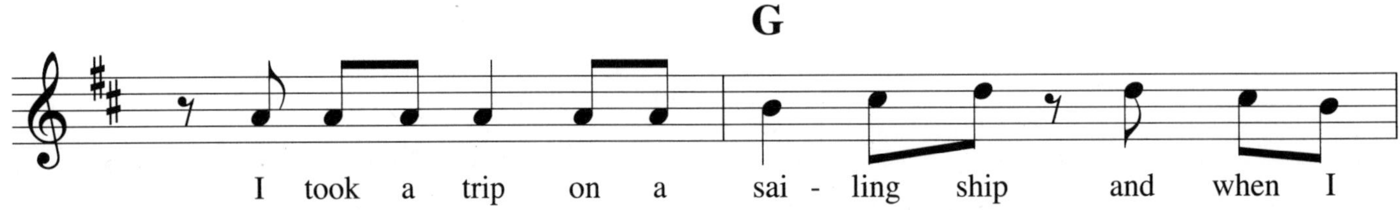

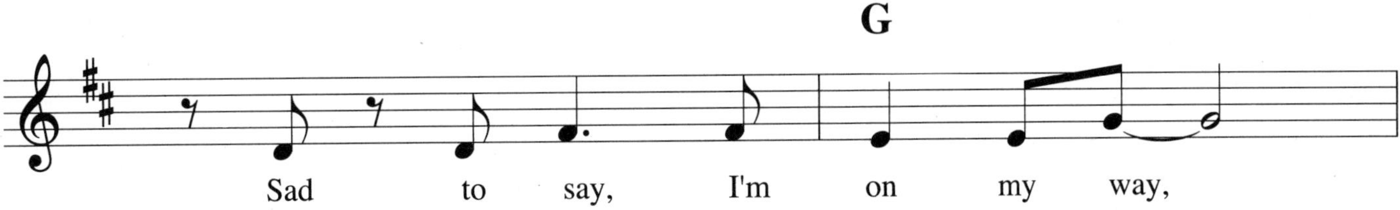

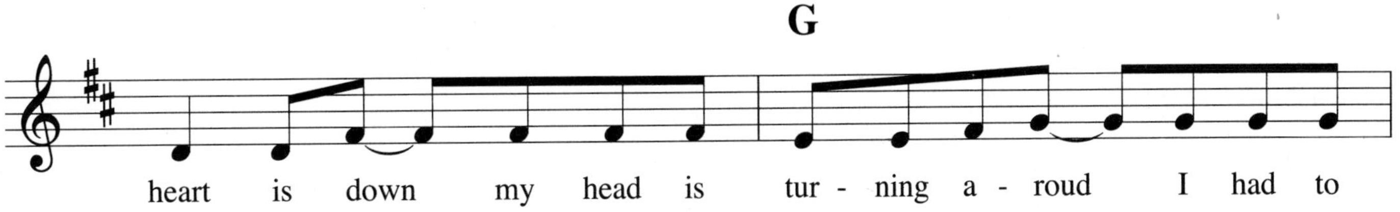

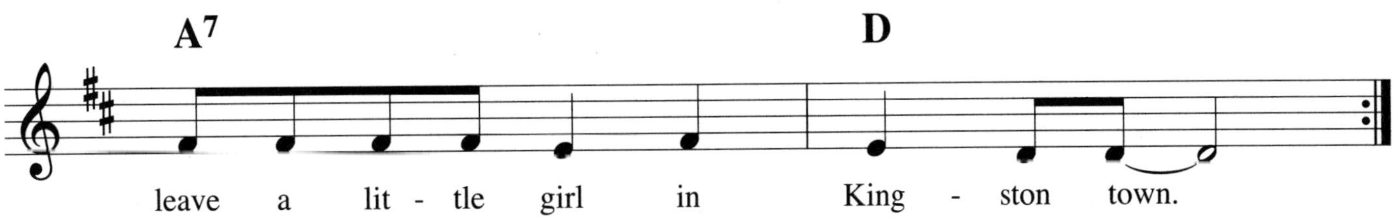

2. Sounds of laughter everywhere,
And the dancing girls sway, to and fro,
I must declare my heart is there,
Though I've been from Maine to Mexico, but I'm
Sad to say, I'm on my way, etc.

3. Down at the markets, you can hear,
Ladies cry out, while on their heads they bear,
Ackie rice, salt fish are nice,
And the rum is fine any time of year, but I'm
Sad to say, I'm on my way, etc.

LESSON FOURTEEN

TRANSPOSING

When you try to sing a melody for the first time, you will often find that parts of it are too high or too low for your personal voice range. In such cases it is necessary to know how to **transpose** the melody to another key. Transposing (or transposition) means changing the key of a piece of music. This can apply to a scale, a phrase, a short melody, or an entire song. The ability to transpose is an essential skill for all singers to develop.

The easiest way to transpose is to write the **scale degrees** under the original melody and then work out which notes correspond to those scale degrees in the key you want to transpose to. You should work towards being able to do this in your head instantly, without the need for notated scale degrees. Written below is a short melody played by a guitar in the key of **C** and then transposed to the keys of **F** and **G**. Listen to the CD and notice that the melody sounds the same, but the overall pitch is higher or lower.

71.0 Key of C

CD 1

71.1 Key of F

CD 1

71.2 Key of G

Here is the melody in C again, but with sol-fa syllables instead of scale degrees.

As mentioned previously, sol-fa syllables can be applied to any major scale. Here is the same melody in the key of F, with its accompanying sol-fa syllables.

Here it is again in the key of G.

Now try transposing this short melody in C major with its accompanying sol-fa syllables to other major keys. Try the same technique with other melodies you know. The more you do this, the easier it gets; and the better you are at transposing, the easier it will be to sing and read music in any key.

CD 1 **72.**

The transposing process is the same regardless of whether you are transposing a short phrase or a whole song. The following song is in the key of **C major**. This key may be comfortable for you or it may be too high or too low. On the facing page you will see 16 bars of empty staves. These are for you to transpose the song to whichever key best suits your voice range. Use the method shown in the previous pages and write the appropriate sharps or flats as a key signature.

CD 1 **73. Get to Know You** **Peter Gelling**

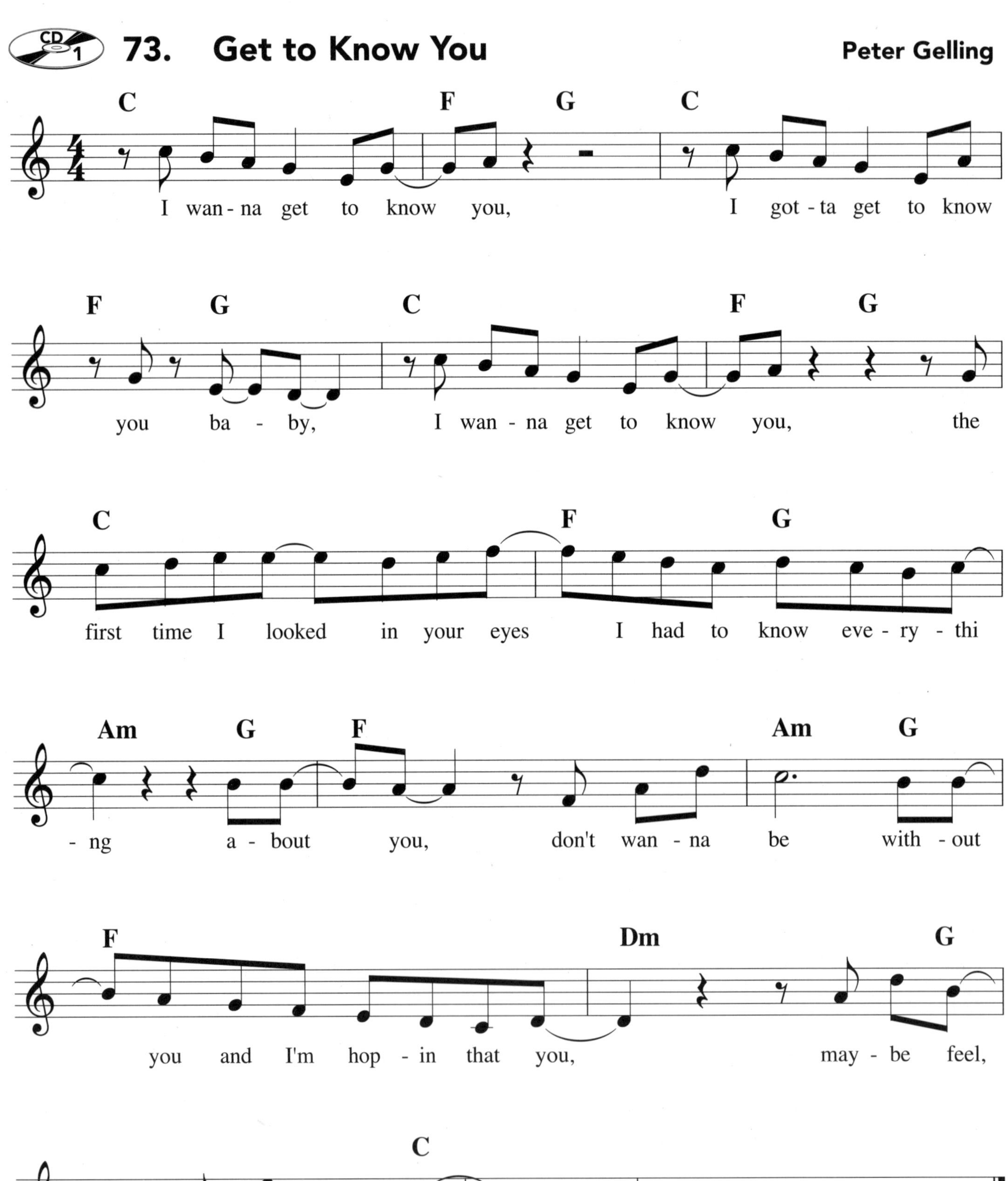

Get to Know You

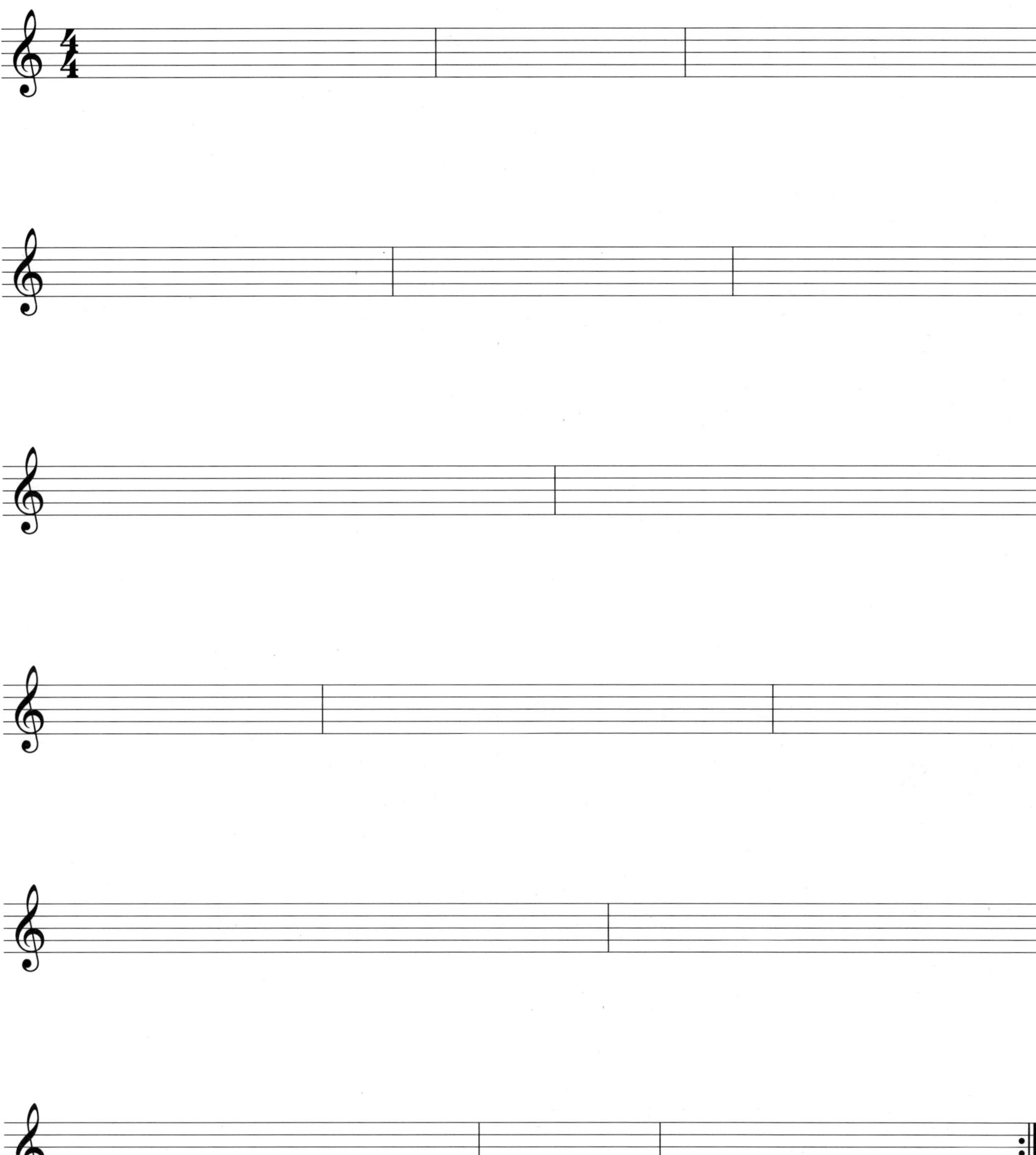

LESSON FIFTEEN

MINOR KEYS AND SCALES

So far, everything has been discussed in terms of **major** keys. However, there is another common type of key called a **minor key**. Minor keys are often described as having a "sadder" sound than major keys. Songs in a minor key use notes taken from a minor scale. There are several types of minor scales. The three most common are the **natural minor**, the **harmonic minor** and the **melodic minor**. Each one has its own distinctive pattern of tones and semitones. Here are the three **A minor** scales, along with the appropriate pattern of tones and semitones. The degrees of each scale as they would relate to the major scale are written under the note names.

74.0 A Natural Minor

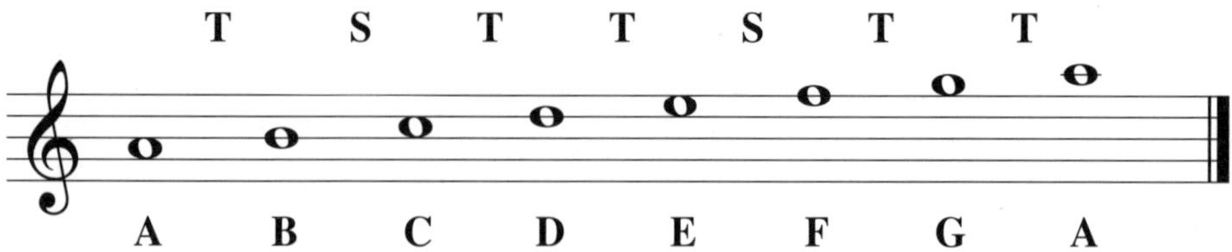

74.1 A Harmonic Minor

Notice the distance of 1½ tones (three semitones) between the 6th and 7th degrees of the harmonic minor scale. This scale is often described as having an 'Eastern' sound.

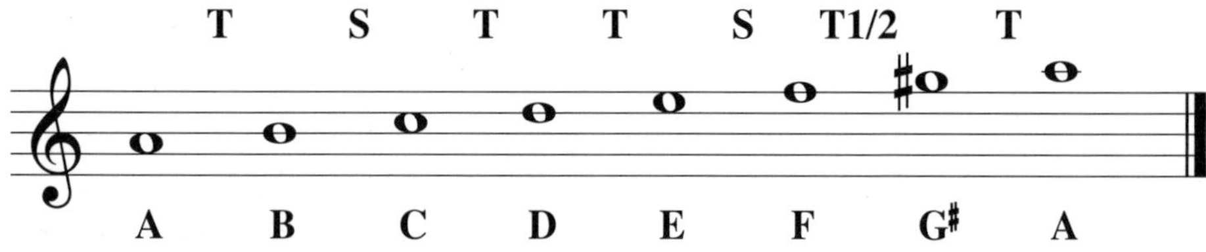

74.2 A Melodic minor

In Classical music the **6th** and **7th** notes of the melodic minor scale are sharpened when ascending and returned to natural when descending. However, in Jazz and other modern styles, the melodic minor descends the same way it ascends. An easy way to think of this scale is as a major scale with a flattened third degree.

RELATIVE MAJOR AND MINOR KEYS

For every key signature there are two keys, one major and one minor. Keys which share a key signature are called **relative keys.** The minor scale used to determine key signatures for minor keys is always the **natural minor scale**.

For **every** major scale there is a **relative minor scale** which is based upon the **6th note** (degree) of the major scale. This means that if you sing the C major scale starting and finishing on **A** (A B C D E F G A) instead of C, it becomes the **A natural minor scale.** Therefore, these two scales contain exactly the same notes. The only difference is that they start (and finish) on different notes. This chart shows the relative minor of all twelve major keys.

MAJOR KEY (I)	C	D♭	D	E♭	E	F	F♯	G♭	G	A♭	A	B♭	B
RELATIVE MINOR KEY (VI)	Am	B♭m	Bm	Cm	C♯m	Dm	D♯m	E♭m	Em	Fm	F♯m	Gm	G♯m

Both the major and the relative minor share the same key signature.

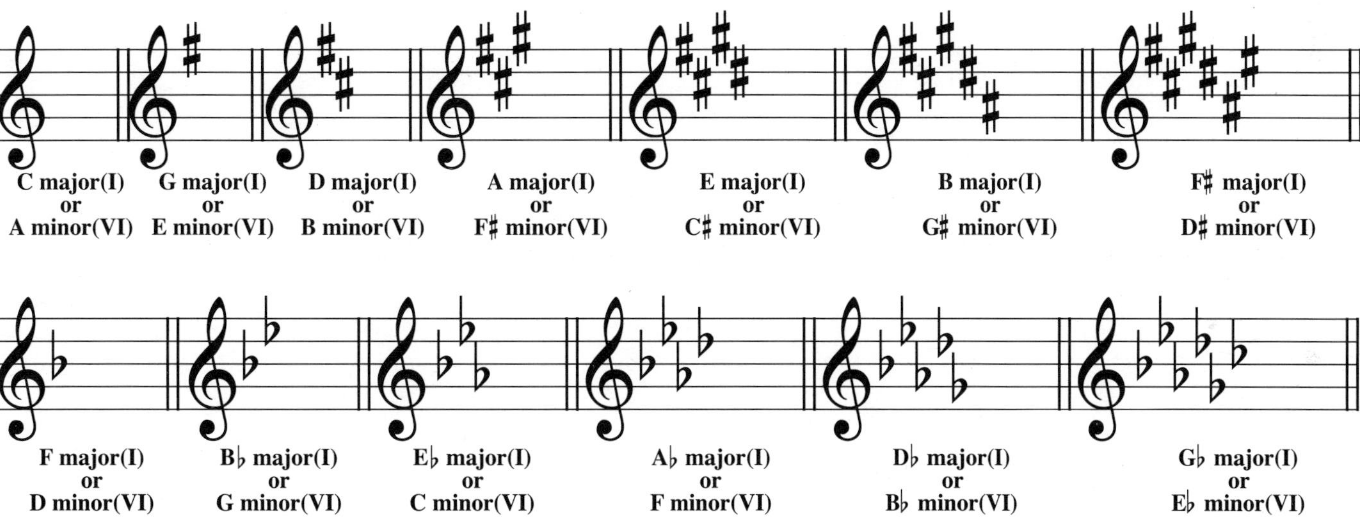

The sharpened **7th** note that occurs in the relative minor key is never included as part of the key signature. Because each major and relative minor share the same key signature, you will need to know how to distinguish between the two keys. For example, a song with the key signature of **F♯** thus

could indicate either the **key of G major** or its relative, **E minor**. The most accurate way of determining the key is to look through the melody for the sharpened **7th** note of the **E minor** scale (**D♯**). The presence of this note will indicate the minor key. If the **7th** note is present, but not sharpened, then the key is more likely to be the relative major (i.e. **D** natural notes would suggest the **key of G major**).

Another method is to look at the first and last chords of the progression. These chords usually (but not always) indicate the key of the piece. If the piece starts and/or finishes with **Em** chords then the key is more likely to be **E minor**.

 75. Scarborough Fair

Traditional

Scarborough Fair is an example of a song in a minor key. Because there is no key signature written at the start of the song, the song is in either C major or A minor. It is usually possible to tell which of two possible keys (major or relative minor) a song is in by looking at the note on which the melody ends, and often the starting note as well. This melody begins and ends on the note A, so this tells us that the key is A minor. Another indication is the chords which accompany the melody. The first and last chord symbol here is **Am** which indicates an A minor chord.

Notice the use of the note F sharp (**F♯**) in this song. When sharps or flats occur that are not part of the key signature, they are called **accidentals**. An accidental is a temporary alteration to the pitch of a note and is cancelled by a bar line. Notice also the use of **ties**.

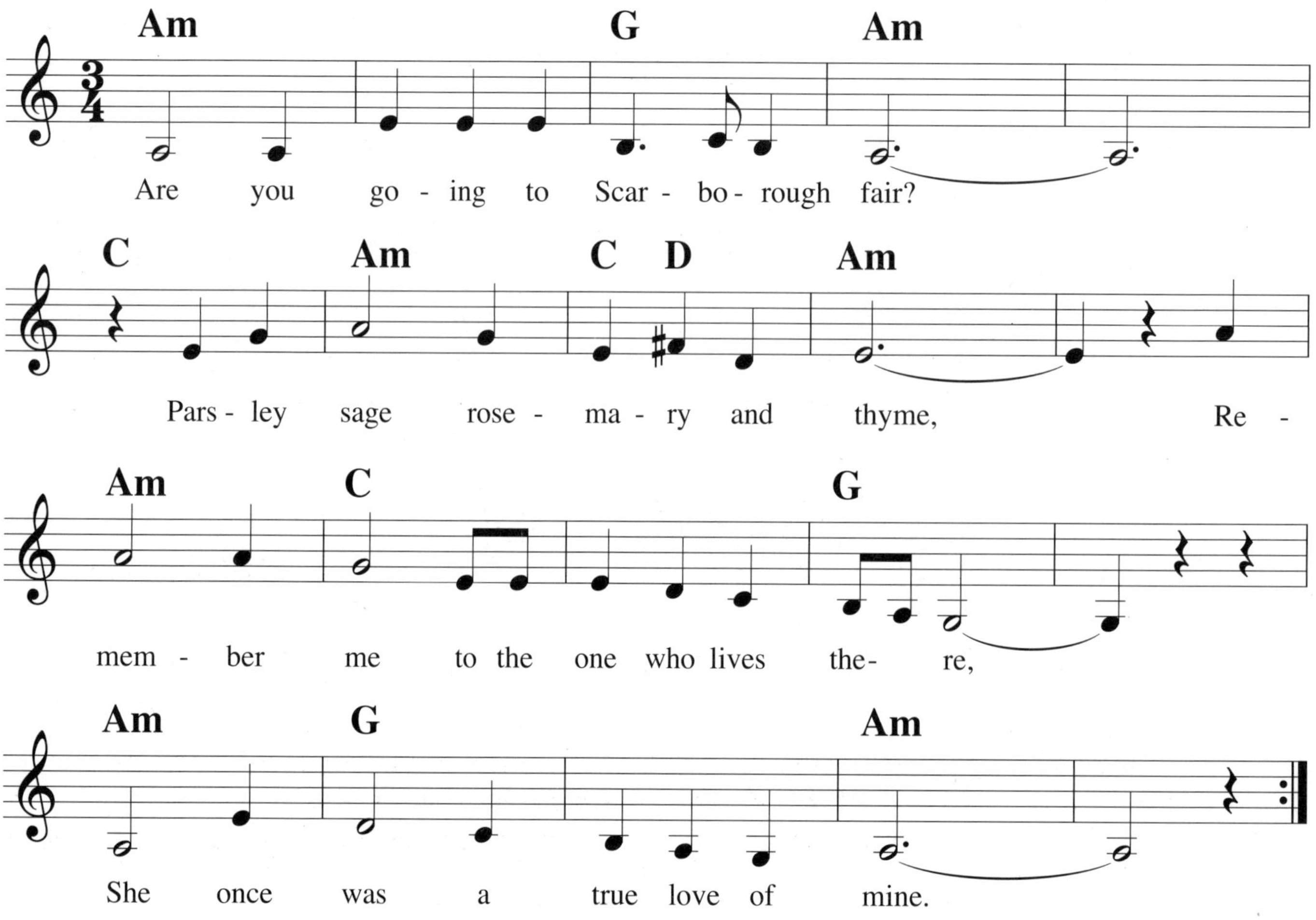

Am G Am
Are you go - ing to Scar - bo - rough fair?

C Am C D Am
Pars - ley sage rose - ma - ry and thyme, Re -

Am C G
mem - ber me to the one who lives the- re,

Am G Am
She once was a true love of mine.

2. "Tell her to make me a cambric shirt,"
Parsley, sage, rosemary, and thyme;
"Without any seam or needlework,
For once she was a true love of mine."

3. "Tell her to wash it in yonder well,"
Parsley, sage, rosemary and thyme;
"Where never spring water nor rain ever fell,
For once she was a true love of mine."

4. "Now he has asked me questions three,"
Parsley, sage, rosemary and thyme;
"I hope he will answer as many for me,
For once he was a true love of mine."

5. "Tell him to find me an acre of land,"
Parsley, sage, rosemary and thyme;
"Betwixt the salt water and the sea sand,
For once he was a true love of mine."

 76. Scarborough Fair (Male Vocalist)

This version is in the key of **C minor**, as can be seen from the key signature (3 flats). This key was chosen because it suited our male vocalist. As mentioned earlier, everybody has a different voice range, so some people will prefer to sing any given song in one key, while others will prefer a different key. The key chosen depends on the range of notes used in that particular melody and whether they feel comfortable for the singer. Often (in a choir, for example) many different singers, both male and female will sing a song in the same key in unison, or in harmony in different octaves. The vocal exercises in this book are sung by male and female voices in the same key, but in different octaves. However, there are times when changing the octave moves the melody too far up or down for an individual's range. In this situation, finding a new key between the two octaves is usually the solution.

Cm B♭ Cm

Are you go- ing to Scar- bo- rough fair?

E♭ Cm E♭ F Cm

Pars - ley sage rose - ma - ry and thyme, Re -

Cm E♭ B♭

mem - ber me to the one who lives the- re,

Cm B♭ Cm

She once was a true love of mine.

LESSON SIXTEEN

THE LEAD-IN

Sometimes a song does not begin on the first beat of a bar. Any notes which come before the first full bar are called **lead-in** or **pick-up notes**. When lead-in notes are used, the last bar is also incomplete. The notes in the lead-in and the notes in the last bar add up to one full bar. The song **Greensleeves** on the facing page contains one lead-in note.

When lead-in notes are used, it means that the melody begins before the accompaniment. This means you will probably need a reference pitch for your starting note in order to be sure you are singing the correct pitch. Before you begin the song, get somebody to play first the note or chord of the key, and then the starting note on an instrument. Hum the starting note to yourself for a few seconds until you are confident of the note and then begin counting the song in. On the CD we do this for you, as in this introduction to **Greensleeves**. The chord is an **E minor** chord because the song has been recorded in the key of E minor and the lead-in note is also an **E** note.

77.

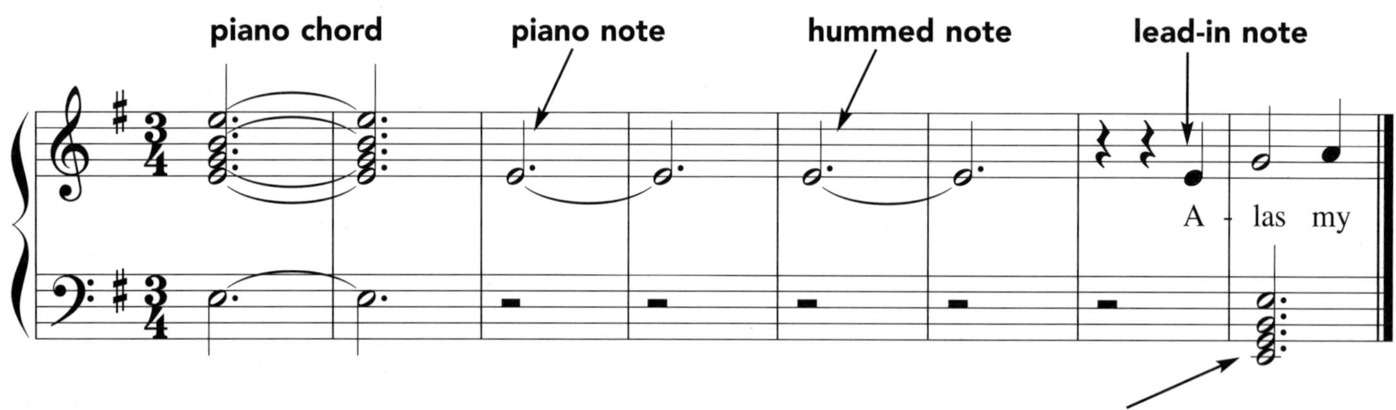

FIRST AND SECOND ENDINGS

Greensleeves contains **first and second endings**. The **first** time you sing through the verse, sing the **first ending** (1.), then go back to the beginning. The **second** time you sing through the verse, sing the **second ending** (2.) instead of the first.

78. Greensleeves

Traditional

This arrangement of the traditional English folk song is in the key of **E minor**, which is the relative minor of G major. It is in $\frac{3}{4}$ time and begins with a lead-in note. Notice the **F♯** in the key signature, which reminds you to treat all F notes as F♯. Notice also the frequent use of extra **accidental** sharps in this song. Both our male vocalist and our female vocalist found E minor a comfortable key for singing this song. Once again, the difference is that they are singing the same notes in different octaves.

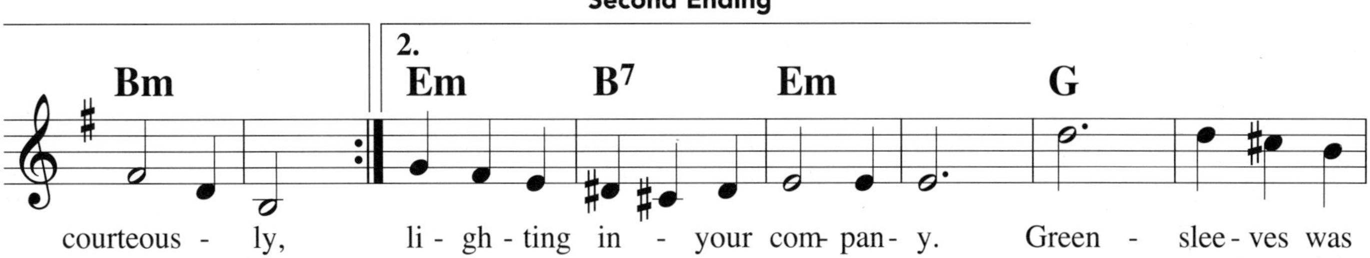

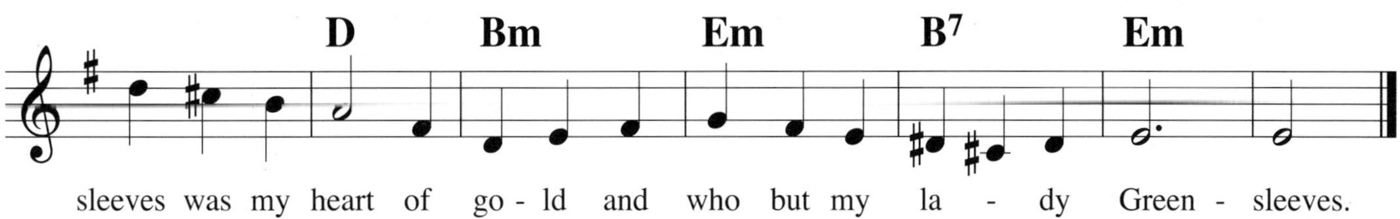

2. I have been ready at your hand
To grant whatever you would crave,
I have both wagered life and land,
Your love and good will for to have.

3. I bought thee petticoats of the best,
The cloth so fine as it might be,
I gave thee jewels for the chest,
And all this cost I spent on thee.

4. Well, I will pray to God on high,
That thou my constancy may'st see,
For I am still thy lover true;
Come once again and love me.

This Rock song contains three lead-in notes. The melody contains both ties and eighth rests. Listen to the CD while watching the music. This will help you get a feel for the rhythms and the pitches of the notes.

79. Up on Stage

Peter Gelling

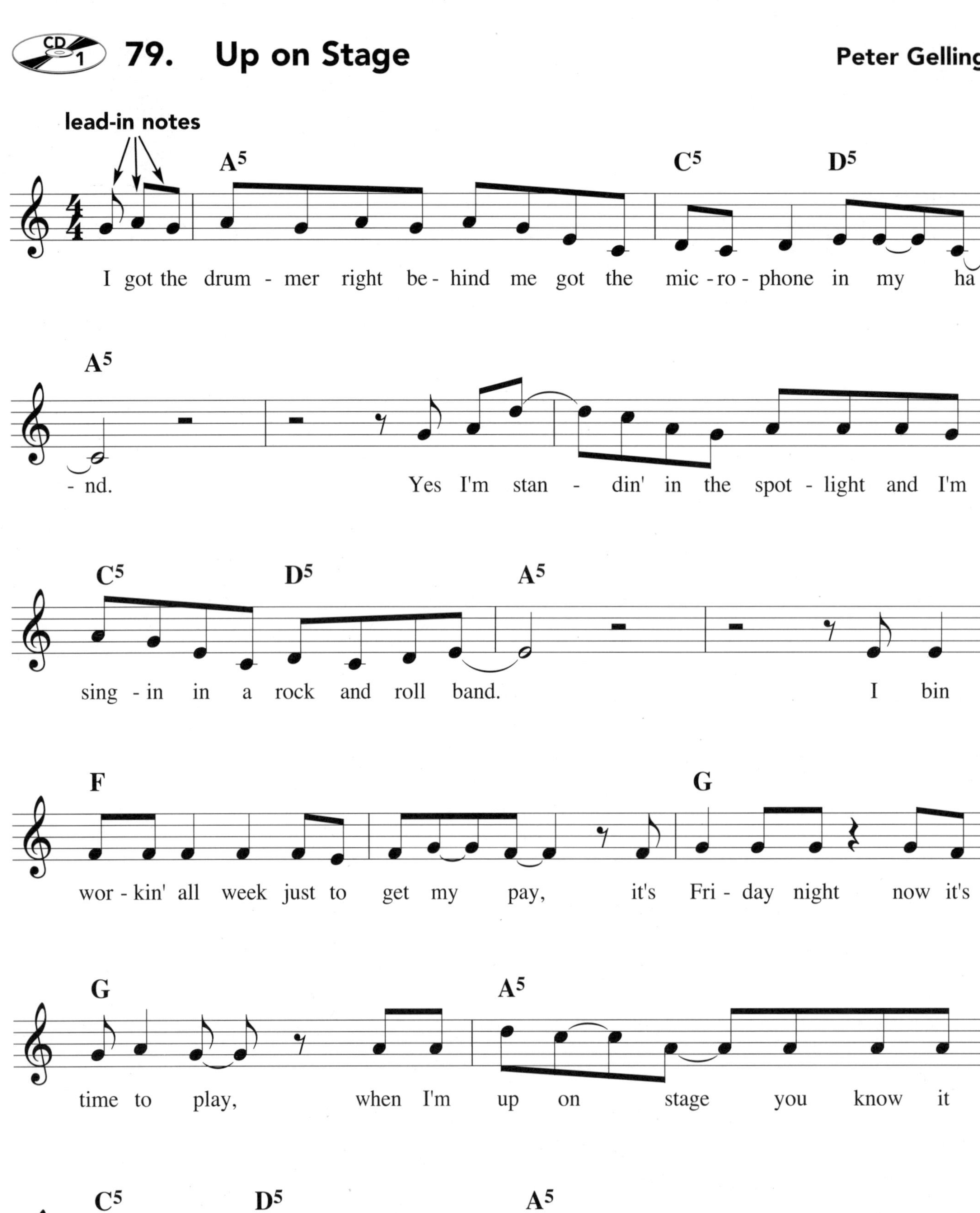

Section 2

LESSON SEVENTEEN

DEVELOPING YOUR SENSE OF PITCH

One of the most essential elements of singing is the ability to hear and sing pitches accurately. The best way to develop this ability is train your ear by studying **intervals.** An interval is the distance between two musical notes. **All melodies and harmonies are made up of a series of intervals**. Intervals are calculated by counting the number of letter names (**A B C D E F G A**) between and including the notes being measured. Within an octave, intervals are: **Unison** (two notes of the same pitch played or sung together or consecutively), **2nd**, **3rd**, **4th**, **5th**, **6th**, **7th** and **Octave** (two notes an octave apart). Thus **A** to **B** is a **2nd** interval, as is B to C, C to D etc. **A** to **C** is a **3rd** interval, **A** to **D** is a **4th**, **A** to **E** is a **5th**, **A** to **F** is a **6th**, **A** to **G** is a **7th** and **A** to the next **A** is an **octave**.

Intervals may be **melodic** (two notes played consecutively) or **harmonic** (two notes played at the same time). Hence two people singing at the same time are said to be singing in harmony.

INTERVAL QUALITIES

Different intervals may have different qualities.

Quality	***Can be applied to the Intervals:***
Perfect	Unisons, 4ths, 5ths and Octaves
Major	2nds, 3rds, 6ths and 7ths
Minor	2nds, 3rds, 6ths and 7ths
Augmented	All intervals
Diminished	All intervals

Interval qualities can be best explained with the aid of a chromatic scale. If you look at the one below, it is easy to see that since **intervals are measured in semitones**, they may begin or end on a sharp or flat rather than a natural note.

A A♯/B♭ B C C♯/D♭ D D♯/E♭ E F F♯/G♭ G G♯/A♭ A

Perfect intervals are **4ths**, **5ths** and **octaves**. If you **widen** a perfect interval by a semitone it becomes **augmented** (added to). E.g. if you add a semitone to the perfect 4th interval **C** to **F**, it becomes the **augmented 4th interval C** to **F♯**. Notice that the letter name remains the same – it is not referred to as C to G♭.

If you **narrow** a perfect interval by a semitone it becomes **diminished** (lessened). E.g. if you lessen the perfect 5th interval **D** to **A** by a semitone, it becomes the **diminished 5th interval D to A♭**. Again, the letter name remains the same–it is not referred to as D to G♯.

Major intervals become minor if narrowed by a semitone and **minor** intervals become major if widened by a semitone. A **diminished** interval can be created by narrowing a perfect or minor interval by a semitone. An **augmented** interval can be created by widening a perfect or major interval by a semitone.

INTERVAL DISTANCES

In summary, here is a list of all common intervals in an octave, measured in semitones. Each new interval is one semitone further apart than the previous one. Notice that the interval of an octave is exactly twelve semitones. This is because there are twelve different notes in the chromatic scale. Notice also that the interval which has a distance of six semitones can be called either an augmented 4th or a diminished 5th. This interval is also often called a **tritone** (6 semitones = 3 tones).

Minor 2nd - One semitone
Major 2nd - Two semitones
Minor 3rd - Three semitones
Major 3rd - Four semitones
Perfect 4th - Five semitones
Augmented 4th or Diminished 5th - Six semitones
Perfect 5th - Seven semitones
Minor 6th - Eight semitones
Major 6th - Nine semitones
Minor 7th - Ten semitones
Major 7th - Eleven semitones
Perfect Octave - Twelve semitones

Here are are the above intervals ascending within one octave, starting and ending on the note **C**.

80.

IDENTIFYING INTERVALS BY EAR

Since **all melodies are made up of a series of intervals**, you need to be able to identify intervals by ear and then reproduce them at will with your voice. If you can sing something accurately, it means you are hearing it accurately. Here are some ways of improving your ability to identify and reproduce intervals. The first two exercises both use a minor 3rd, but it is essential to go through these processes with **all** intervals.

Intervals Exercise 1.

Choose an interval you wish to work on (e.g. minor 3rds). Play any starting note (e.g. C) on a keyboard (or guitar) and sing it. Then sing the name of the note which is a minor 3rd up from that note (E♭). Hold the note with your voice while you test its accuracy on the keyboard. Then choose another starting note and repeat the process. Keep doing this until you are accurate every time. The next step is to sing the interval (in this case a minor 3rd) downwards from your starting note. Again, do this repeatedly until you are accurate every time.

81.

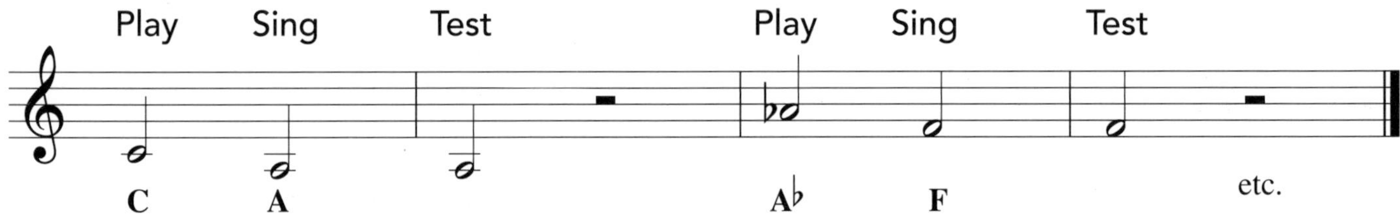

Intervals Exercise 2.

Sing the same interval consecutively upwards and then downwards several times. E.g. start on C and sing a minor 3rd up from it (E♭). Then sing a minor 3rd up from E♭ (G♭). Then another minor third up from G♭ (B♭♭ – which is enharmonically the same as A). Then up another minor 3rd (C an octave higher than the starting note). Once you can do this, reverse the process (start on C and sing a minor 3rd down to A, then another minor 3rd down and then another, etc.).

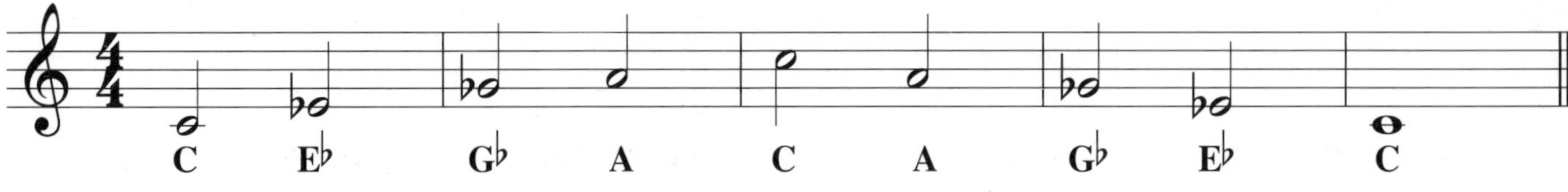

Intervals Exercise 3.

Play and sing a starting note (e.g. C) and then think of it as the first degree of the chromatic scale – sing "one". Now sing the flattened second degree of the scale – sing 'flat two'. This note is a minor 2nd up from your C note (a D♭ note). Then sing the C again ('one'). Then sing the second degree of the scale (a D note - sing 'two'). Next, sing your C Note again ('one'). Continue in this manner all the way up the chromatic scale until you reach C an octave above. The entire sequence goes: 1, ♭2, 1, 2, 1, ♭3, 1, 3, 1, 4, 1, ♭5, 1, 5, 1, ♭6, 1, 6, 1, ♭7, 1, 7, 1, 8, 1. As with the previous exercises, once you can do this accurately (check your pitches on keyboard), reverse the process and sing downwards from the top of the scale, working your way down the chromatic scale again. The downward sequence goes 1(8), 7, 1, ♭7, 1, 6, 1, ♭6, 1, 5, 1,♭ 5, 1, 4, 1, 3, 1, ♭3, 1, 2, 1, ♭2, 1, 1, 1(8).

Intervals Exercise 4.

As well as hearing intervals melodically (one note at a time), it is important to be able to hear them harmonically (two notes played together). A good way to develop this is to have a friend play random harmonic intervals on either guitar or keyboard while you identify them. Keep your back to the instrument while you do this, so that you cannot identify the intervals by sight.

It is important to work at these things regularly until they become easy. Do not get frustrated if you cannot hear intervals accurately at first. Most people have trouble with this. If you work at it for several months, you will see a dramatic improvement in your musical hearing, and will be able to improvise much more freely as well as being able to work out harmonies off CDs more easily.

As mentioned at the start of this lesson, intervals can be melodic or harmonic. Here are some examples of 3rd intervals written melodically in repetition on various pitches (a sequence) and harmonically (a melody harmonised in 3rds).

✏ Write the following intervals above each note.

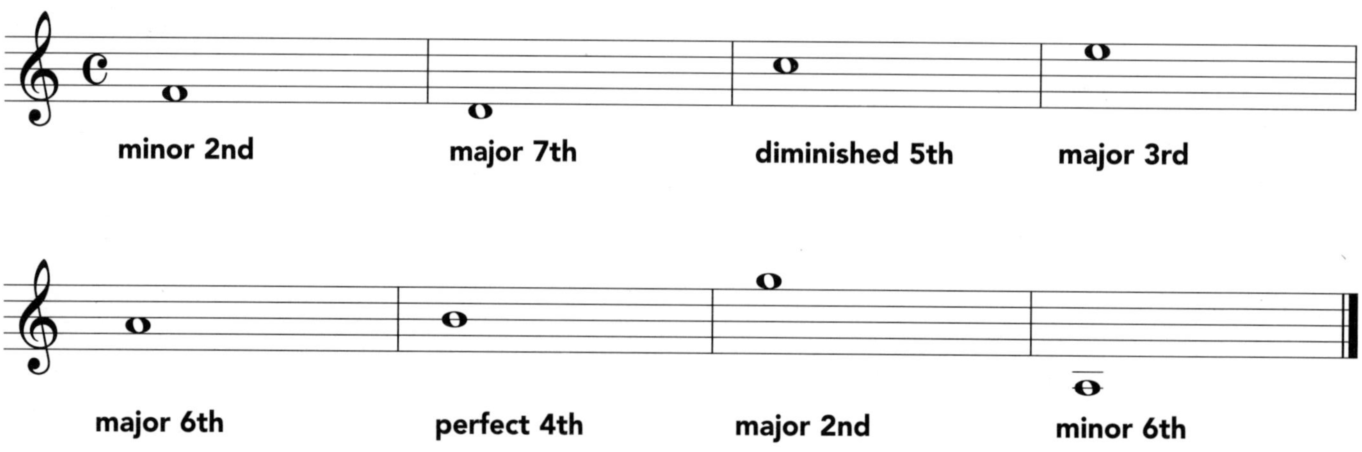

✏ Write the correct name below each interval.

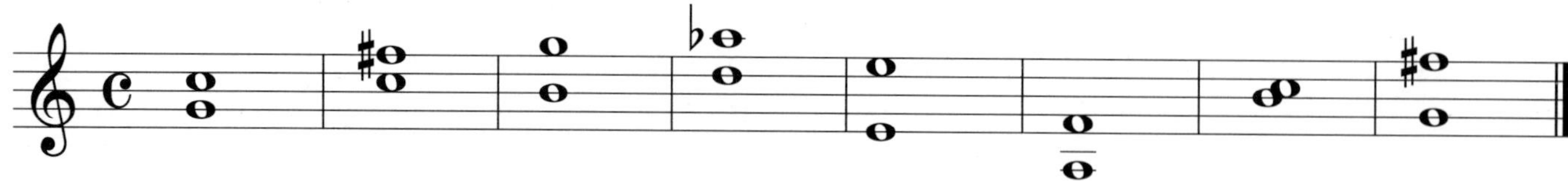

✏ Here are some examples of harmonic intervals (two notes played together). Write the name of each interval above or below the notation and and then sing them as melodic intervals. Make sure you are familiar with the sound of each interval.

✏ For more practice with intervals, write and sing the intervals indicated above each of these notes.

LESSON EIGHTEEN

ENHARMONIC NOTES

The 'in between' notes in the chromatic scale can be described as either sharps or flats. Because of the way scales and chords are constructed, flats are used more often than sharps. Here once again is the C chromatic scale with scale degrees written under the notes. The scales degrees written here relate to the natural notes and the flat notes. The sharps and flats are **enharmonic equivalents**, which means they are the same pitch (e.g **C♯** =**D♭** and **F♯** =**G♭**).

C	C♯/D♭	D	D♯/E♭	E	F	F♯/G♭	G	G♯/A♭	A	A♯/B♭	B	C
1	♭2	2	♭3	3	4	♭5	5	♭6	6	♭7	7	1

ACCIDENTALS

Many melodies use notes from outside the scale, particularly in styles such as Rock, Funk, Blues and Jazz. These 'outside notes' are called **accidentals**. An accidental is a temporary alteration to a note or notes from a particular key.

Therefore, if you have a piece of music in the key of C which contains notes which are not in the C major scale, you can relate these notes to the **C chromatic scale**.

CD 1 82.0 Key of C

On the recording, this melody is played by a guitar. Sing along with it until you can match the pitches and then sing it from memory without the CD. Singing melodies containing accidentals takes a bit of practice, But it is a great way to improve your sense of pitch.

The next two examples are the same melody transposed to the keys of F and G. Once again, you should transpose this melody to all the other keys in the key cycle. It is worth learning to sing the chromatic scale starting on any note of the key cycle. Once you can do this, it will be easier to learn more complex melodies in any key and also easier to transpose any melodies from one key to another to suit your voice.

CD 1 82.1 Key of F

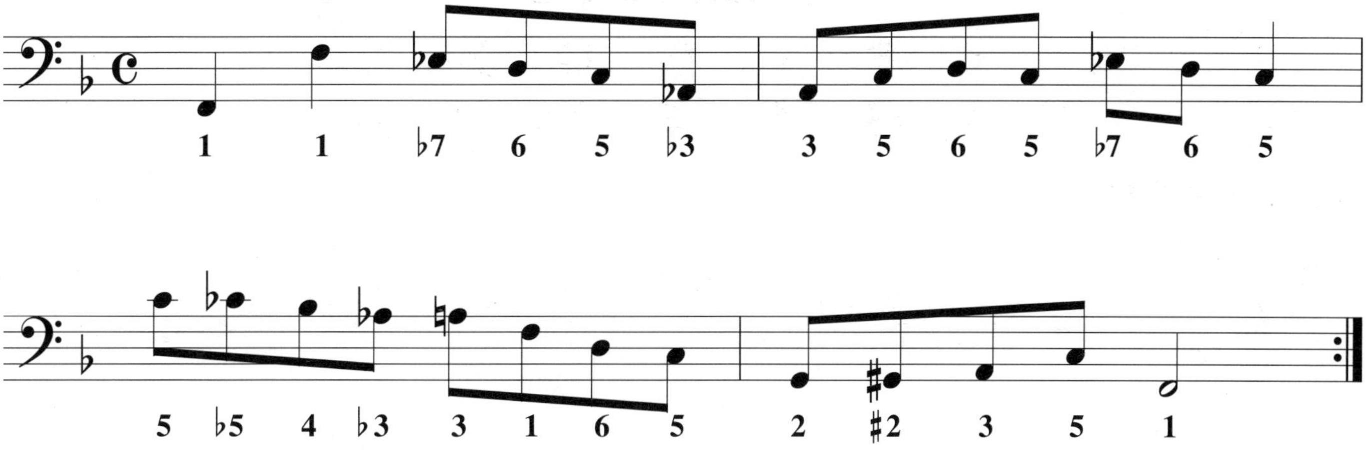

1 1 ♭7 6 5 ♭3 3 5 6 5 ♭7 6 5

5 ♭5 4 ♭3 3 1 6 5 2 ♯2 3 5 1

CD 1 82.2 Key of G

1 1 ♭7 6 5 ♭3 3 5 6 5 ♭7 6 5

5 ♭5 4 ♭3 3 1 6 5 2 ♯2 3 5 1

CD 1 82.3

Here is another melody in the key of C. Analyze its degrees and then transpose it to all twelve keys.

THE BLUES SCALE

One of the most common scales used in modern popular music is the **Blues scale**. The notes and degrees of the **C** Blues scale are written below along with a demonstration of the sound. Listen to the CD and sing along with it. You may recognise the sound.

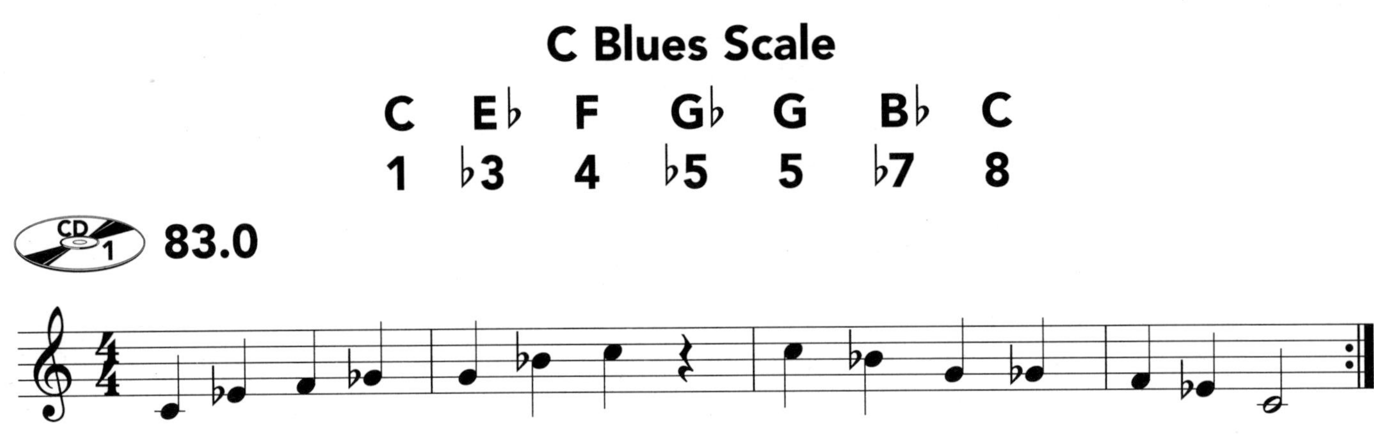

SINGING SCALE DEGREES

A good way to become familiar with the notes and sound of any new scale is to sing the scale degrees along with the pitches. Sing the degrees of this C Blues scale along with the CD and then practice it until you can confidently sing the scale without listening to the CD first.

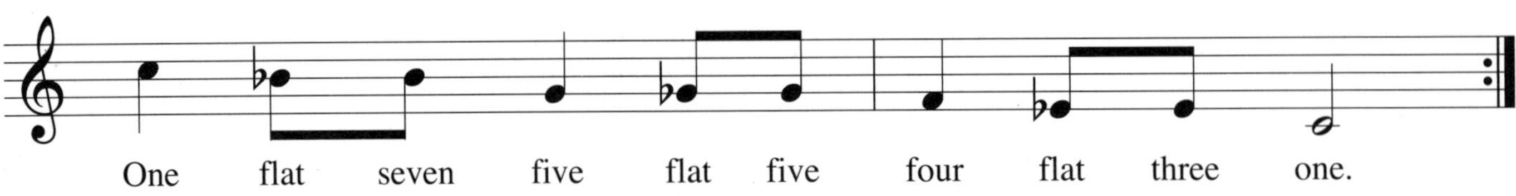

Another useful technique for becoming familiar with a new scale is to sing from the first note of the scale to every other note of the scale, returning to the first degree between each pitch.

CD 1 83.2

One flat three one four one flat five one five

one flat seven one one one one.

One flat seven one five one flat five one four

one flat three one one one.

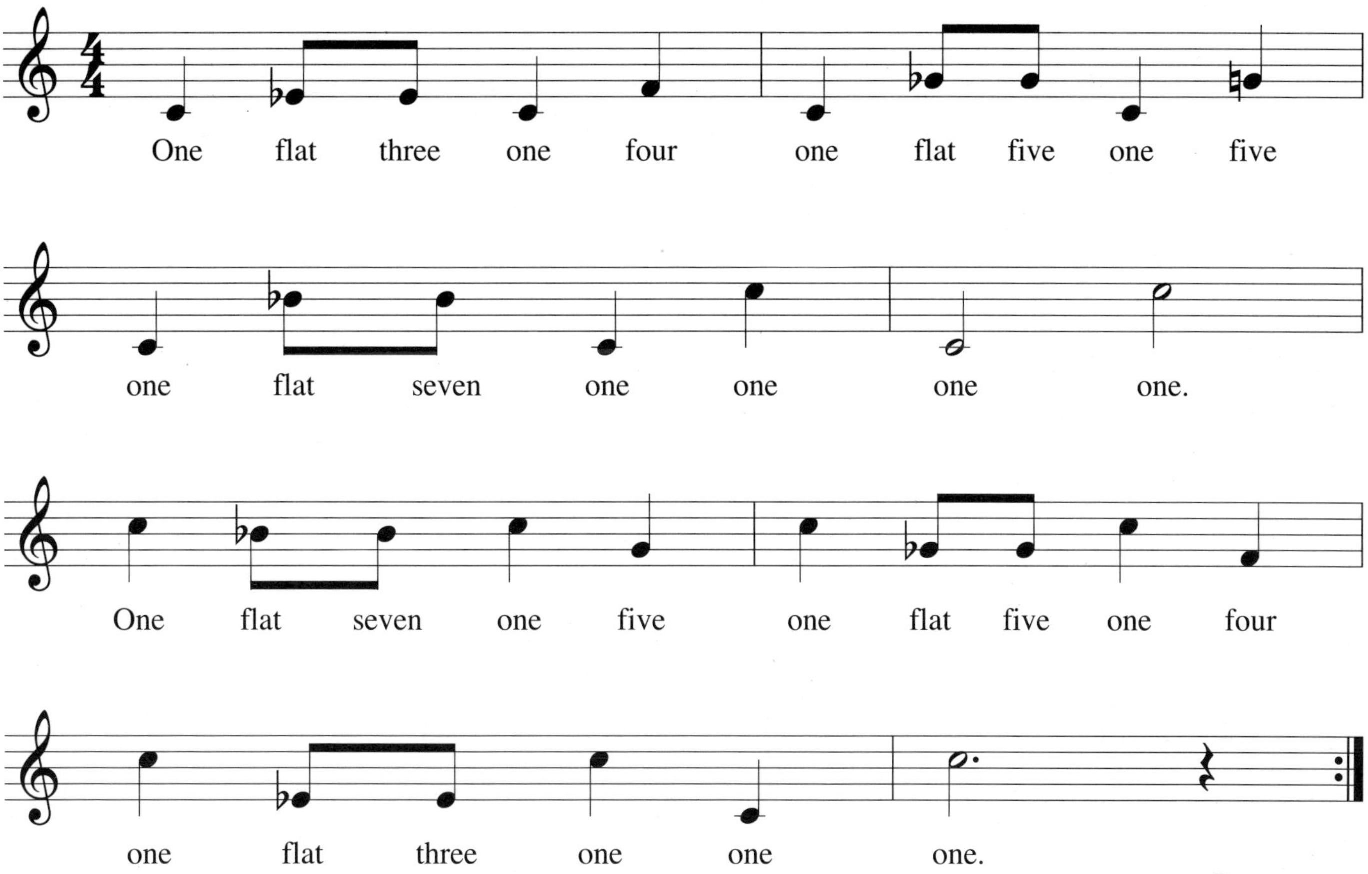

LESSON NINETEEN

THE TRIPLET

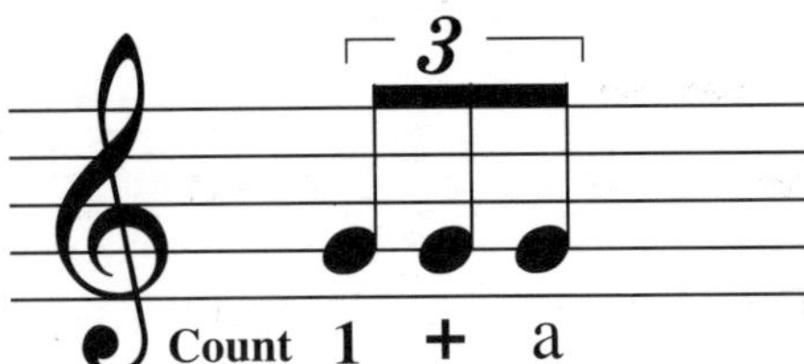

A **triplet** is a group of **three** evenly spaced notes sung within one beat. **Eighth note triplets** are indicated by three eighth notes grouped together by a bracket (or a curved line) and the numeral ***3***. The eighth note triplets receive one third of a beat each. Triplets are easy to understand once you have heard them played. Listen to this example to hear the effect of triplets.

CD 1 84.0

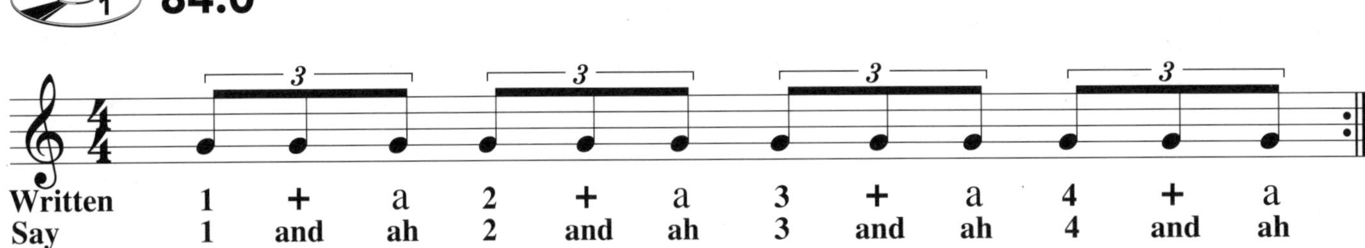

Triplets sound great when combined with the notes of the Blues scale. Notice in this example that the note **F♯** is used instead of **G♭**. This can be done because the two notes are enharmonically the same. The degree is still the flattened fifth (**♭5**).

CD 1 84.1

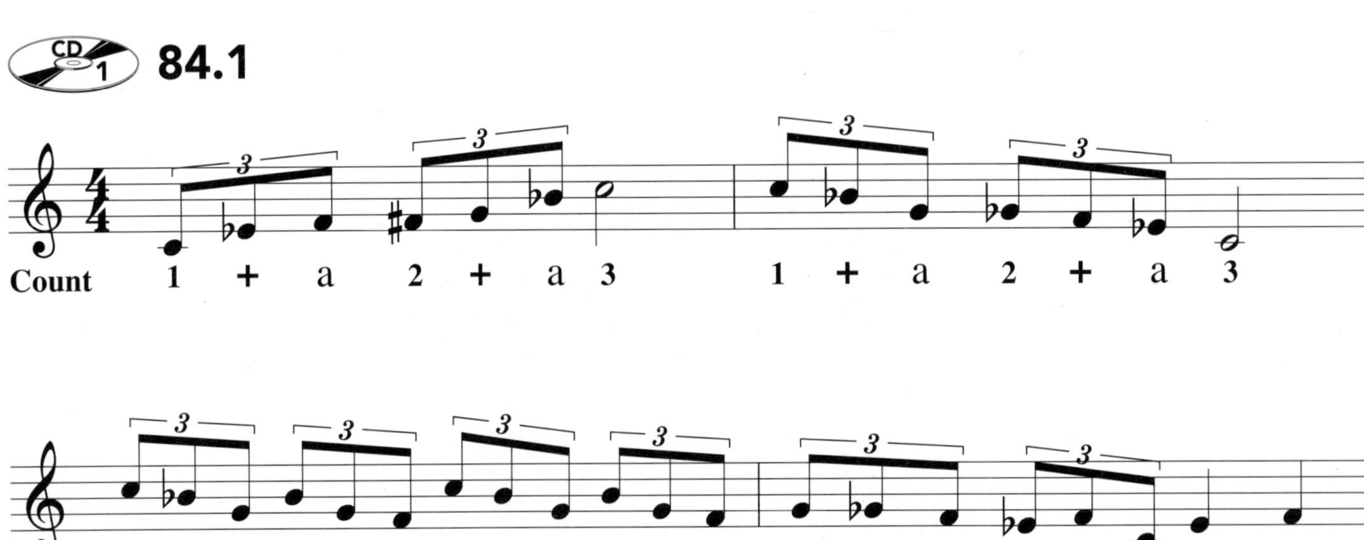

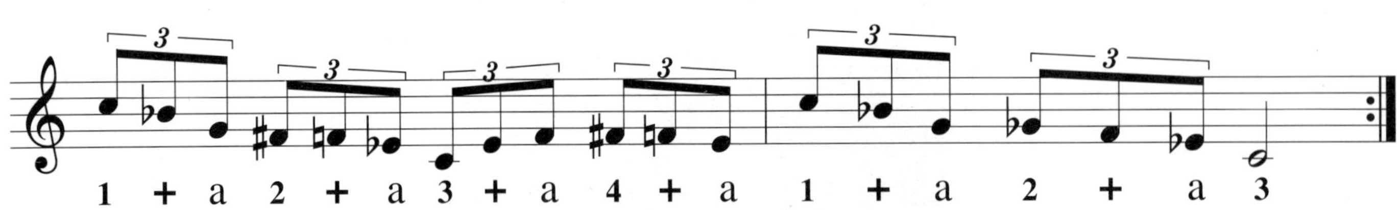

85. Amazing Grace

This traditional Gospel song contains triplets in bars 1, 5, 9 and 13. It is in $\frac{3}{4}$ time and in the key of **C** major. First clap the rhythm while counting and tapping your feet on the beat, then sing along with the CD. Remember to continue tapping your foot as you sing.

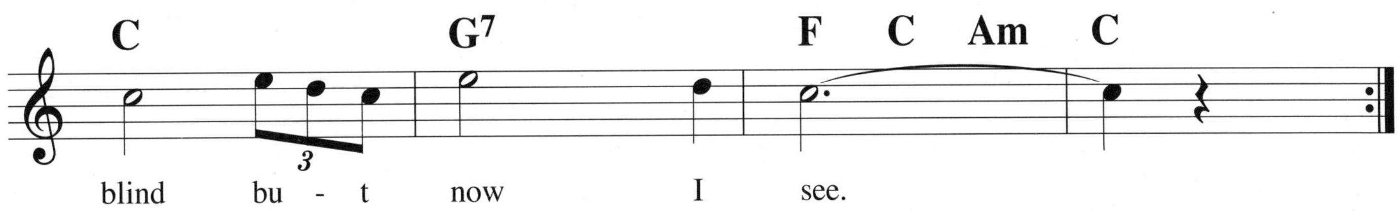

2. 'Twas grace that taught my heart to fear,
   And grace my fears relieved.
   How precious did the grace appear,
   The hour I first believed.

3. Thro' many dangers, toils and snares,
   I have already come.
   'Tis grace hath bro't me safe thus far,
   And grace will lead me home.

SWING RHYTHMS

A **swing rhythm** can be created by playing or singing only the first and third notes of a triplet. There are several ways of writing swing rhythms. First, using the syllable **ba.** Sing this example which contains eighth note triplets.

86.0

86.1

In this variation has the first and second notes of the triplet group are tied. This creates a swing feel.

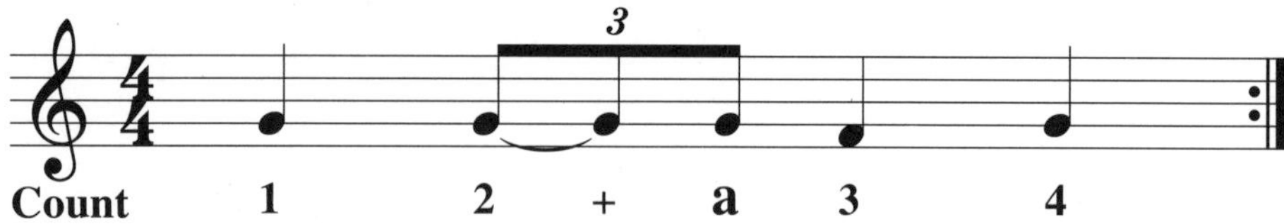

86.2

The two eighth note tied together in Example 86.1 can be replaced by a quarter note.

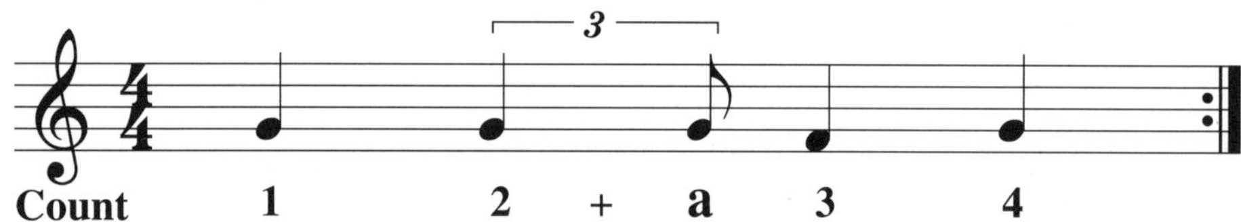

To simplify notation, it is common to replace the with , and to write at the start of the piece = .

86.3

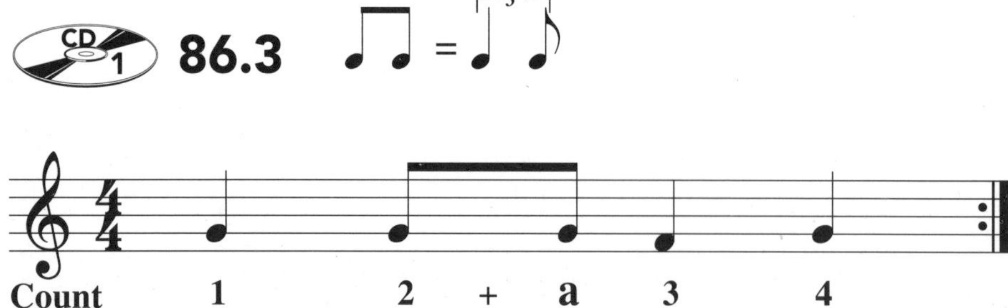

The previous three examples sound exactly the same. They are simply different ways of notating the same melody.

87. St James Infirmary

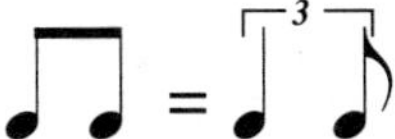

Traditional

This song was made famous by Louis Armstrong. It is played and sung with a swing feel. This means that all the eighth notes in the song are swung. Many songs in various styles have a swing feel. They are particularly common in Blues and Jazz as well as Gospel, Rock and Country music.

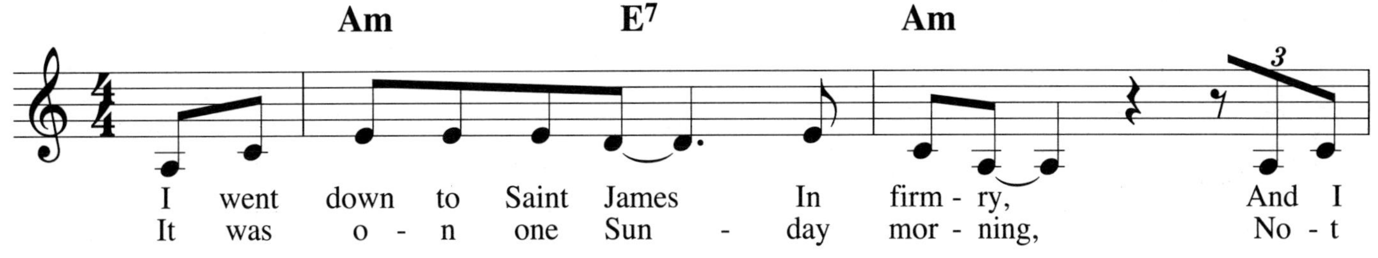

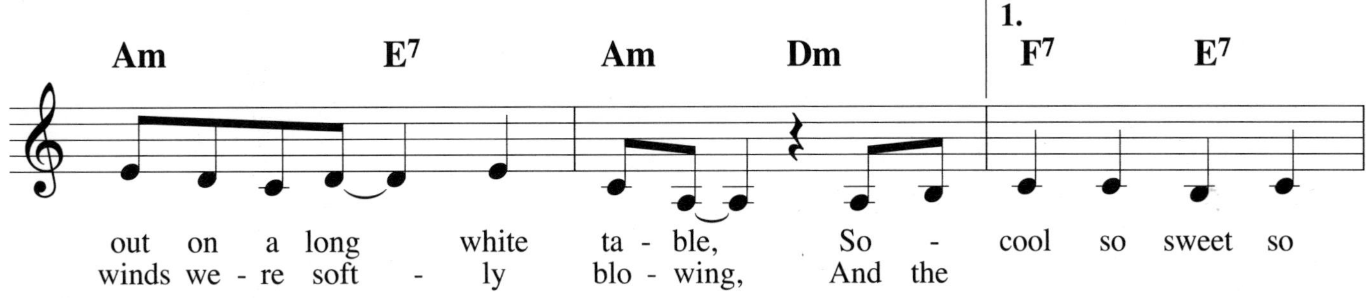

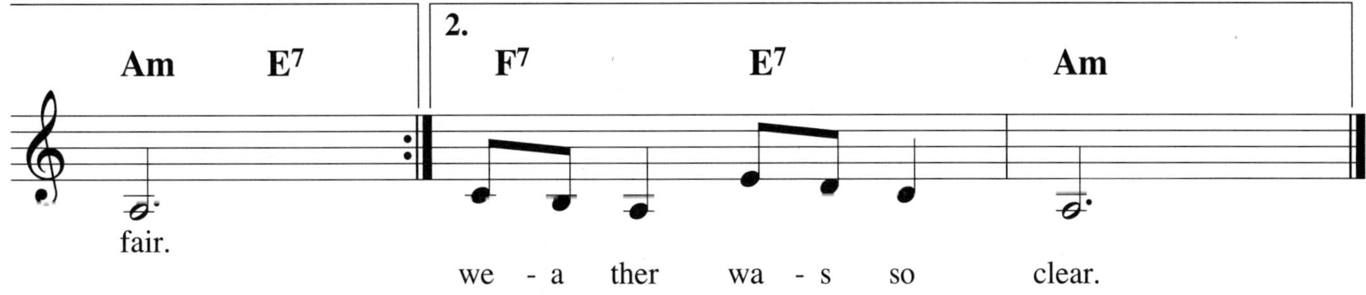

88. St James Infirmary (Version 2)

The second version of this song on the recording is in the key of E minor. Once again, there are slight differences in phrasing between the two versions. Sing along with the version that feels most comfortable for your vocal range.

The following example contains some common rhythms using triplets and swing eighth notes. As with previous rhythm exercises, clap the rhythms while counting and tapping your foot on the beat. Then sing the rhythms along with the CD using the syllable **ba** and then sing them from memory while tapping your foot on each beat.

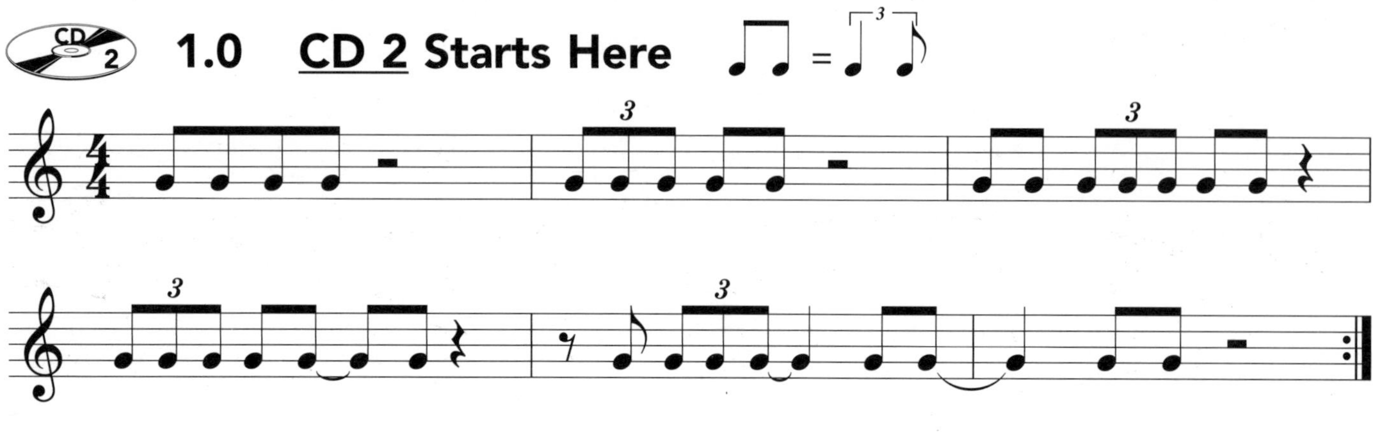

Now try these phrases which apply the above rhythms to the **C** Blues scale. On the recording, the syllable **ba** is used, but try these phrases with other syllables as well.

CALL + RESPONSE

Call and response is sometimes described as a **question and answer** style. It is found in almost all styles of music and originally comes from African music, and the Blues. In Gospel music, the 'call' is made by the preacher and the 'response' is made by the congregation. The simplest form of call and response is direct imitation. The following example gives you an opportunity to practice responding to a phrase by ear. It is not notated, but on the recording a space is left after each phrase so you can respond to what you have just heard.

CD 2 — 2. Call and Response

LESSON TWENTY

12 BAR BLUES

12 Bar Blues is a sequence of chords which repeats every twelve bars. There are hundreds of well known songs based on this chord progression, i.e., they contain basically the same chords in the same order. 12 bar Blues is commonly used in Rock music and is the basis of Blues music. There have been many hit songs by artists such as Chuck Berry, The Beatles, Elvis Presley, Little Richard, The Beach Boys, B.B King, Jimi Hendrix, Led Zeppelin, AC/DC, Van Halen, Joe Satriani, Gary Moore, Robert Cray, Stevie Ray Vaughan and Eric Clapton which are based on this progression. Here are some well known songs which are based on the 12 bar Blues progression.

Original Batman TV Theme
Hound Dog - Elvis Presley
Rock Around the Clock - Bill Haley
Good Golly Miss Molly - Little Richard
Blue Suede Shoes - Elvis Presley
Rock In Peace - ACDC
Sweet Home Chicago - Blues Brothers
Johnny B Goode - Chuck Berry
Roll Over Beethoven - Chuck Berry
Surfin' USA - The Beach Boys
Killing Floor - Jimi Hendrix
Give Me One Reason - Tracy Chapman
Pride and Joy - Stevie Ray Vaughan
Why Didn't You Call Me? - Macy Gray

CD 2 3. 12 Bar Blues in C

Listen to this typical 12 bar Blues. The progression is in the key of C.The symbol ⁒ which appears above some of the bars is a bar repeat sign. It indicates that this bar is identical to the previous one. The last two bars of the progression are called the **turnaround**, an ending which leads to the next verse.

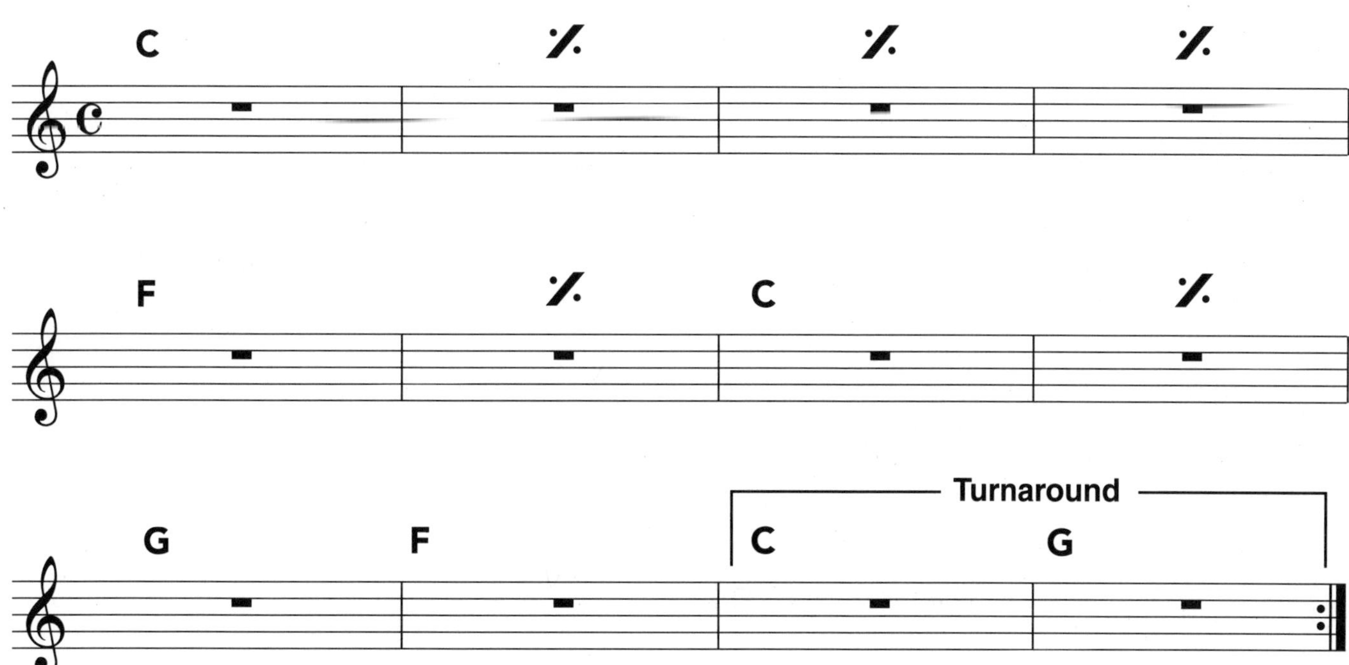

BLUES SINGING

Although Blues is based on African American music, it has influenced almost every style of music since the beginning of the 20th century. Call and Response is central to the blues. Listen to the following song and notice how the guitar plays a response after each vocal phrase. Blues is often sung with a rougher, more 'gutsy' sound than most other styles. This often involves growling sounds made from the throat, along with various slides and bends between notes. Be careful when using these sounds and keep the throat relaxed, otherwise you may risk vocal damage if you do it regularly. If you intend to sing a lot of Blues, it is recommended that you consult a singing teacher.

CD 2 **4. Come Back Darlin'** **Peter Gelling**

Many people think of the Blues as 'sad', but in reality it expresses every mood and emotion in life. The Blues is essentially storytelling music. The following song tells a story of the Blues itself. Listen to the recording and notice how the vocalist interacts with the musicians during the 12 bar introduction, setting up the mood of the song before the first verse. This call and response continues throughout the song. Notice also how the vocalist uses the basic melody as a framework and sings variations on it. This kind of improvisation is common in Blues and is also central to Jazz. There are more verses on the recording. Write out the lyrics and then sing along with the recording. This is a great way to pick up new influences and techniques. The more you do it, the easier it gets.

5. If it Wasn't for the Blues

Peter Gelling

Learning any musical style well involves lots of listening. To get a good feel for the blues style, listen to singers like BB King, Bobby Bland, John Lee Hooker, Lightnin' Hopkins, Bessie Smith and Koko Taylor. There are many other great Blues singers as well.

For recordings by Peter Gelling, visit: **www.bentnotes.com**

LESSON TWENTY ONE

SIXTEENTH NOTES

This is a **sixteenth note**.
It lasts for **one quarter** of a beat.
There are **four** sixteenth notes in one beat.
There are **16** sixteenth notes in one bar of $\frac{4}{4}$ time.

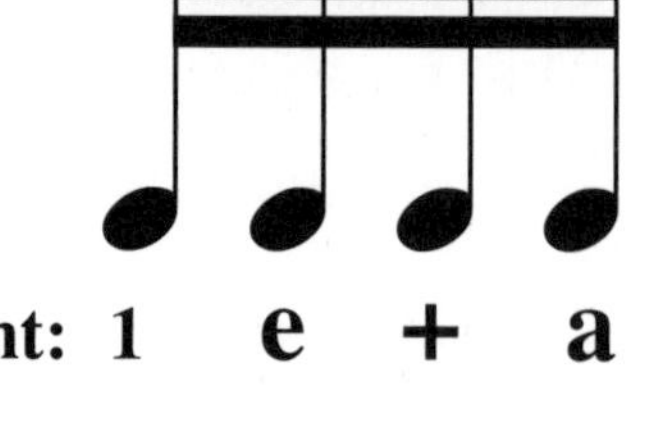

Say: one 'ee' and 'ah'

 6.0 Counting Sixteenth Notes

Tap your foot on each beat to help you keep time as you sing this example.

6.1

Often in songs you will find two sixteenth notes grouped together with an eighth note.

 6.2

Now try this example which combines sixteenth notes with some of the other note values you have learnt. Notice the dotted eighth note and sixteenth note grouping. The dotted eighth note lasts for three quarters of a beat and the sixteenth note makes up the last part of the beat. Once you understand sixteenth notes, you have covered all the common note types and basic rhythms used in song melodies.

Here are some phrases to practice which contain sixteenth notes. As with previous examples, clap the rhythms while counting if you have trouble with them.

7.0

7.1

THE SIXTEENTH NOTE TRIPLET

Triplets can be created on any note value. A sixteenth note triplet is three sixteenth notes sung evenly across the space usually taken by two sixteenth notes. This means that the triplet grouping lasts for the same duration as an eighth note. It is common for two sixteenth note triplets to occur together as a group of six notes across one quarter note beat. The example below demonstrates sixteenth note triplets on one note. As with previous note values, practice it with your metronome. To count a sixteenth note triplet, say **ta ka ta**, for two sixteenth note triplets across a beat, say **ta ka ta ta ka ta**. Sixteenth note triplets are often used in Rap and Hip-hop.

8.0

8.1

Now try these phrases.

INTERPRETATION AND IMPROVISATION

Every singer has his or her own way of interpreting a song. Two singers rarely sing a song exactly the same way. Often a singer will learn a new song by getting the basic melody from another vocalist's version and then changing it to suit their own style. This may mean varying the length of notes, changing the rhythms, changing a few notes to different pitches, or even totally changing the melody. As long as the new melody fits with the lyrics, this is perfectly OK. In fact, some of the greatest recordings of songs have come about by the vocalist completely changing the melody and the accompanying musicians fitting their parts to the new version of the melody. Another situation where improvising comes in handy is in writing songs, particularly when you already have some lyrics and need to put a melody to them. There is always more than one way of doing this. Here are two different ways of phrasing the same lyrics.

9.0

In many melodies there is a natural accent on the first beat of the bar. This can be used to stress particular words in a song. In the first phrase of this example, the emphasis is on the word You.

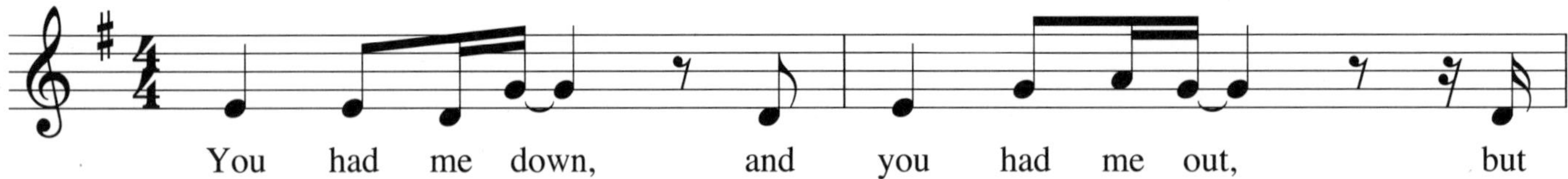

9.1

In this version, there is a rest on beat one, and the first word sets up a different rhythm. You may prefer one approach or the other, but the two versions show that there is more than one way of approaching a lyric, a melody or a rhythm. In styles such as Rock, Blues, Jazz, Gospel and Hip-hop, improvisation is a large part of the vocalist's art. Experiment with improvising on other songs you know.

REPETITION AND VARIATION

Here is another song to help you practice improvising. There are two bars of melody followed by two bars of backing only. You can improvise over this section. This happens three times during the song. Each two bar melody is based on several of the rhythms you have been learning. There is also much repetition of rhythms. Repetition is important because it helps a listener to keep track and make sense of what you are singing. It also helps the other musicians you are playing with to follow you and complement what you are doing. Many of the best melodies ever written are based on the elements of repetition and variation. The 16th notes in this solo are swung. Try swinging the 16th notes in other examples you have learned.

CD 2 10. Hangin' Out

Peter Gelling

11. Swing Low, Sweet Chariot

Traditional

The first version of this song is in the key of E, as shown by the key signature (four sharps). The second half contains several examples of improvisation. If you have trouble with the timing, practice the rhythm figures on one note, as in the earlier rhythm examples. Also try singing along with the recording and try to feel the timing and then imitate it.

E A E
Swing low, sweet cha - ri - o - t, Com - in for to ca - rry me

B7 E A E
home, Swi - ng low, sweet cha - ri - o - t,

B7 E
Com- in for to ca - rry me home. I looked o - ver Jor - dan and

A E
what did I see - - com - in for to ca - rry me

B7 E
home, A ba - nd of An - - gels

A E B7 E
com - in af - ter me - - com - in for to ca- rry me - - home

2. If you get there before I do,
Coming for to carry me home,
Tell all my friends I'm coming too,
Coming for to carry me home.

3. The brightest day that ever I saw,
Coming for to carry me home,
When Jesus wash'd my sins away,
Coming for to carry me home.

12. Swing Low, Sweet Chariot (Version 2)

The second version of this song is in the key of G. This version also contains improvised phrases in the second half. As with previous songs, use the version which best suits your particular vocal range.

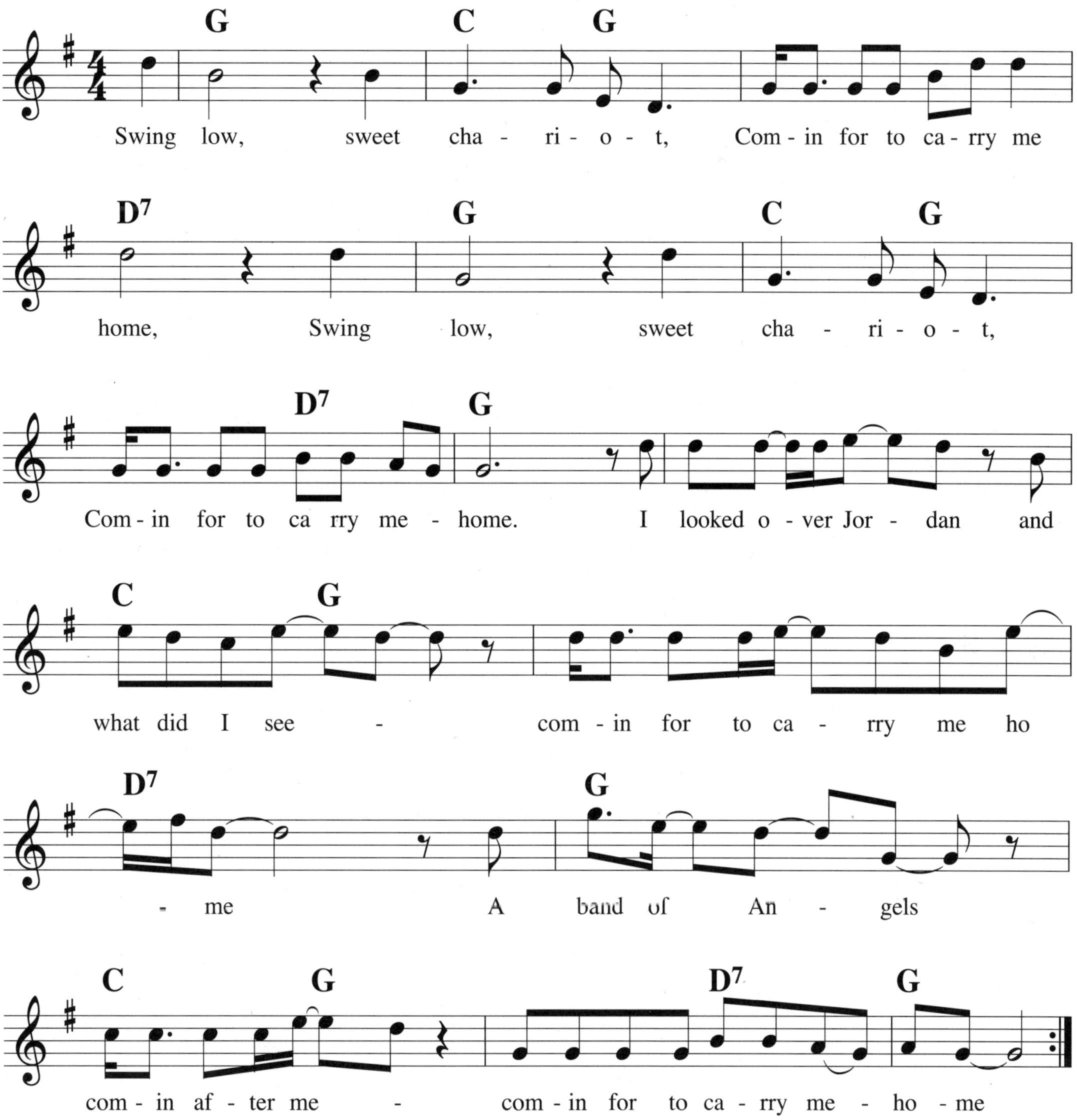

Swing low, sweet cha - ri - o - t, Com - in for to ca - rry me

home, Swing low, sweet cha - ri - o - t,

Com - in for to ca rry me - home. I looked o - ver Jor - dan and

what did I see - com - in for to ca - rry me ho

- me A band of An - gels

com - in af - ter me - com - in for to ca - rry me - ho - me

LESSON TWENTY TWO

PHRASING AND RUBATO

As you have learnt in the last few lessons, The printed music is often just a starting point for the vocalist to learn a song before giving it their personal interpretation. One of the most common ways a vocalist will change the original timing is to hold a note at the end of a phrase and pause before delivering the next lyric. This is particularly common in ballads. The accompanist(s) will need need advance warning, so they can pause along with the vocalist.

Sometimes a composer will write timing variations into the phrasing. In the following ballad, you will notice an occasional bar of $\frac{2}{4}$ time (two quarter notes per bar). This is to give the vocalist two extra beats to hold the last note of the phrase. This brings attention to the lyrics in a way that would not happen if the timing continued straight ahead in $\frac{4}{4}$.

Listen to the recording and notice that the second time a $\frac{2}{4}$ bar occurs, there is a definite pause by both the vocalist and accompanist. This is indicated by the symbol 𝄐 , which is called a **fermata**. Stretching or altering the timing is referred to as **rubato**. The amount of rubato is up to the individual performer. It is best developed by listening to the way great singers and instrumentalists use it. Once again, this involves a lot of listening.

13. Born to Believe

Ghita Prey/Richard Turner

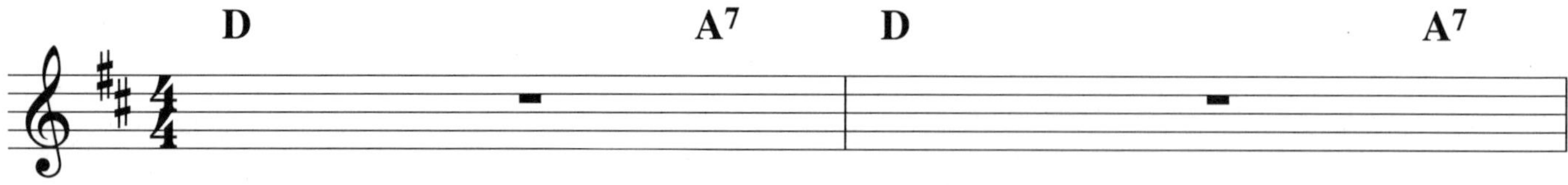

A7
D
vi- sion of my ey - es. I've got the fi - re - and I've got the drive,

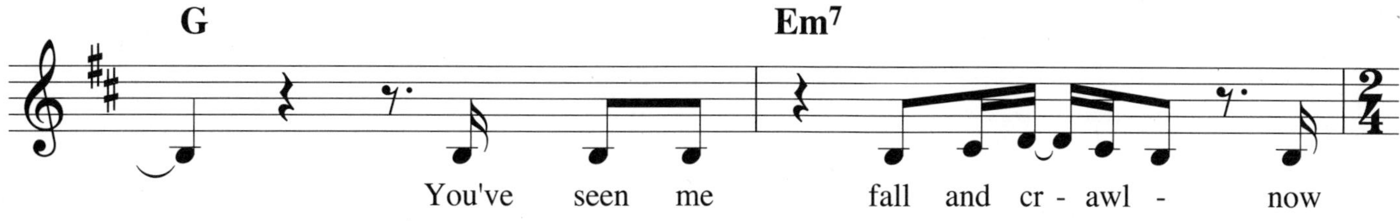
G
Em7
You've seen me fall and cr - awl - now

Em7/A
A7sus4
watch me come a - live. I do it for

D
G
you, and I do it for me - I do it for the

Em7
Em7/A
A7
dream in - side that shines i - n me - - I do it for the

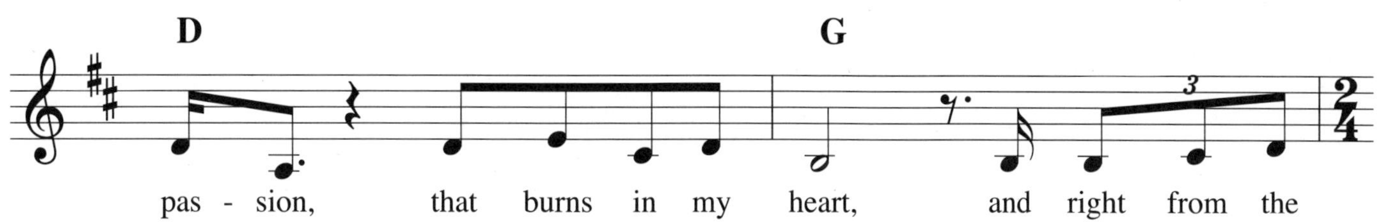
D
G
pas - sion, that burns in my heart, and right from the

Em7
A7sus4
D
ve - ry start, I was born to be - lieve.

LESSON TWENTY THREE

THE SIX EIGHT TIME SIGNATURE

$\begin{matrix}6\\8\end{matrix}$ This is the **six eight** time signature.
There are six eighth notes in one bar of $\begin{smallmatrix}6\\8\end{smallmatrix}$ time.
The six eighth notes are divided into two groups of three.

When playing or singing $\begin{smallmatrix}6\\8\end{smallmatrix}$ time there are **two** beats within each bar, with each beat having the value of a **dotted quarter note.** This is different from $\begin{smallmatrix}4\\4\end{smallmatrix}$ and $\begin{smallmatrix}3\\4\end{smallmatrix}$ time where each beat is a quarter note.

CD 2 14. House of the Rising Sun

This traditional American song is in $\begin{smallmatrix}6\\8\end{smallmatrix}$ time and is written here in the **key of E minor**.

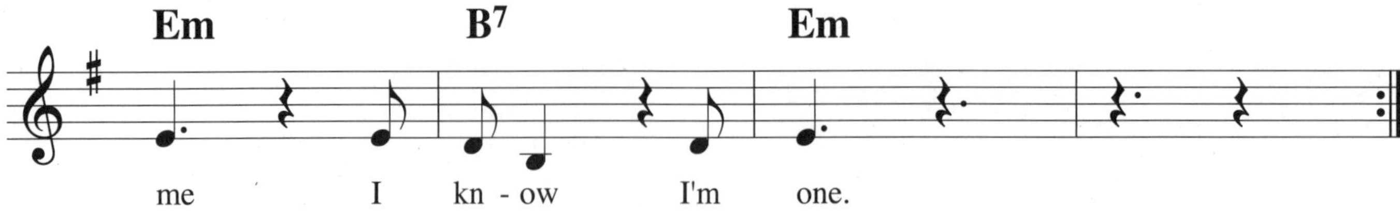

15. House of the Rising Sun (Version 2)

The second version of this song is in the key of B♭ minor, which means it has been transposed up an interval of a diminished 5th from the key of E minor. A good knowledge of intervals is particularly useful for transposing, as well as helping you to learn songs more quickly by sight or by ear.

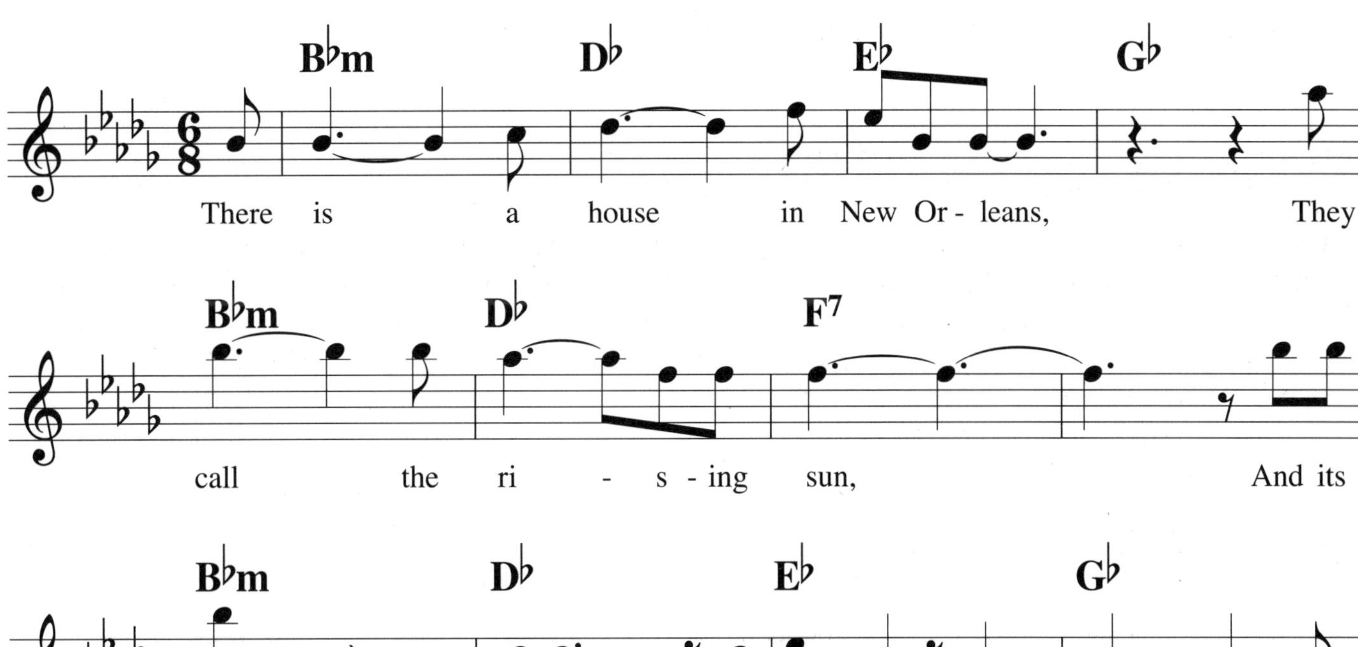

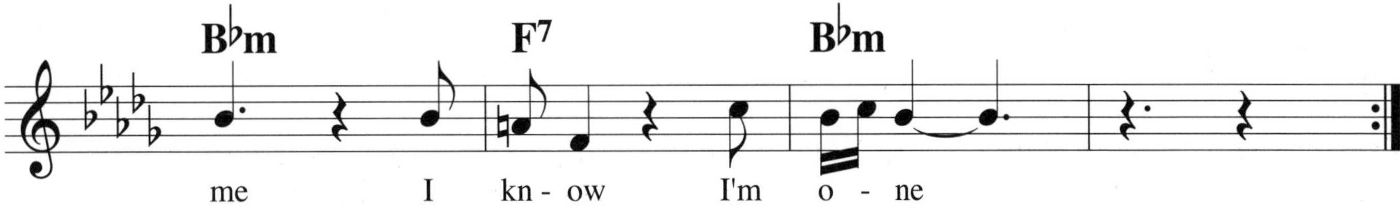

2. My mother she's a tailor
She sews those new blue jeans
My husband he's a gamblin' man,
Drinks down in New Orleans.

3. My husband he's a gambler,
He goes from town to town
And the only time he's satisfied
Is when he drinks his liquor down.

4. Now, the only thing that a gambler needs
Is a suitcase and a trunk
And the only time he's ever satisfied
Is when he's on a drunk.

5. He fills his glasses up to the brim
And he passes the cards around
And the only pleasure he gets out of life
Is ramblin' from town to town.

6. Go tell my baby sister
Not to do what I have done
Shun that house in New Orleans
They call the risin' sun.

7. If I had listened to what my mother said
I'd have been at home today
But I was so young and foolish
I let a rambler lead me astray.

8. Well it's one foot on the platform
And the other foot on the train
I'm goin back to New Orleans
To wear that ball and chain.

9. I'm goin back to New Orleans
My race is nearly run.
I'm goin back to end my life
In the house of the risin sun.

SIMPLE AND COMPOUND TIME

Time signatures fall into two basic categories – simple time and compound time. **Simple time** is any time signature where the basic beat is **divisible by two**. E.g. in $\frac{4}{4}$, $\frac{3}{4}$, and $\frac{2}{4}$ the basic beat is a quarter note, which may be divided in half to become two eighth notes per beat. Any time signature where the basic beat is **divisible by three** (eg. a dotted quarter note) is called **compound time**. The most common example of compound time is **six eight** time. Other examples of compound are $\frac{9}{8}$ and $\frac{12}{8}$. In each case, the basic beat is felt as a dotted quarter note which can be divided by three.

TWELVE EIGHT TIME ($\frac{12}{8}$)

Another popular time signature is **twelve eight time** ($\frac{12}{8}$), which means that there are **twelve eighth note beats** in each bar. A bar of eighth notes in twelve eight time sounds the same as a bar of triplets in four four time. This is because the twelve individual beats are grouped into threes and counted as four pulses (**1** 2 3 **2** 2 3 **3** 2 3 **4** 2 3). Many Blues songs and Ballads are written in $\frac{12}{8}$ time.

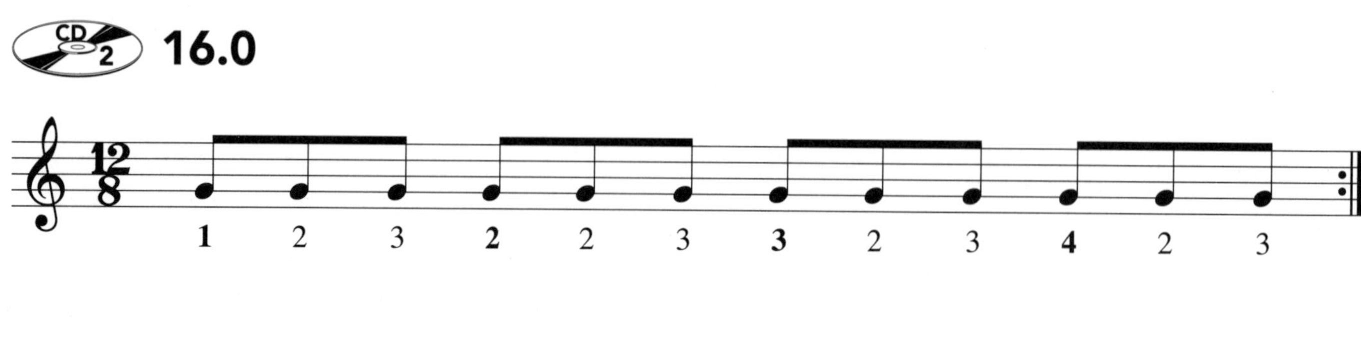

16.1 (CD 2)

This melody uses of 16th notes in $\frac{12}{8}$ time. Write counting numbers under the notes and notice that each main beat adds up to the equivalent of a dotted quarter note.

GROUPING NOTES IN COMPOUND TIME

Another common compound time signatures is **nine eight time**. In all compound time signatures, eighth notes are grouped in threes. Remember that a group of three can be made up of quarter note followed by an eighth note or a dotted quarter note. These were both used in the melody on the previous page. Some correct and incorrect groupings are shown below.

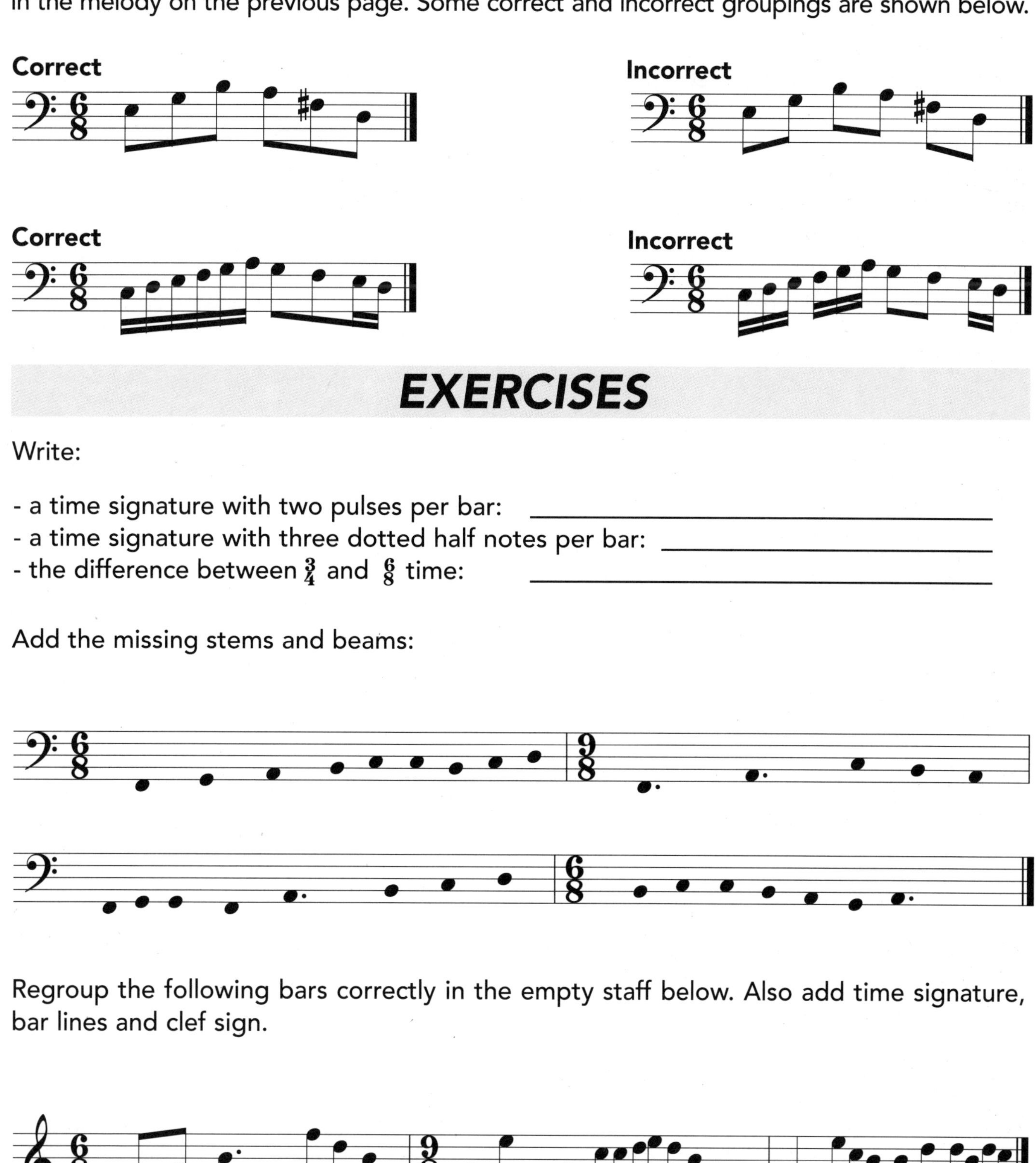

EXERCISES

✏ Write:

- a time signature with two pulses per bar: ______________________
- a time signature with three dotted half notes per bar: ______________________
- the difference between $\frac{3}{4}$ and $\frac{6}{8}$ time: ______________________

✏ Add the missing stems and beams:

✏ Regroup the following bars correctly in the empty staff below. Also add time signature, bar lines and clef sign.

LESSON TWENTY FOUR

HARMONY SINGING

One of the greatest sounds in music is two or more voices singing in **harmony**. This means more than one note being sung at the same time. Harmony can range from a melody harmonized with a single interval to a whole choir singing many different notes together.

The simplest form of harmony involves a second voice following the melody using a particular interval. The most common intervals used for harmonizing melodies are major and minor **thirds**. The second voice simply sings a **third interval** above every note of the melody line. Here is the C major scale harmonized in thirds. All the harmony notes come from the scale itself.

17.

Here is a melody in the key of C harmonised in thirds.

18.0

If the person singing the harmony part has a lower voice range than the person singing the melody, an interval of a **sixth** below the melody may be used. The notes are then the same notes as for a third above the melody, but each one is an octave lower.

18.1

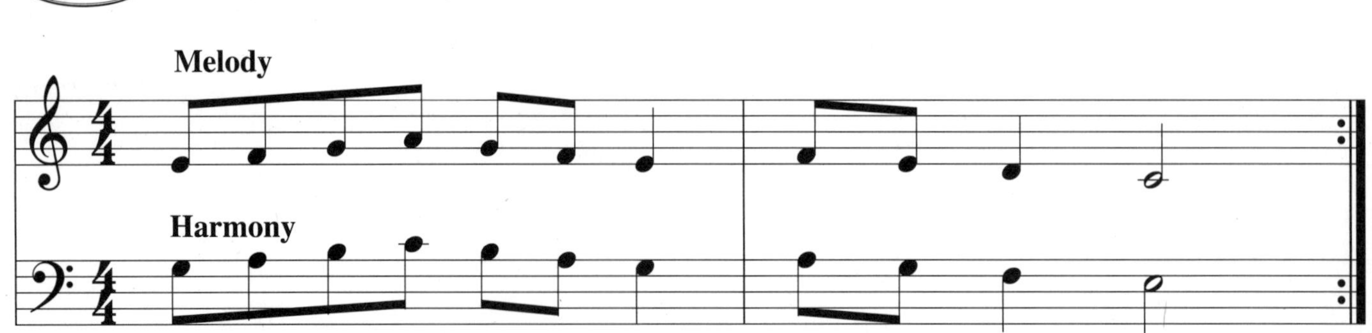

Harmonies sung in 3rds and 6ths sound great on simple songs in both major and minor keys. Many people learn to sing these harmonies by ear, without needing to refer to sheet music. Listen to this song on the CD and try imitating the harmony by ear. Then sing it along with the recording Try to absorb the **sound** of the harmony. If this harmony is too high for your voice, try singing it an octave lower.

CD 2 19. Banks of the Ohio

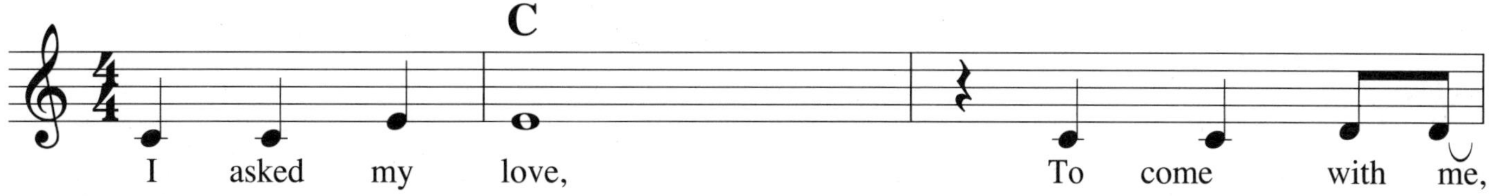

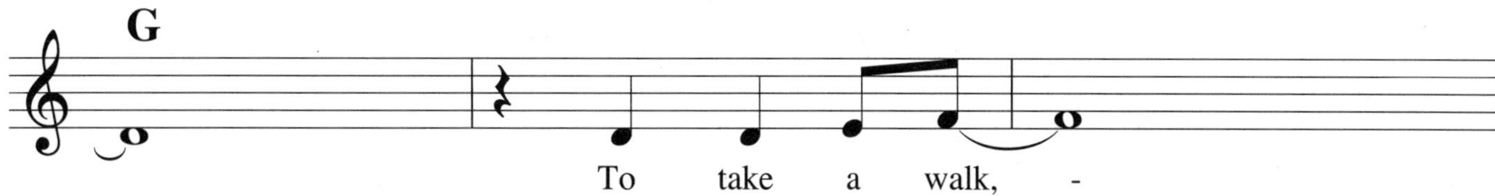

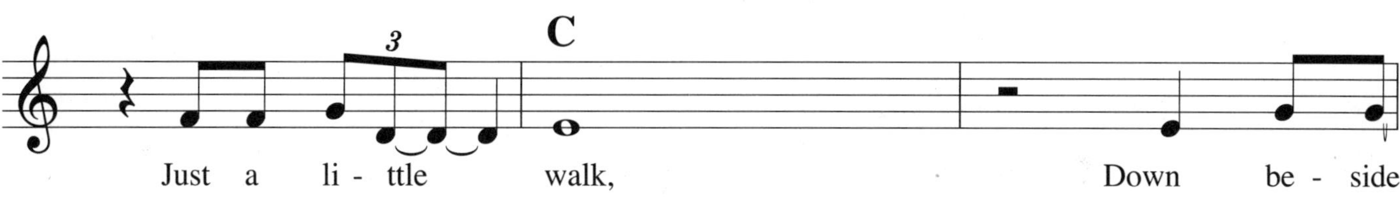

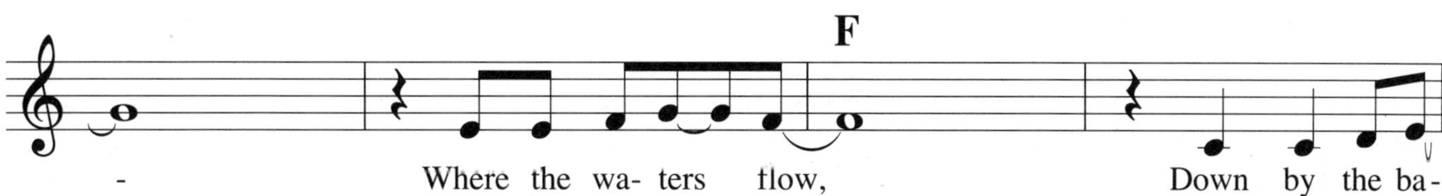

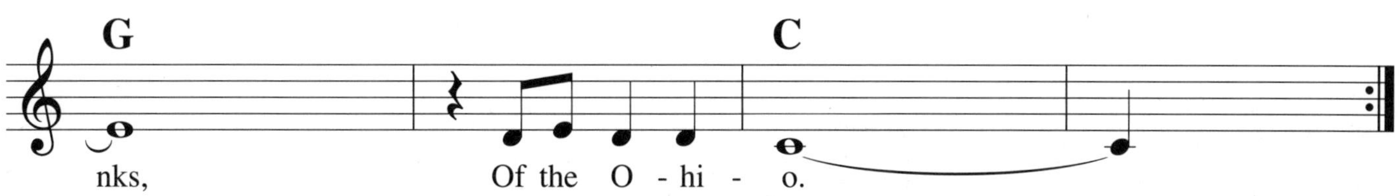

Here is **Banks of the Ohio** again, this time with the harmony part written above the melody. This harmony mostly consists of **3rd** intervals above the melody, but in bar 6**,** the harmony voice changes to a 5th above the melody (on the second beat of the triplet). Then in bar 8 the harmony voice departs from 3rds again and sings several different intervals above the melody, before returning to 3rds on the last note of bar 12. These other notes all come from the chords which the band is playing to accompany the melody.

Banks of the Ohio (With Harmony)

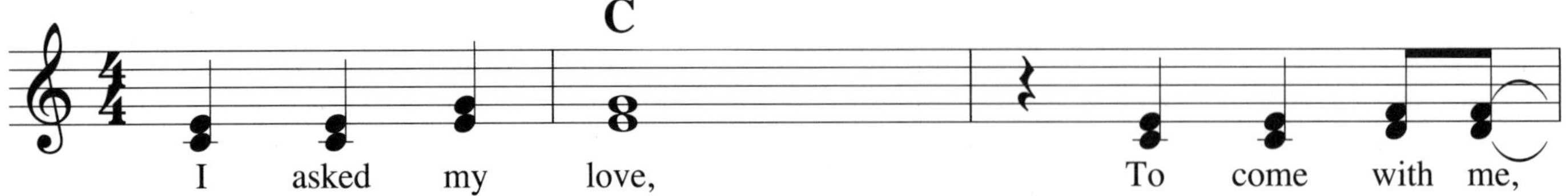

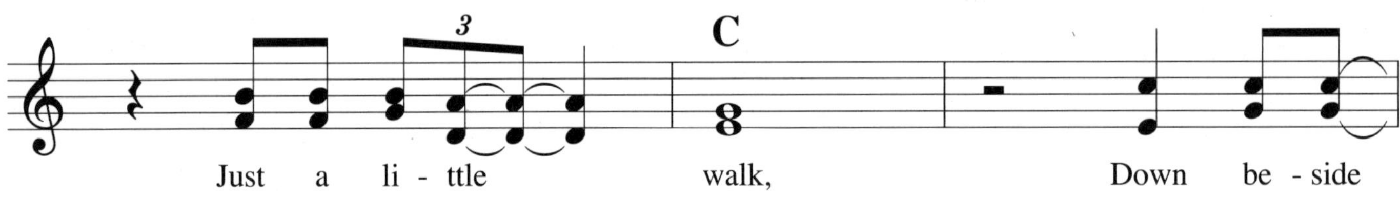

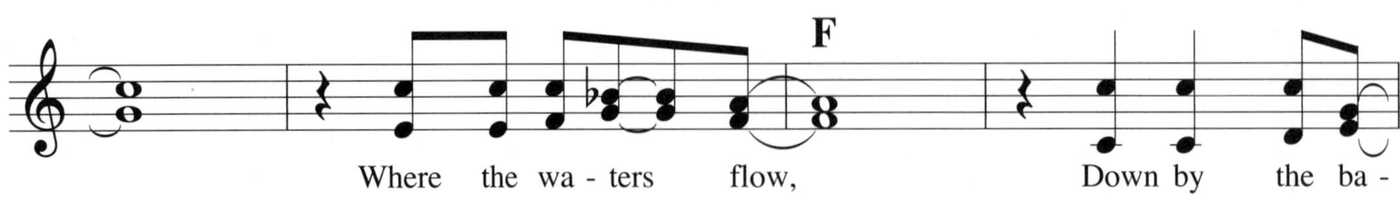

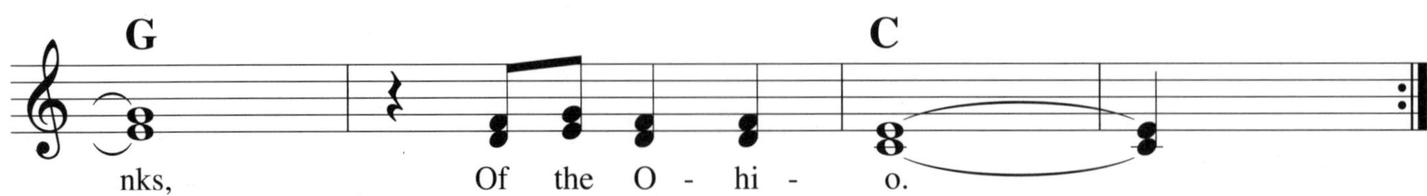

HARMONY AND CHORDS

Harmony can be thought of as the notes that support and add character to a melody. The basic building blocks of harmony are **chords**. A chord is a group of three or more notes played simultaneously (e.g. strumming on a guitar). There are many different types of chords, the most common being the **major chord**. All major chords contain three notes, taken from the major scale of the same letter name. These three notes are the 1 (first), 3 (third) and 5 (fifth) notes (degrees) of the major scale, so the **chord formula** for the major chord is: **1 3 5**. If these notes are taken from the C major scale the chord is a **C major chord**, usually just called a **C chord**. Chords are represented by symbols placed above the vocal melody on sheet music. The symbol for a C chord is the letter **C**. The symbol for a D (major) chord is the letter **D**. The symbol for an E flat chord would be **E♭**.

Chord Symbol

C

The C Major Chord

Notes in Chord

C	E	G
1	3	5

The C major chord is constructed from the C major scale. Using the chord formula **1 3 5** on the C major scale, it can be seen that the C major chord contains the notes C, E and G.

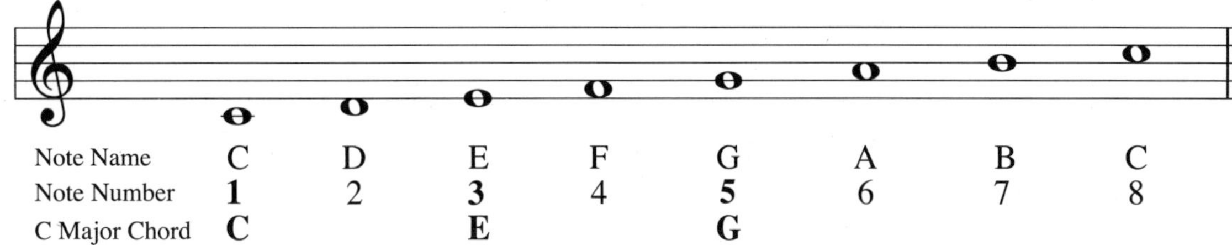

Here is a C chord in the bass staff, along with a keyboard diagram demonstrating the notes.

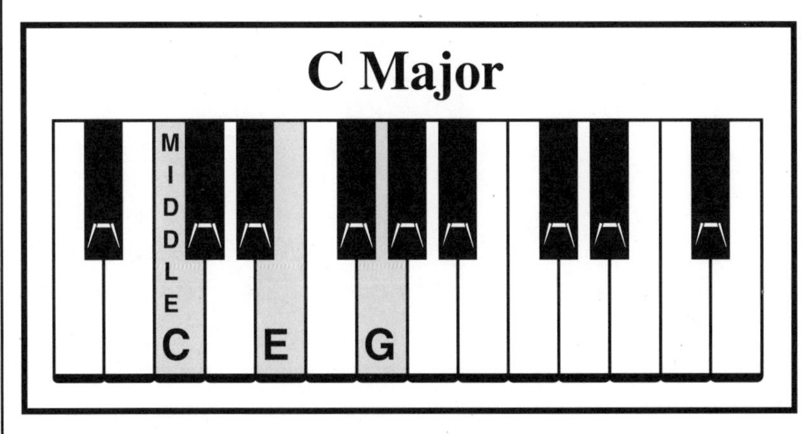

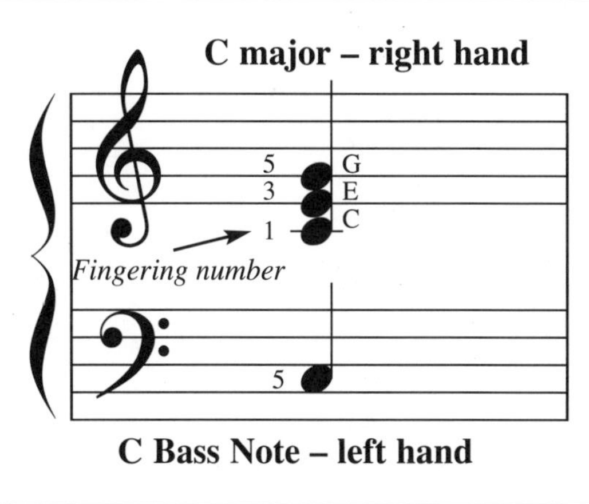

Look again at the first two bars of **Banks of the Ohio** (Version 2) and notice that all the notes in both the melody and harmony are contained within the C chord. Notice also the **C** chord symbol telling the band or accompanist that this is the right chord to play at this point in the song.

CHORD PROGRESSIONS

Chords are usually played in a repeating sequence called a **chord progression**. A chord progression may repeat every 2, 4, 8, 12 or 16 bars. This could mean that the progression is repeated many times within a verse (as in many Rock songs), or that it may be the same length as the verse. The best way to learn about chords and chord progressions is to learn a bit of basic guitar or keyboard. Many singers like to accompany themselves on guitar or keyboard, so a little knowledge in this area can have a practical value as well as helping you learn more about music. ***Progressive Beginner Guitar*** and ***Progressive Beginner Piano*** will provide a good introduction to these instruments.

If you read through the music to **Banks of the Ohio** you will notice three different chord symbols – **C**, **F** and **G**. These chords all work for melodies in the key of C, because the chords themselves are created from the notes of the C major scale. Shown below are the chords F and G as they would be played on a keyboard. Look at the notes involved in these chords. If you add up all the different notes in **C**, **F** and **G**, you end up with all the notes of the C major scale. This means that you can use any notes from these three chords to **harmonize** any melody created from the C major scale.

Chord Symbol

The F Chord

An **F Major** chord (usually just called an **F** chord) is made up of the notes **F**, **A** and **C**.

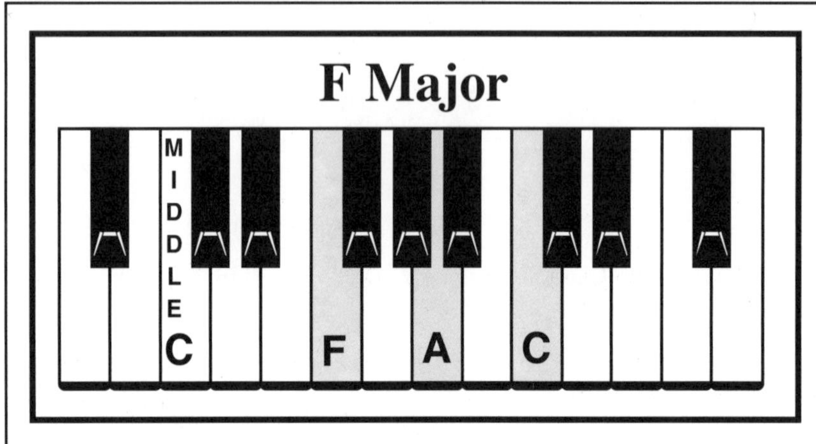

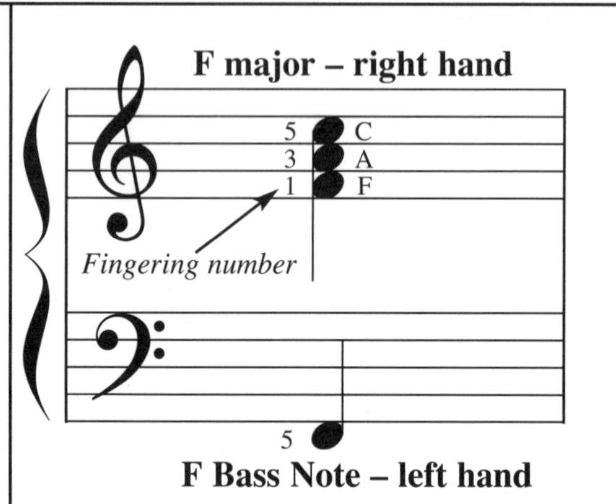

Chord Symbol

The G Chord

An **F Major** chord (usually just called an **F** chord) is made up of the notes **F**, **A** and **C**, as shown in the diagram.

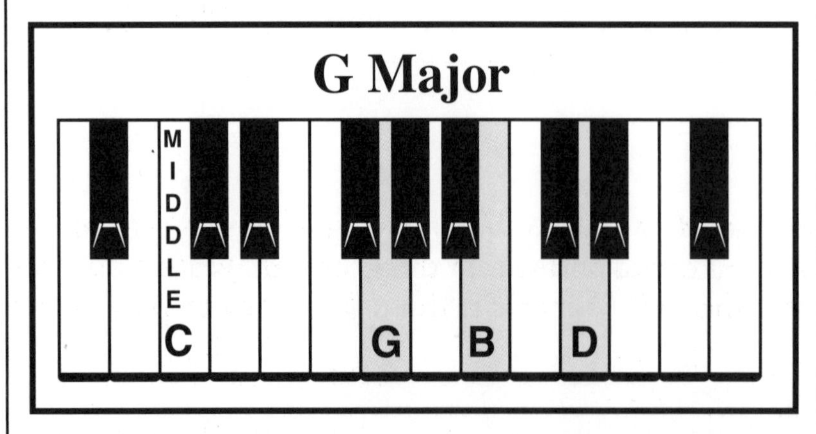

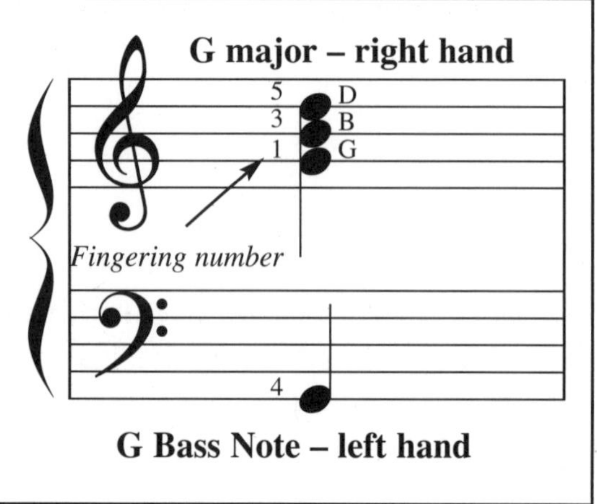

20.

Here is the C Major Scale harmonized with the chords **C**, **F** and **G**. The notes of the chords have been re-arranged so that they are close together on the keyboard. This produces a smoother sound. Different arrangements of the notes of chords are called **inversions**.

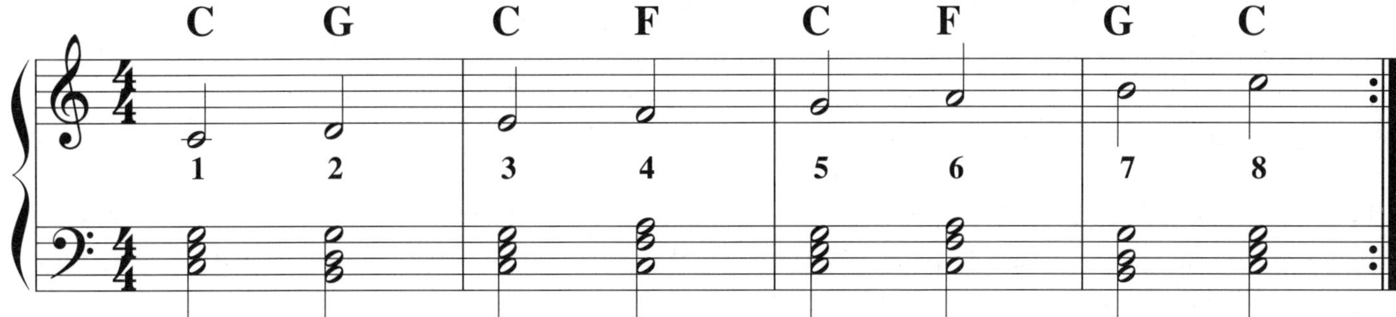

HARMONIZING MELODIES

To harmonize a melody, the musician simply plays a chord on the **first beat of each bar** that contains the melody note that occurs on that beat. In $\frac{4}{4}$ time it is also possible to add another chord on the third beat of the bar. The **Banks of the Ohio** is harmonized with the chords **C**, **F** and **G**. This is a good starting point for finding vocal harmonies for the song. If you play guitar or keyboard, you could experiment using notes from these chords until you find a harmony that suits your voice.

Banks of the Ohio (With Chords)

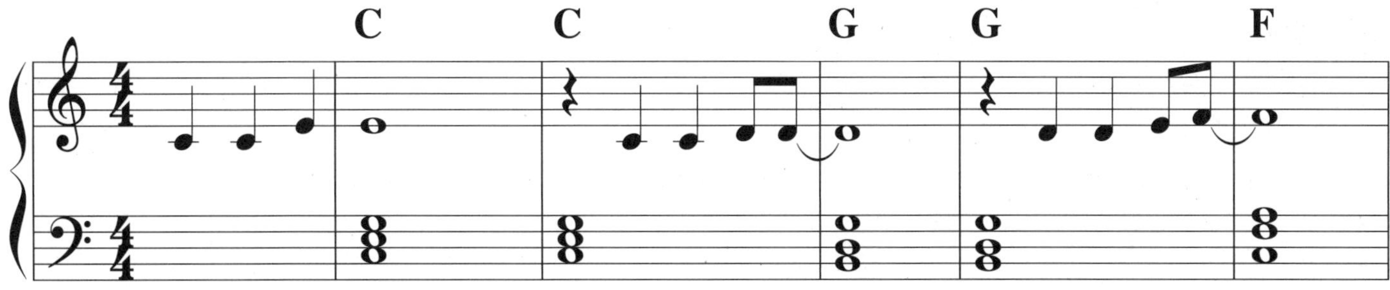

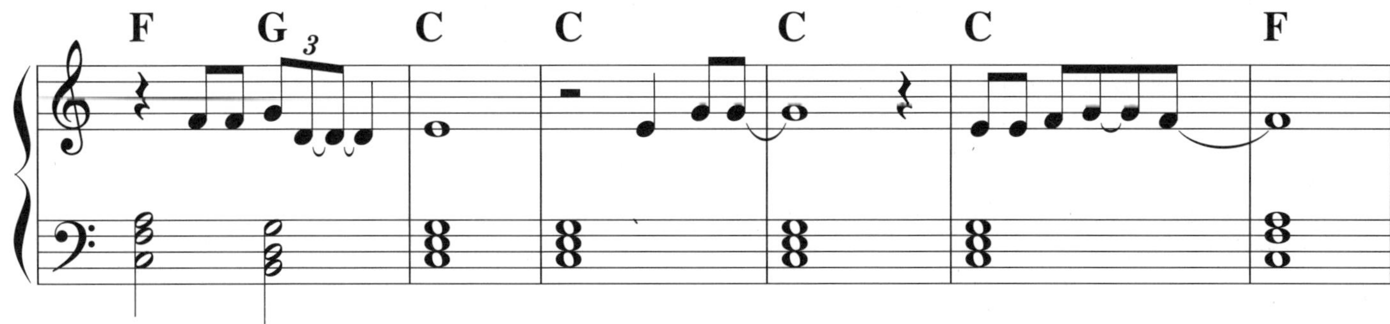

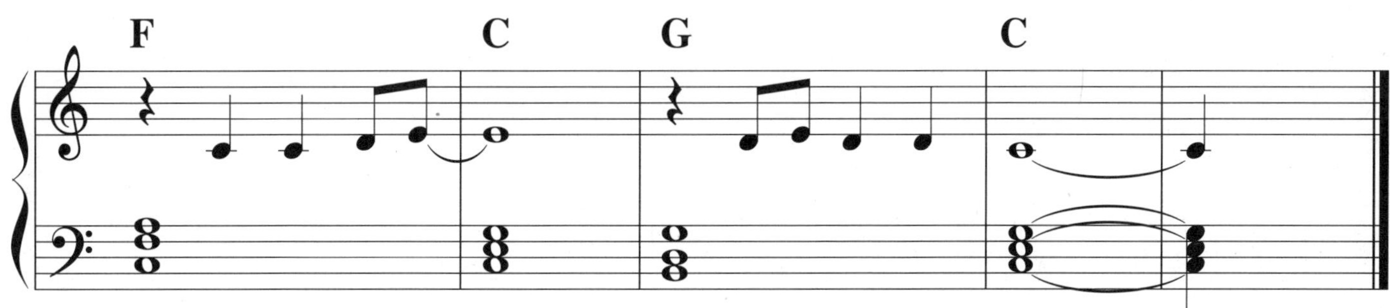

LESSON TWENTY FIVE

WRITING VOCAL PARTS

Although chords are the main source of harmonies, a singer can only deliver one note at a time. This means that the notes of a chord must be shared between voices. In the case of a simple harmony based on 3rd intervals, it is possible to select just one chord tone for a harmony, but if more than one note is desired, the chord must be split and written on different staves. Here is the chord progression **C F G C** written on three staves. The top two are for **Soprano (S)** and **Alto (A)** voices and use a treble staff, while the bottom notes for a **Baritone (B)** voice are on the bass staff.

CD 2 **21.**

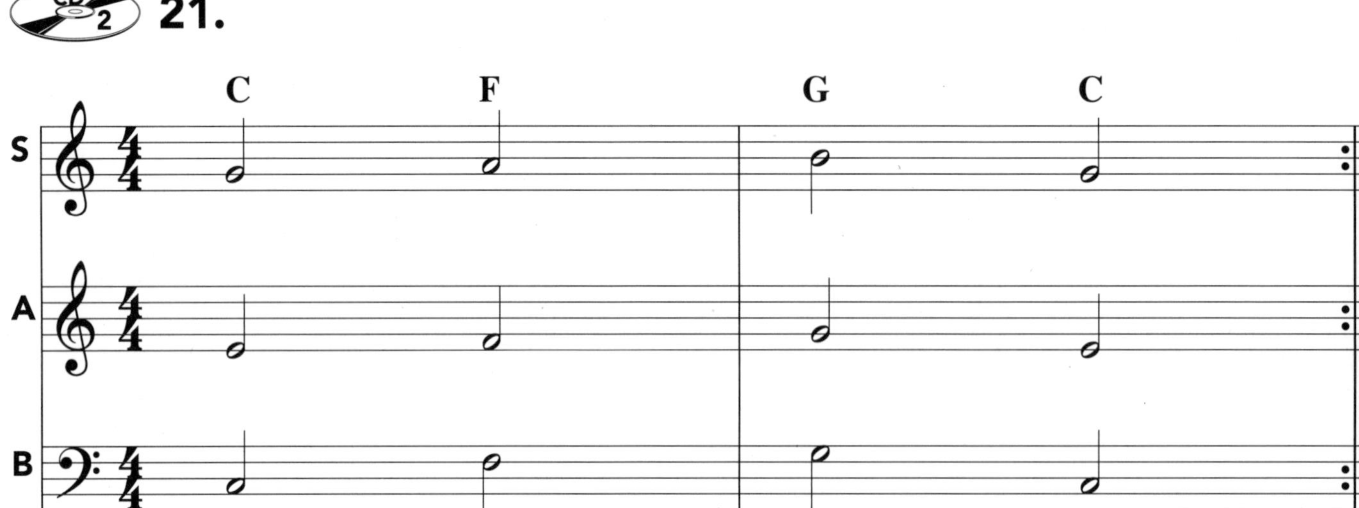

When writing harmonies, the harmonising voices can either follow every note of the melody, or sing single sustained chord tones (notes of the chord) while the melody moves between them. Sometimes one approach works best and sometimes the other. In the example below, the melody is in the Bass and the Soprano and Alto voices harmonise every note. In this situation, any notes from the scale of the key can be used. As long as you do not use notes from outside the key, the notes will harmonize. The first option would be to use two thirds one above the other – i.e. a Soprano note one third interval above the Alto note, which is a third interval above the melody.

CD 2 **22.**

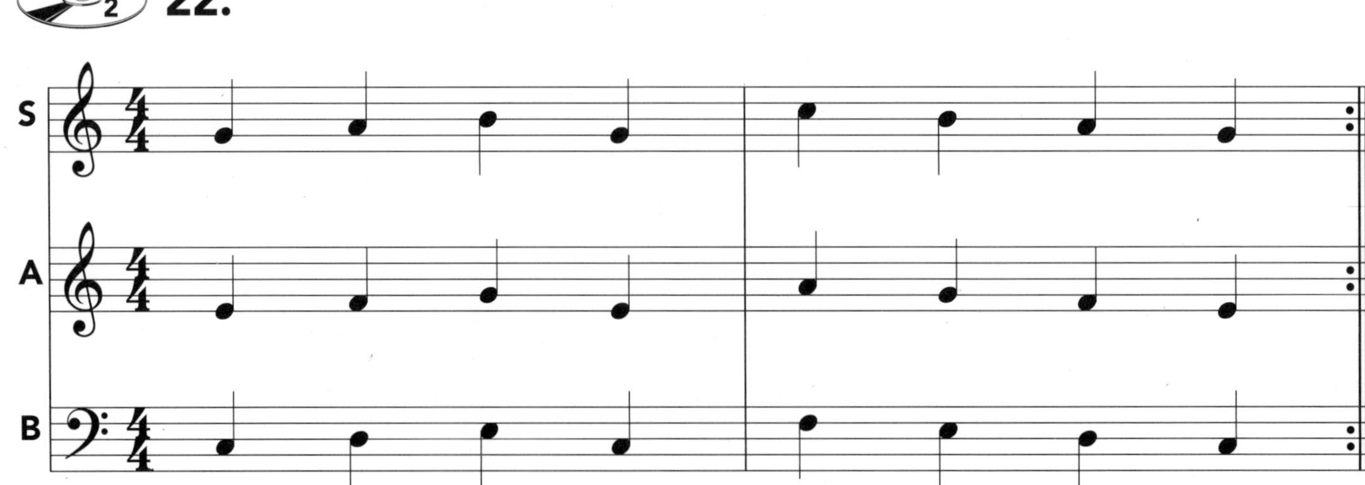

FOUR PART HARMONY

The tradition of writing **four part harmony** for four voices stretches back for many centuries. The voice ranges – Soprano (S), Alto (A), tenor (T) and Bass (B) – can be shortened to **S A T B**. When writing SATB harmonies, it is often necessary to double chord tones so that each part has a note to sing. The most commonly doubled notes are the root and the 5th. The 3rd is rarely doubled. Occasionally it is necessary to triple one of the tones and omit another. If a note is omitted, it is usually the 5th of the chord, and the root is tripled in its place.

There are many conventions and rules in four part writing. It is beyond the scope of this book to discuss them all. If you are interested in four part harmony, it is recommended that you study it with a Classical harmony teacher. With or without a teacher, it is also recommended that you study the vocal music of J.S. Bach, as well as listening extensively to choral music.

23.

In this simple example, Soprano, Alto and Tenor voices sing chord tones together, independently of the melody sung by the Baritone. This kind of harmony is often used in the chorus of a Pop or Rock song. It has been used by everyone from the Beach Boys to Boy Bands.

In lesson 37 there is a fully scored vocal arrangement of a traditional song for four female voices.

LESSON TWENTY SIX

CHORD CONSTRUCTION – TRIADS

Chords are usually made up of combinations of major and minor third intervals. As mentioned previously, the simplest chords are **triads** made up of three notes. There are **four** basic types of triads: **major**, **minor**, **augmented** and **diminished**. Examples of each of these are shown below along with the appropriate **chord formula** and intervals.

C Major Chord

Chord Symbol

C

	5	**G**
Minor Third		
	3	**E**
Major Third		
	1	**C**

Notes in Chord

C	E	G
1	3	5

C Minor Chord

Chord Symbol

Cm

	5	**G**
Major Third		
	♭3	**E♭**
Minor Third		
	1	**C**

Notes in Chord

C	E♭	G
1	♭3	5

C Augmented Chord

Chord Symbol

C+

	♯5	**G♯**
Major Third		
	3	**E**
Major Third		
	1	**C**

Notes in Chord

C	E	G♯
1	3	♯5

C Diminished Chord

Chord Symbol

Cdim or C°

	♭5	**G♭**
Minor Third		
	♭3	**E♭**
Minor Third		
	1	**C**

Notes in Chord

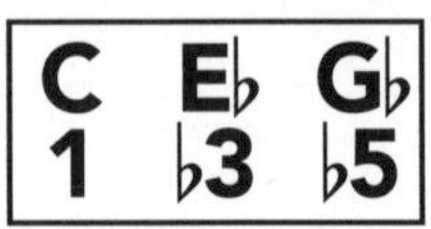

C	E♭	G♭
1	♭3	♭5

Using the formulas on the previous page, you can easily work out the notes for any type of triad beginning on any note. E.g, to form a **A major** chord you would begin with the note **A** and then add a **major 3rd** (four semitones) above it (**C♯**) and then a **minor 3rd** (three semitones) above that (**E**). To form a **D♯ diminished** chord, you would begin with a **D♯** note and then add a **minor 3rd** above it (**F♯**) and then another minor 3rd above that (**A**). To help you become more familiar with the four types of triads, write the required notes above the root notes shown below to create the triads indicated.

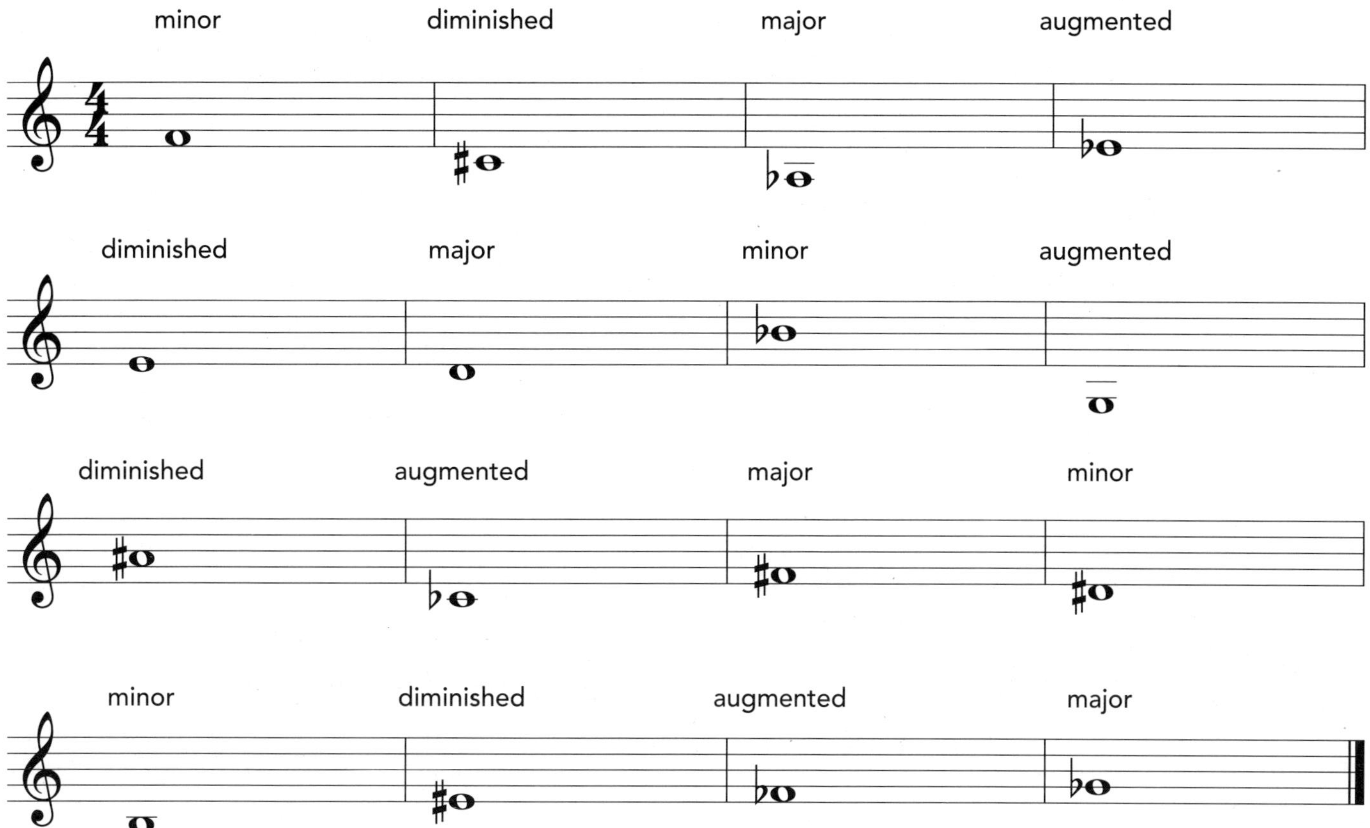

DOUBLE SHARPS AND DOUBLE FLATS

Sometimes in music, particularly when notating chords it is necessary to use double sharps (indicated by 𝄪) and double flats (indicated by 𝄫). The reason for this is the spelling of the intervals. E.g. a **B** augmented triad would contain the notes **B**, **D♯** and **F** 𝄪. You will notice **F double sharp** is the same as **G natural**. The reason F double sharp is used is that the interval of a major 3rd above **D♯** must contain the letter **F** and not the letter **G**; The same principle applies with double flats. E.g. an **E♭** diminished triad would contain the notes **E♭**, **G♭** and **B𝄫** . The **B double flat** would be used instead of **A natural** because the minor 3rd interval above **G♭** must contain the letter **B** and not **A**. These are more examples of **enharmonic** notes. You may also have noticed the use of notes such as **C♭**, **F♭**, **B♯** and **E♯** in some of the previous examples. Although they are not common, these notes are used in music and are therefore worth learning.

UNDERSTANDING CHORD SYMBOLS

Chords are indicated by a **chord symbol** above the music notation. In the case of major chords, the symbol consists only of the letter name of the chord. E.g. a **C major chord** is indicated by the **letter C**, an **A major chord** is indicated by the letter **A**, a **B♭ major chord** is indicated by the symbol **B♭**, etc.

LESSON TWENTY SEVEN

CHORD INVERSIONS

All triads contain three different notes. These notes can be duplicated and/or played in a different shape. When the lowest note in each of these three chords is the root note, the shape given is called the **root position**. When the third (3) is the lowest note of the chord shape, the chord is said to be the **first inversion**. Here are the three inversions of a G major chord, which contains the notes G, B and D.

G Major Chord Inversions

These three diagrams illustrate the root position (1 3 5), first inversion (3 5 1), and second inversion (5 1 3) of the G chord.

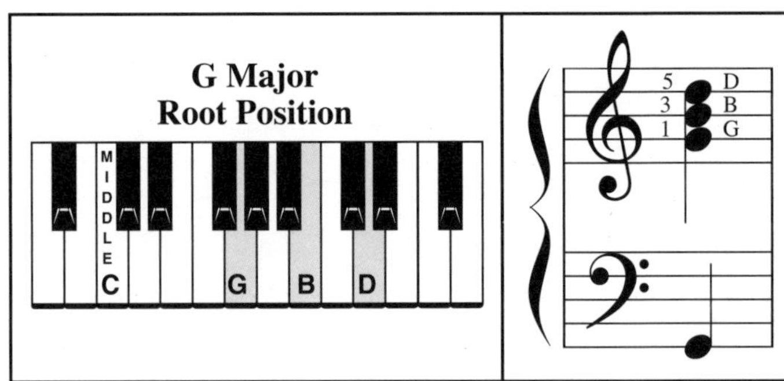

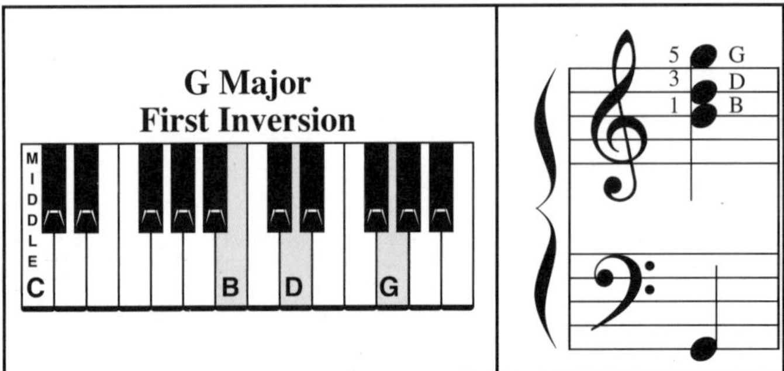

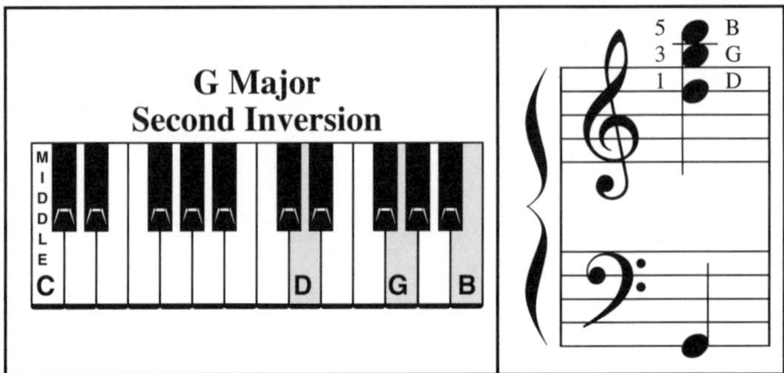

24.0

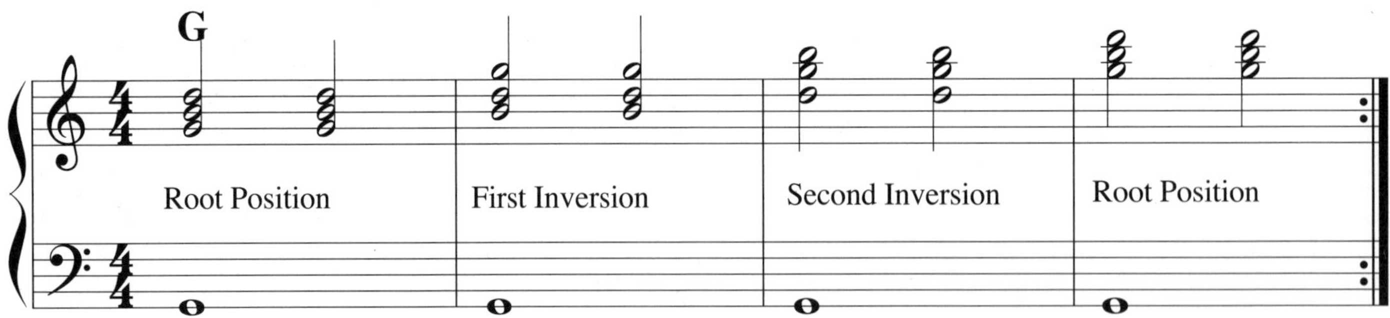

✏ Name the following inversions.

All chord types can be inverted. The following example uses the root position, first inversion, second inversion, and an octave of the root position of the **C minor** chord.

24.1

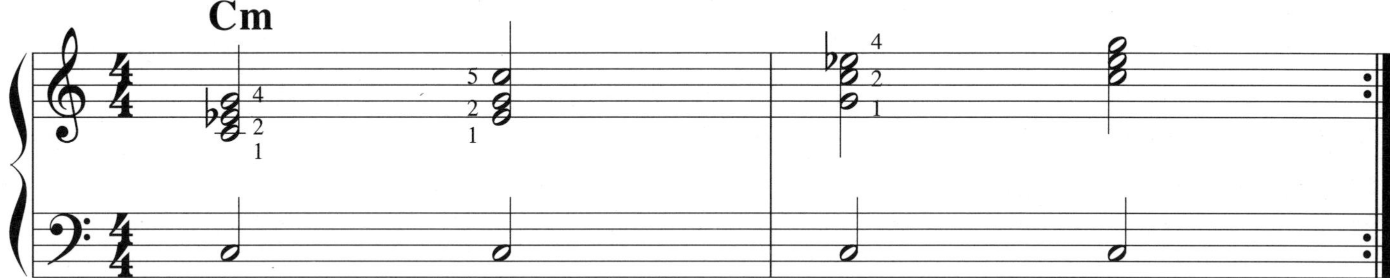

25.0

Here is a keyboard part making use of the **first inversion** of the **C minor chord (E♭ G C)**. The use of the inversion allows the root note to become the highest note in the chord.

25.1

One of the reasons inversions are so useful is that they enable you to find chords which are close together on instruments such as keyboard or guitar, and to write vocal parts which are easy to sing. Here the **C** chord appears in **root position**, the **F** chord is in **second inversion** and the **G** chord is in **first inversion**. The left hand plays the root note of each chord. When you play inversions which are close together, the chord changes sound smoother and often contain common tones, e.g. the chords **C** and **F** both contain the note **C**.

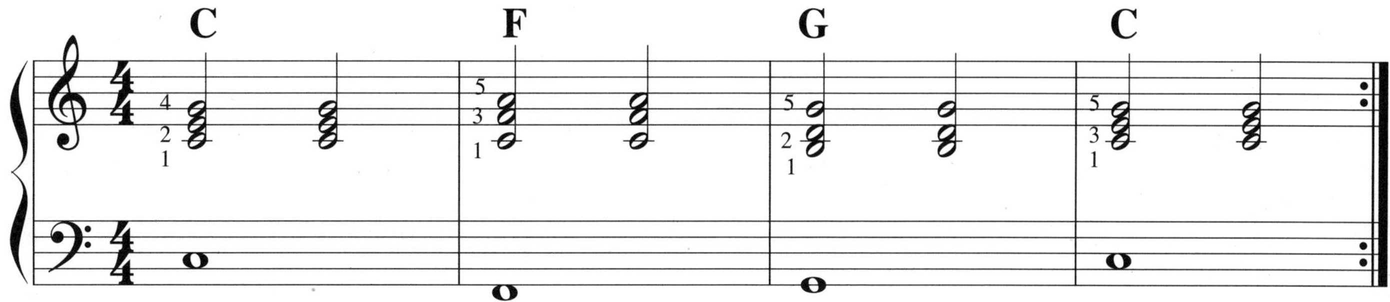

VOICE PARTS ON THE GRAND STAFF

This is a traditional church melody arranged as a **chorale** (choir or **choral** piece) by 19th century composer **Robert Schumann**. The chords are made up of four individual voice parts written on the grand staff – Soprano and Alto on the treble staff, Tenor and Baritone on the bass staff. The parts are determined by their stem directions. i.e Soprano and Tenor parts have their stems pointing up, while the Alto and Bass parts have their stems pointing down. This arrangement contains extensive use of chord inversions. Listen to how smoothly the voices move between the chords.

CD 2 26. Chorale

Robert Schumann

ARPEGGIOS

An **arpeggio** is a chord sung or played one note at a time. As it is not possible to sing two notes simultaneously with one voice, singing an arpeggio is the only way a singer can sing a chord. The value of arpeggios is that they enable you to create melodies and parts which fit chord progressions perfectly, since every note of an arpeggio is a note of the accompanying chord. The **C major arpeggio** below consists of the notes **C**, **E** and **G**. These are the **root**, **third** and **fifth** of a **C major chord**.

CD 2 **27.0**

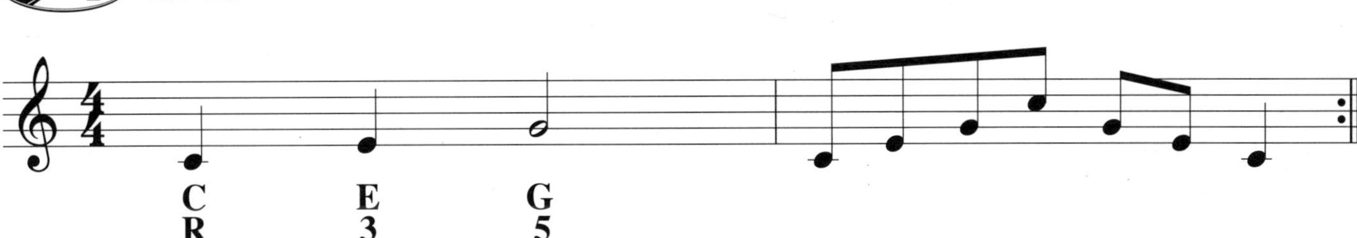

For every type of chord there is a corresponding arpeggio. Shown below is a **C minor arpeggio** which consists of the notes **C**, **E♭** and **G**–the **root**, **flattened third** and **fifth** of a **C minor chord**.

CD 2 **27.1**

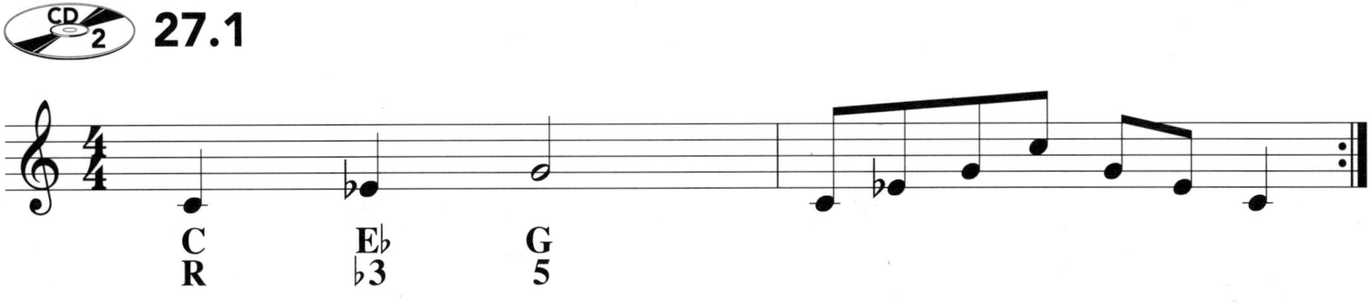

✏ Write out the following arpeggios using the same note values as in bar 2 of the example above. Revise the formulas on page 128 if you need to.

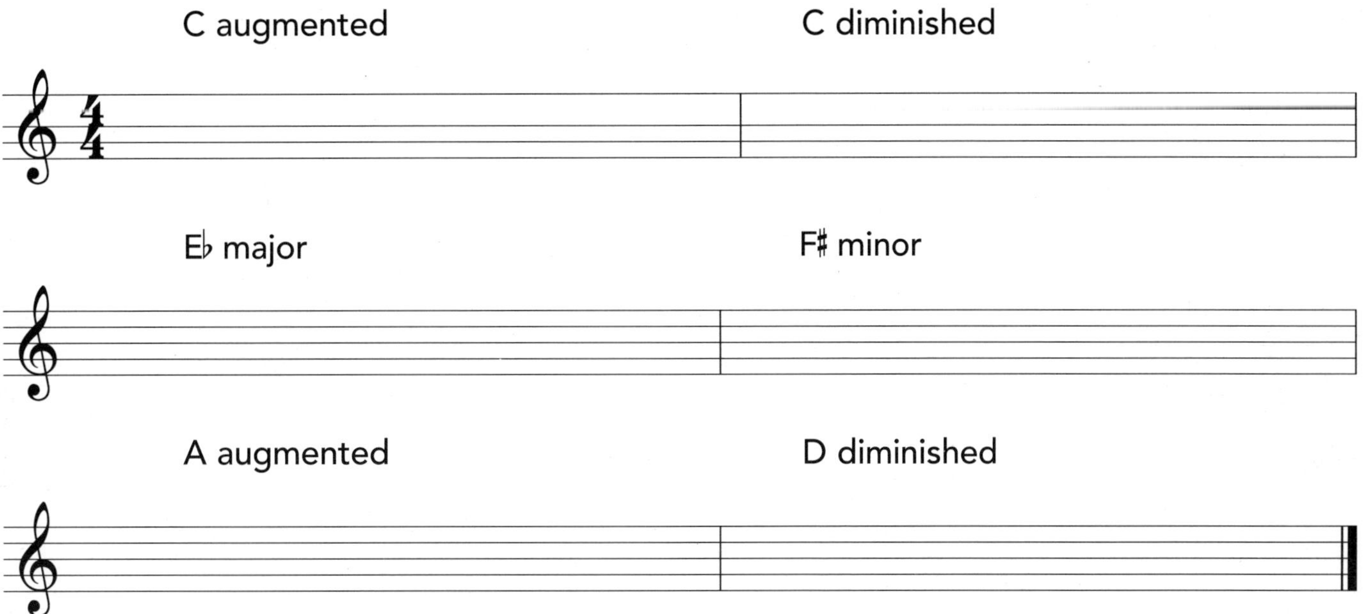

LESSON TWENTY EIGHT

SCALE TONE CHORDS

In any key it is possible to build chords on each degree of the scale. This means that for every major scale there are seven possible chords which can be used for harmonising melodies. These are the seven **scale tone chords**. It is common practice to describe all the chords within a key with **Roman numerals** as shown in the seven scale tone triads in the key of C major.

 **28.**

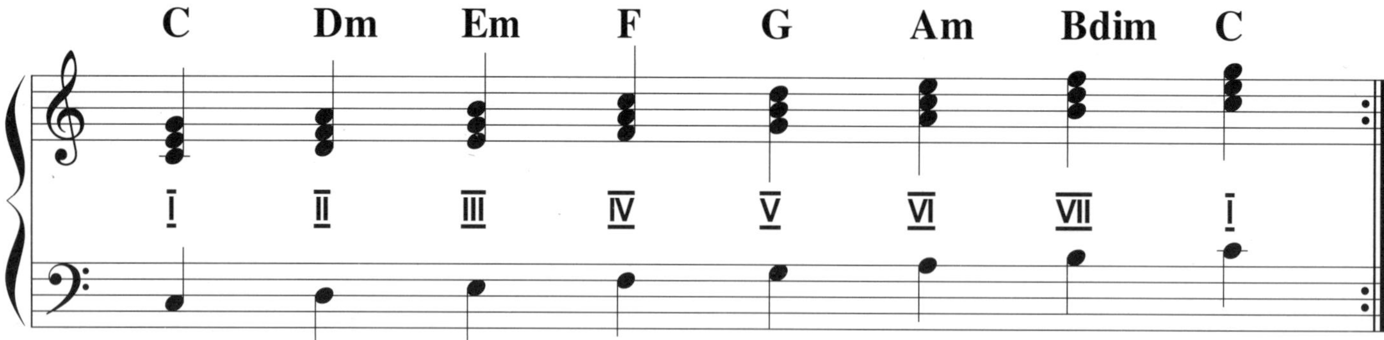

MORE ON CHORD PROGRESSIONS

In most songs there is an underlying harmonic pattern consisting of one chord moving to another and eventually coming to rest or beginning again on the first chord of the key. This chordal movement can be seen in most **chord progression**. If you look at a simple chord progression in the key of C major, it is easy to see how the system of Roman numerals works. The following example contains the chords C, F and G. Since these chords correspond to the first, fourth and fifth degrees of the C major scale, the progression could be described as I IV V I in the key of C.

29.

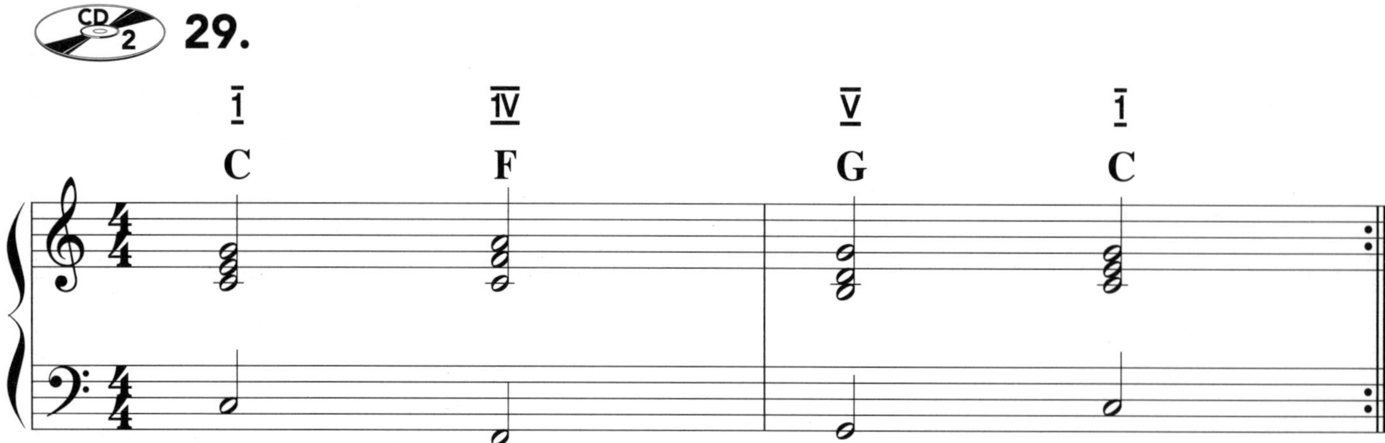

RHYTHM NOTATION

As well as traditional music notation you may sometimes come across **rhythm notation**, in which the notes have a diagonal line instead of a notehead. This tells you that instead of playing individual notes, either the guitar or the keyboard will be playing chords with a specific rhythm pattern.

30.

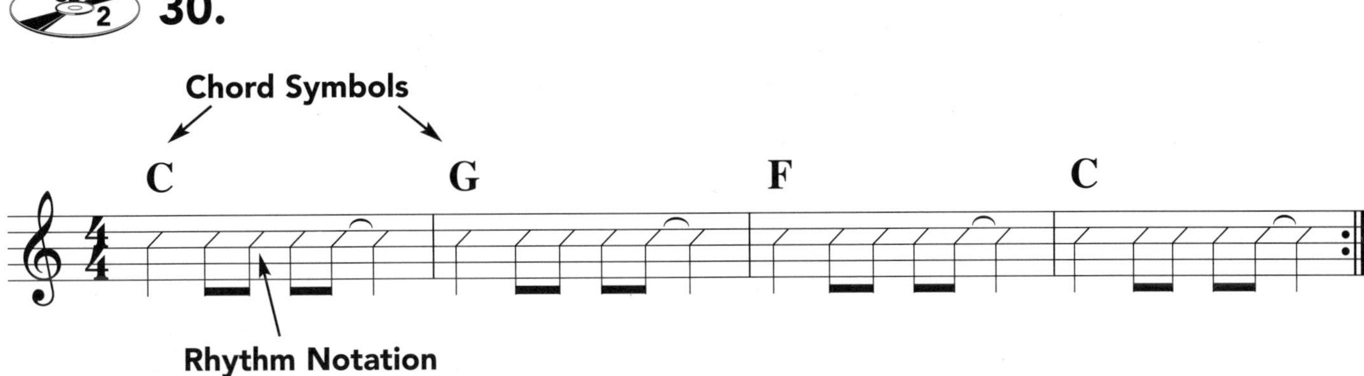

WRITING HARMONIES FROM CHORD CHARTS

As mentioned earlier, once you know the notes which make up chords, you can use any inversion or fingering you know to play them. This may involve re-arranging the order of the notes or doubling some of the notes, but as long as the chord contains only the three note names involved in that particular chord, you are still playing the right chord. The following example demonstrates the above progression written as an **S A T B** arrangement. Any time you see a chart containing chord symbols like the one above, you can write a vocal harmony arrangement from it in this manner.

31.

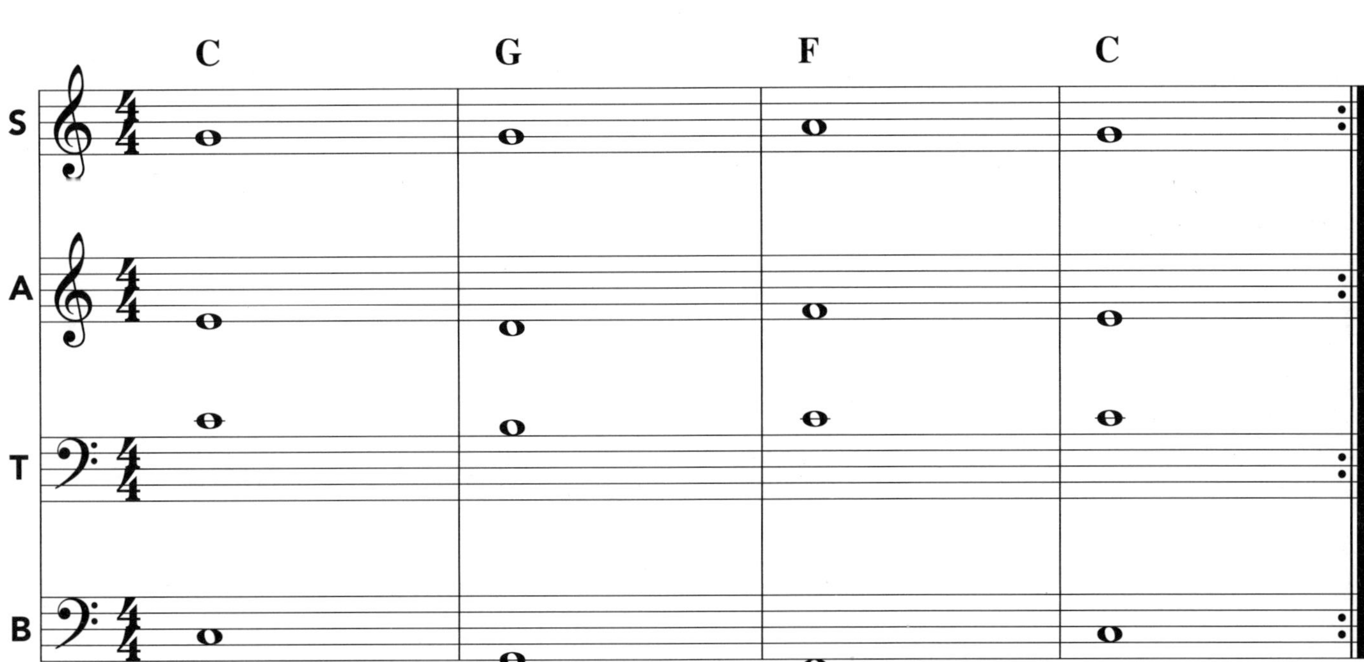

MAJOR KEY TRIAD PATTERN

If you analyse all the scale tone chords in the key of C major you come up with the following pattern:

I	**Major**	**(C Major)**
II	**Minor**	**(D Minor)**
III	**Minor**	**(E Minor)**
IV	**Major**	**(F Major)**
V	**Major**	**(G Major)**
VI	**Minor**	**(A Minor)**
VII	**Diminished**	**(B Diminished)**

This pattern remains the same regardless of the key. This means that if you look at the scale tone triads (three-note chords) in **any major key**, Chord I is **always** major, chord II is always minor, chord III is always minor, etc. The only thing that changes from one key to the next is the letter names of the chords. This can be demonstrated using at the scale tone triads for the key of **G major**.

CD 2 **32.**

CD 2 **33.**

By simply following the roman numerals and remembering which chords are major, minor, etc, it is easy to transpose chords from one key to another. Here is the progression from Example 31 transposed to the key of G.

G D C G

SCALE TONE CHORDS IN ALL KEYS

This chart lists the scale tone triads (three-note chords) in all major keys.

Summary of Scale Tone Chords

Scale Note:	I	II	III	IV	V	VI	VII	VIII (I)
Chord Constructed:	major	minor	minor	major	major	minor	dim	major
C Scale	C	Dm	Em	F	G	Am	B°	C
G Scale	G	Am	Bm	C	D	Em	F♯°	G
D Scale	D	Em	F♯m	G	A	Bm	C♯°	D
A Scale	A	Bm	C♯m	D	E	F♯m	G♯°	A
E Scale	E	F♯m	G♯m	A	B	C♯m	D♯°	E
B Scale	B	C♯m	D♯m	E	F♯	G♯m	A♯°	B
F♯ Scale	F♯	G♯m	A♯m	B	C♯	D♯m	E♯° (F°)	F♯
F Scale	F	Gm	Am	B♭	C	Dm	E°	F
B♭ Scale	B♭	Cm	Dm	E♭	F	Gm	A°	B♭
E♭ Scale	E♭	Fm	Gm	A♭	B♭	Cm	D°	E♭
A♭ Scale	A♭	B♭m	Cm	D♭	E♭	Fm	G°	A♭
D♭ Scale	D♭	E♭m	Fm	G♭	A♭	B♭m	C°	D♭
G♭ Scale	G♭	A♭m(G♯m)	B♭m	C♭ (B)	D♭	E♭m	F°	G♭

COMMON PROGRESSIONS

One of the best ways to become familiar with chords in all keys is to take a simple progression and transpose it to all keys. This may be slow at first, but the more you do it, the easier it gets. Here are some common progressions to learn and transpose. Write them out in all keys, then sing the root notes to hear how they sound.

I IV V I

I VI IV V

II V I

I VI II V

I IV VII III VI II V

EXERCISES

✏ Write the following minor scales on the staves below.

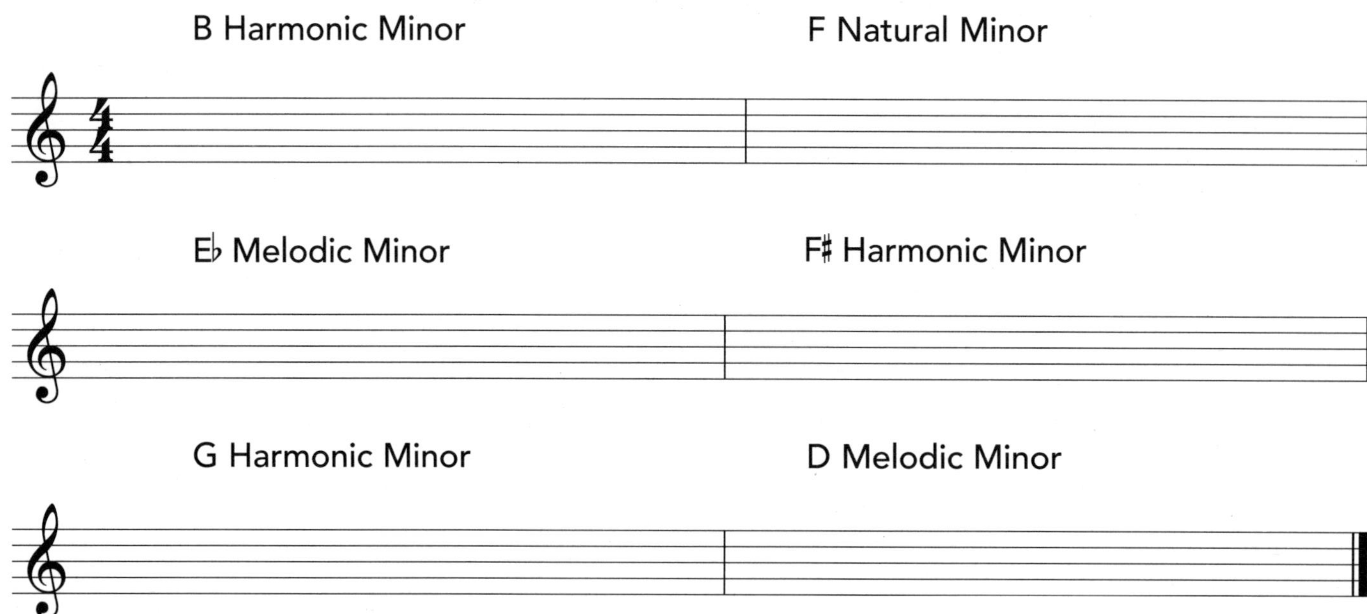

✏ Write the correct chord types for a major key next to the roman numerals below.

✏ Write the correct Roman numerals between the staves to describe the following chord progressions. It may help to write the names of the chords above the treble staff first.

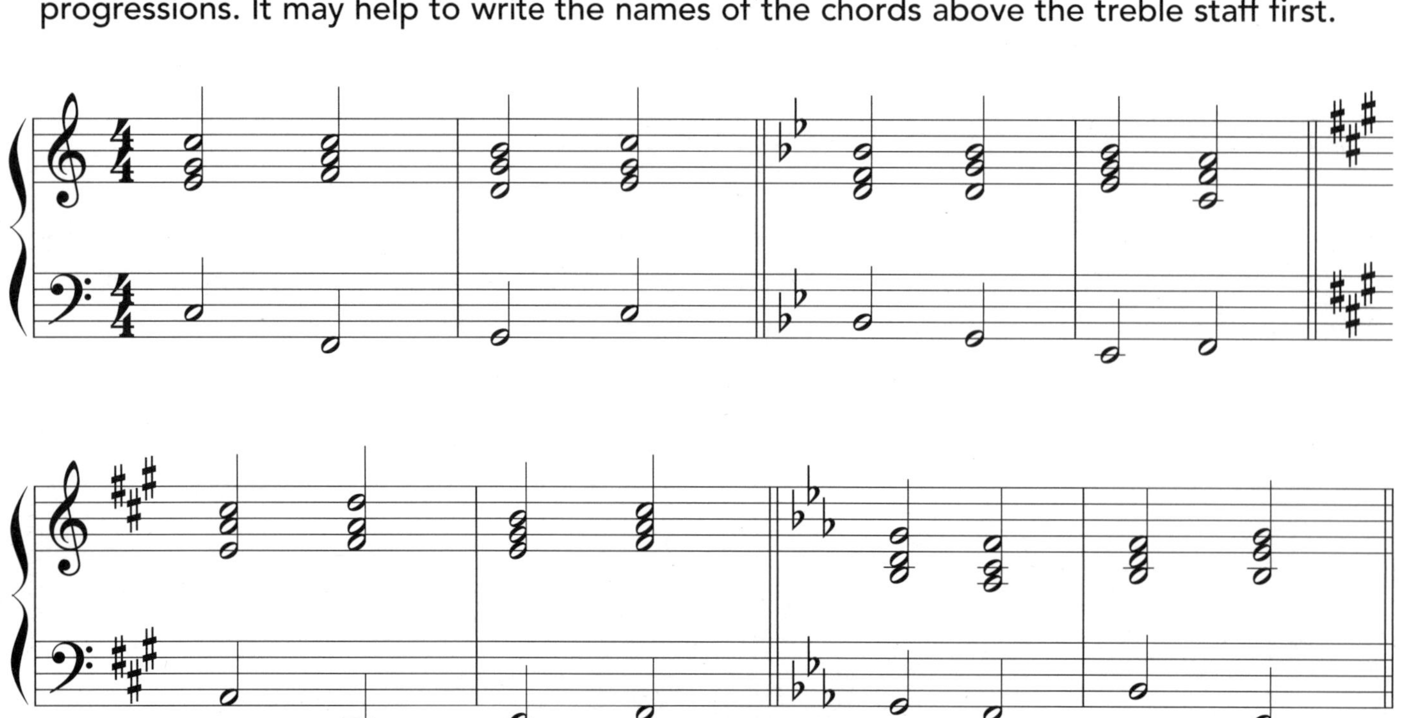

LESSON TWENTY NINE

MORE ABOUT HARMONY

In traditional music theory there are specific names for each degree (note) of the scale and the chords built on them.

1	2	3	4	5	6	7
Tonic	**Supertonic**	**Mediant**	**Subdominant**	**Dominant**	**Submediant**	**Leading Note**

Chords built on the degrees of the scale can be described by the name of each degree, e.g. the tonic triad, the supertonic triad, etc.

PRIMARY TRIADS

When using chords to harmonize melodies, certain chords are more common than others. The most commonly used chords in any key are the **tonic** (I), **subdominant** (IV) and **dominant** (V). With these three **primary triads**, it is possible to harmonize any melody in a key, because between them they contain all the notes (degrees) of the scale, as shown below.

	I	IV	V
Degrees	5	1	2
	3	6	7
	1	4	5
CHORD	**I**	**IV**	**V**

34. Primary Triads in C Major

Here are the primary triads in the key of C major in voicings that are easy to play on the keyboard.

HARMONIZING MELODIES

To harmonize a melody, all you need to do is find chords which contain the same notes as those that occur in the melody on the first beat of each bar.

35.

In $\frac{2}{4}$, $\frac{3}{4}$ or $\frac{3}{8}$ time, there will usually be **one chord per bar**. However, in $\frac{4}{4}$ or $\frac{6}{8}$ there are often **two chords per bar**. In $\frac{4}{4}$ the second chord can be played on the third beat, while in $\frac{6}{8}$ the second chord can be played on the fourth beat. The example below demonstrates another melody in $\frac{4}{4}$ time, with primary chords played on the first and third beats of each bar. Sometimes there is a new chord on the third beat (e.g. bars one and two) and at other times the chord played on the first beat is repeated on the third beat (e.g. bar 3). As a general rule, if the melody note on the third beat is one of the notes contained in the chord on the first beat, the same chord can be repeated, but if the melody note on the third beat is not in the chord from the first beat, a new chord should be used.

36.

MELODIES TO HARMONIZE WITH PRIMARY TRIADS

Here are some melodies in various times and keys for you to harmonize with primary triads. In the beginning, it is a good idea to first write down the notes contained in the primary triads of the key of the melody you are working on. In time, you will know them from memory and this will become unnecessary. Once you have harmonized each melody, experiment until you find the harmony that sounds best.

LESSON THIRTY

SECONDARY TRIADS

Although most melodies can be harmonized using only primary triads, the secondary triads (II III VI VII) can also be used to create different sounds and atmospheres in the music. Here is the melody from Example 35 with secondary triads from the key added to the harmony. Compare the two versions and listen to the different atmosphere created by changing the harmony.

37.

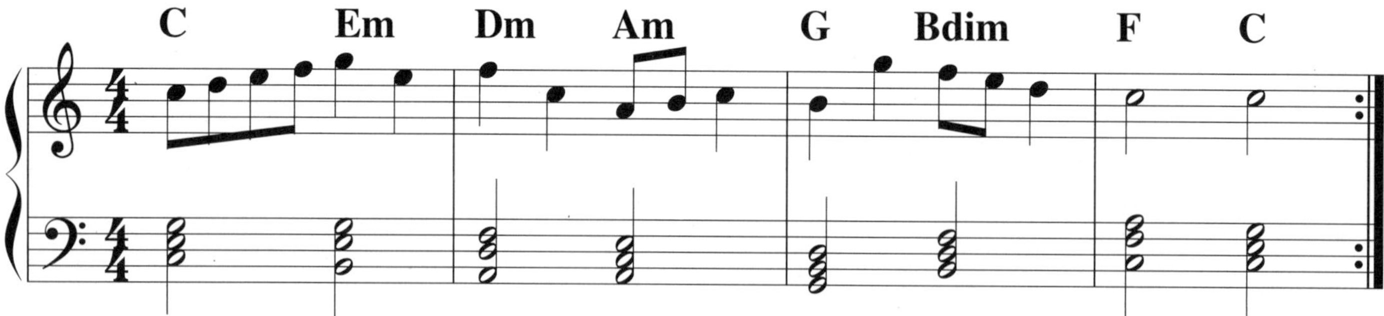

CHORD FUNCTIONS

Once you start using secondary chords, it becomes obvious that there is always more than one chord which can be used to harmonize any note of a melody. Although it is possible to progress form any chord to any other chord, certain progressions sound better than others, and have therefore become part of traditional harmony. Here are the common functions for each chord in a major key.

I Harmonizes degrees **1**, **3** or **5**. Usually ends a progression. Can begin a progression.

II Harmonizes degrees **2**, **4** or **6**. Can substitute for chord IV. Usually leads to chord V.

III Harmonizes degrees **3**, **5** or **7**. Can substitute for I or V. Usually leads to VI or IV.

IV Harmonizes degrees **4**, **6** or **1**. Can substitute for I, II or VI. Usually leads to V or I.

V Harmonizes degrees **5**, **7** or **2**. Can substitute for VII. Usually leads to I or VI.

VI Harmonizes Degrees **6**, **1** or **3**. Can substitute for I or IV. Usually leads to II or IV.

VII Harmonizes Degrees **7**, **2** or **4**. Can substitute for V or II. Usually leads to III or I.

VOICE LEADING

As mentioned in the previous lesson, it is best to use inversions which are close together on the keyboard when harmonizing melodies, as this produces a smoother sound. Each note of a chord can be described as a **voice**. When several chords occur in succession (a chord progression) you end up with a series of voices running through the chords. Unless you are deliberately going for a disjointed, choppy effect, it is desirable to have each of the voices progressing as smoothly as possible. This is called **voice–leading**.

The following example contains two harmonizations of a melody using the same chords. In the first version, the chord inversions are not close together. This is **not** good voice–leading. Compare it with the second version which contains inversions which are close together. Notice how much smoother the second version sounds, and how the whole thing sounds more natural and seems to flow more.

38.

Version 1 – Bad example of voice leading

Version 2 – Good example of voice leading

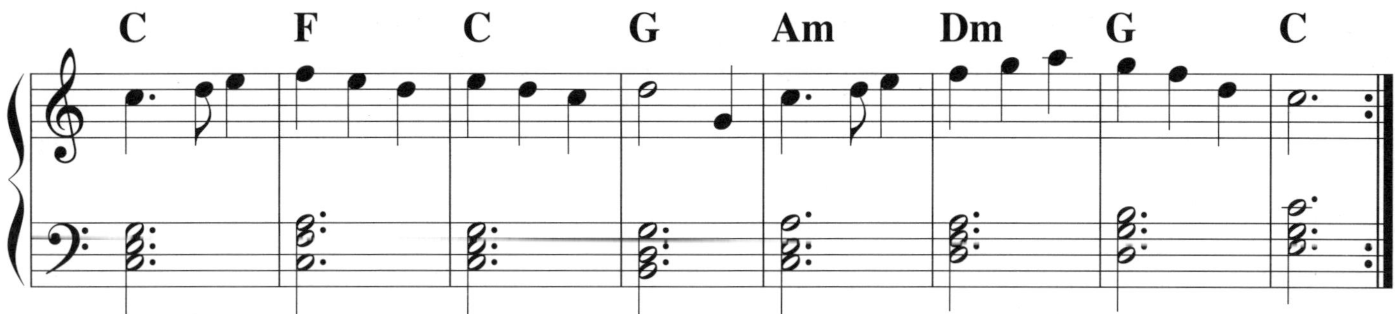

PRACTICE PROGRESSIONS

By learning to play the following progressions **in all keys** using inversions close together on keyboard or guitar, you will develop good voice–leading habits and will also be well prepared for harmonizing most major key melodies. Learn to play the progressions from memory using either hand while playing the root note of each chord with the other hand.

I IV V I   **I VI IV V**   **I III IV V**   **II V I**

I VI II V   **I IV VII III VI II V**

Here is a Chorale in the key of A major, written by the all-time master of voice leading – Johann Sebastian Bach. Listen to the majestic sound he creates with just four human voices. If you are serious about learning harmony, it is recommended that you purchase a book of Bach's Chorales and study some of them with a Classical harmony teacher. This will improve your ability to write and sing harmonies regardless of the style of music you sing.

CD 2 39. Chorale

Johann Sebastian Bach

MELODIES TO HARMONIZE

Here are some melodies to harmonize using both primary and secondary triads. Try two different harmonizations for each one and follow the guidelines for chord functions set out on the first page of this lesson. Remember to use the general voice–leading principle of using chord inversions which are close together.

LESSON THIRTY ONE

MINOR KEY SCALE TONE TRIADS

To find the relative minor of any major key, start on the 6th degree of the major scale. This example shows the scale tone triads for the key of **A minor**, with the chords being derived from the **natural minor** scale. As you will see, the chords are exactly the same as those contained in the key of C major. The only difference is the starting and finishing point. Because the minor scale starts on **A**, A minor will now be chord I instead of VI. As with major keys, notice how the chords are constructed as two lines of 3rd intervals. These can instantly be used as harmonies in the key of A minor.

 **40.**

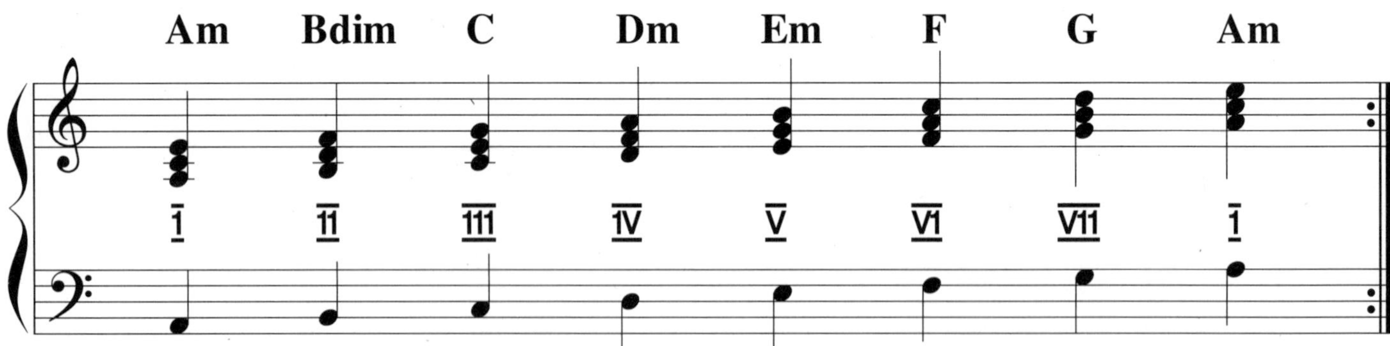

The following progression could be described as VI I V VI IV V VI I V IV V VI in C major or as I III VII I VI VII I III VII VI VII I in A minor. Because the progression has an obvious minor tonality (tonality), musicians would use the second description. Try Writing out the notes of this progression as S A T B voice parts.

41.

CHORDS IN OTHER MINOR KEYS

Here are the scale tone chords for the key of **E natural minor** which is the relative minor of G major. Once again, the chords will be the same as those of its relative, but the starting note is E instead of G, so **Em** will be chord I.

42.

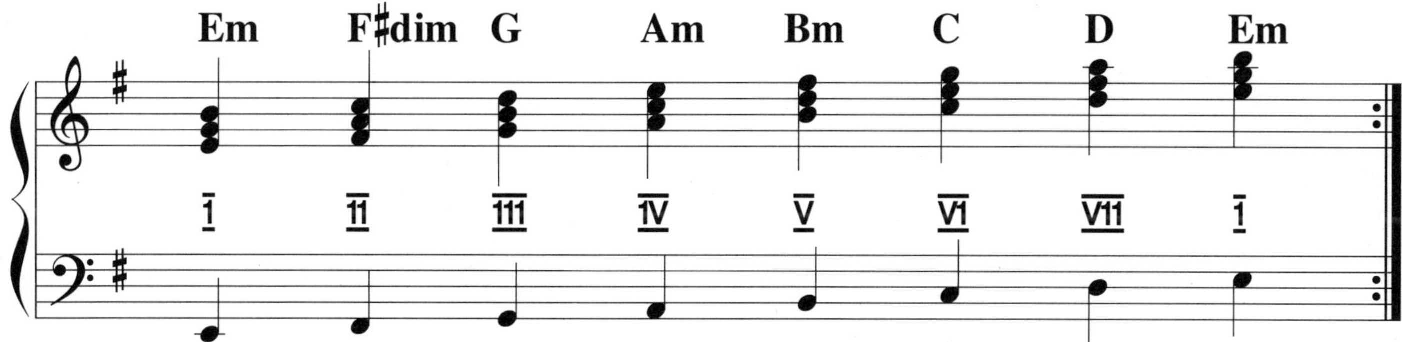

TRANSPOSING IN MINOR KEYS

Just like songs in major keys, songs in minor keys can be transposed to other keys. This example shows the progression from Example 41 transposed to the key of **E minor**.

43.

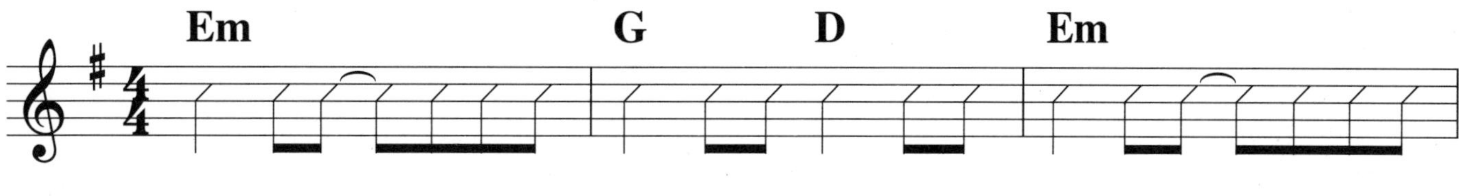

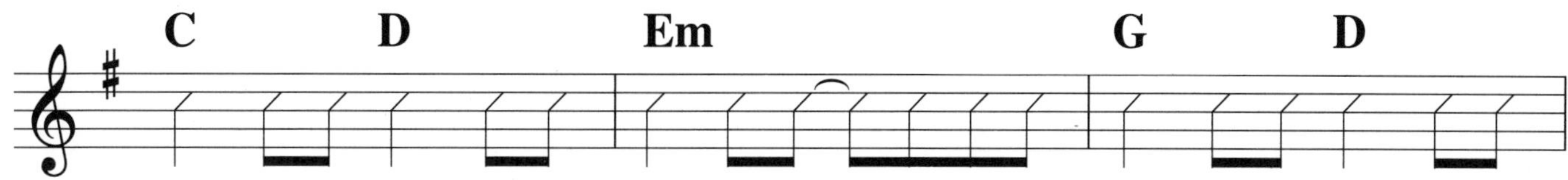

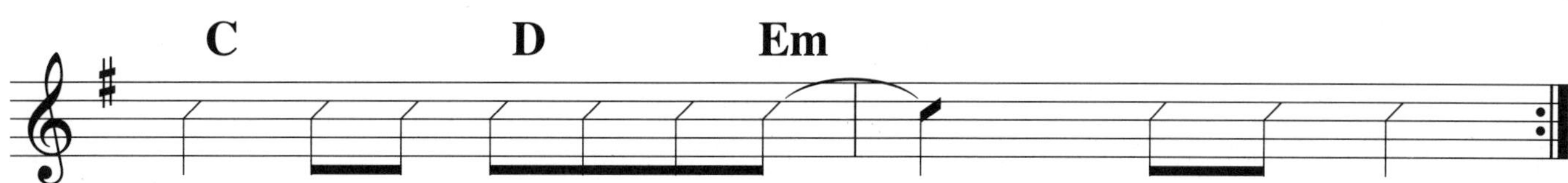

HARMONIC MINOR SCALE TONE CHORDS

Because there are three types of minor scales, it is possible to come up with different sets of chords for a minor key by building chords on the notes of each of the three minor scales. Each variation to the notes of the scale alters the quality of chords built on the scale. The letter names of the chords remain the same, but the chord type may change. Here are the scale tone chords derived from the **A harmonic minor scale**. Notice that chord III is now **augmented** instead of major, and also that chord V is **major** instead of minor and chord VII is **diminished** instead of major. These changes are all brought about by the raising of the 7th degree of the scale from **G** to **G♯**.

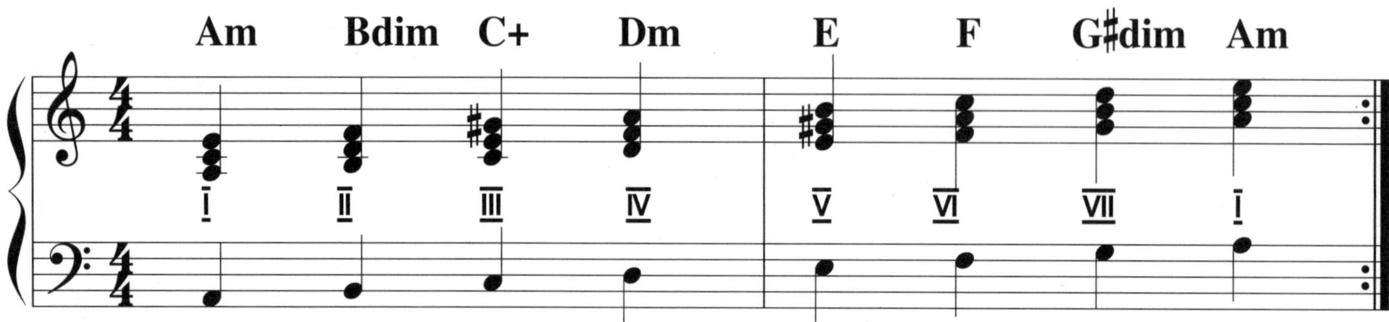

The example below demonstrates a melody and chord progression created from the A harmonic minor scale.

MELODIC MINOR SCALE TONE CHORDS

Now look at the scale tone chords derived from the **A melodic minor scale**. Because of the sharpened 6th degree there will are changes to the types of chords derived from this scale. Notice that chord II is now **minor** instead of major, and also that chord IV is **major** instead of minor and chord VI is **diminished** instead of major. These changes are all brought about by the raising of the 6th degree of the scale from **F** to **F♯**.

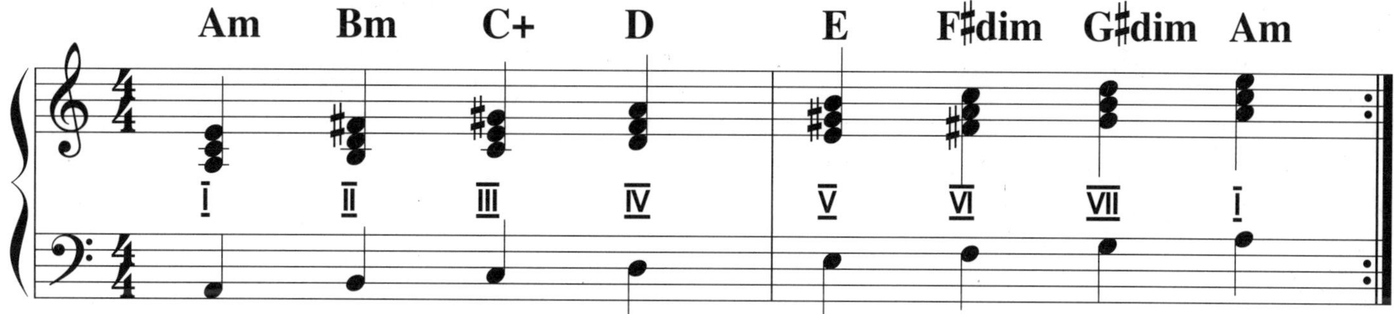

In minor keys, it is common to use chords from all three types of minor scales. A good example of this is the song **House of the Rising Sun**, which is presented here in the key of A minor. Look through the chords and identify which ones come from each type of minor scale. You could also try analyzing other songs in this way, e.g. **Greensleeves** and **Scarborough Fair**.

House of the Rising Sun (Key of A Minor)

Traditional

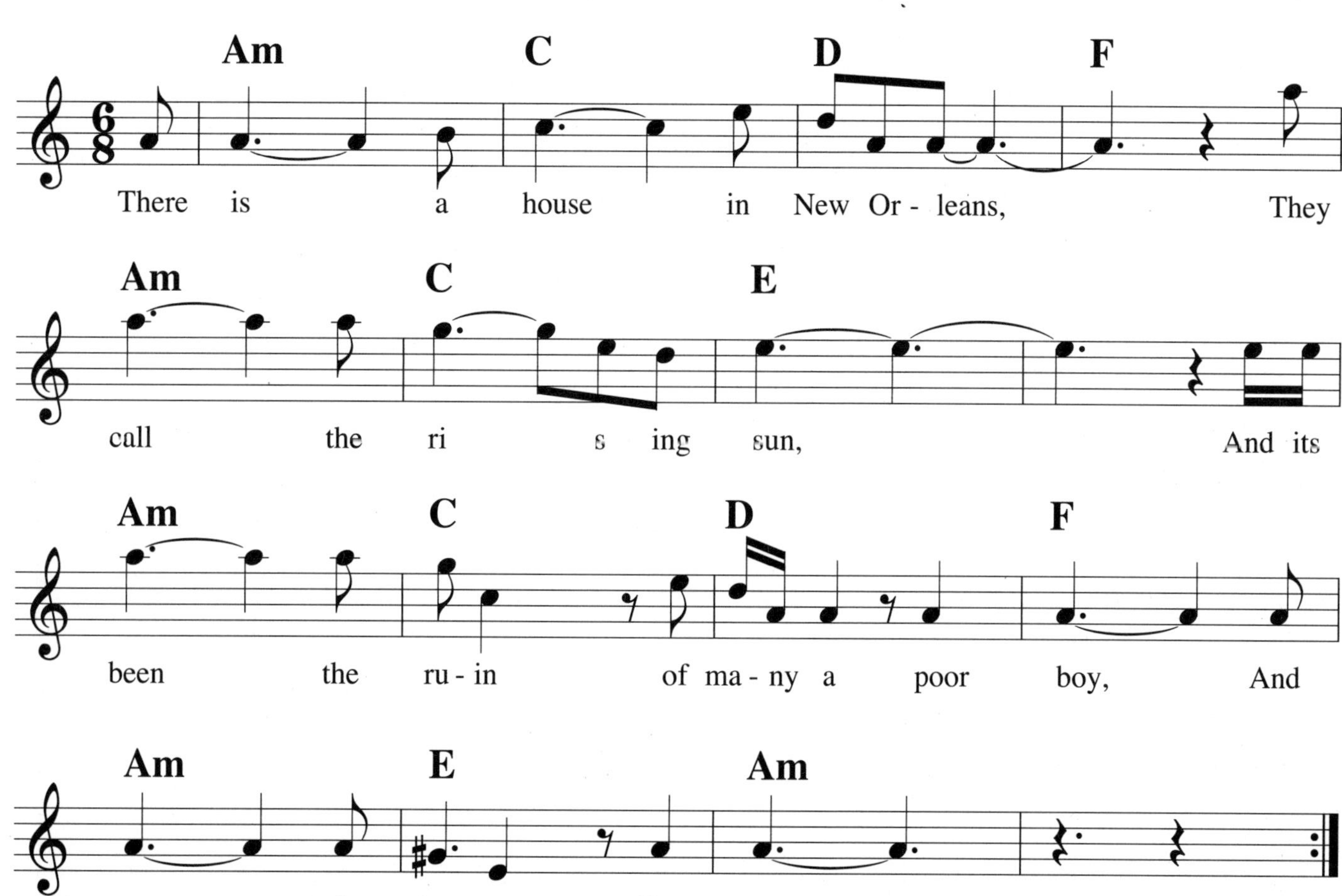

LESSON THIRTY TWO

HARMONIES IN RELATIVE KEYS

Many songs alternate between a major key and its relative minor. In this case it is common to use harmonies from the natural minor scale because it contains the same notes as the relative major scale. If a chord from a different minor scale is desired, there will usually be an indication in the melody, e.g. an accidental. The following progression begins in the key of **G major** and ends in **E minor**. All the notes in these harmonies are found in both the G major scale and the E natural minor scale.

45.

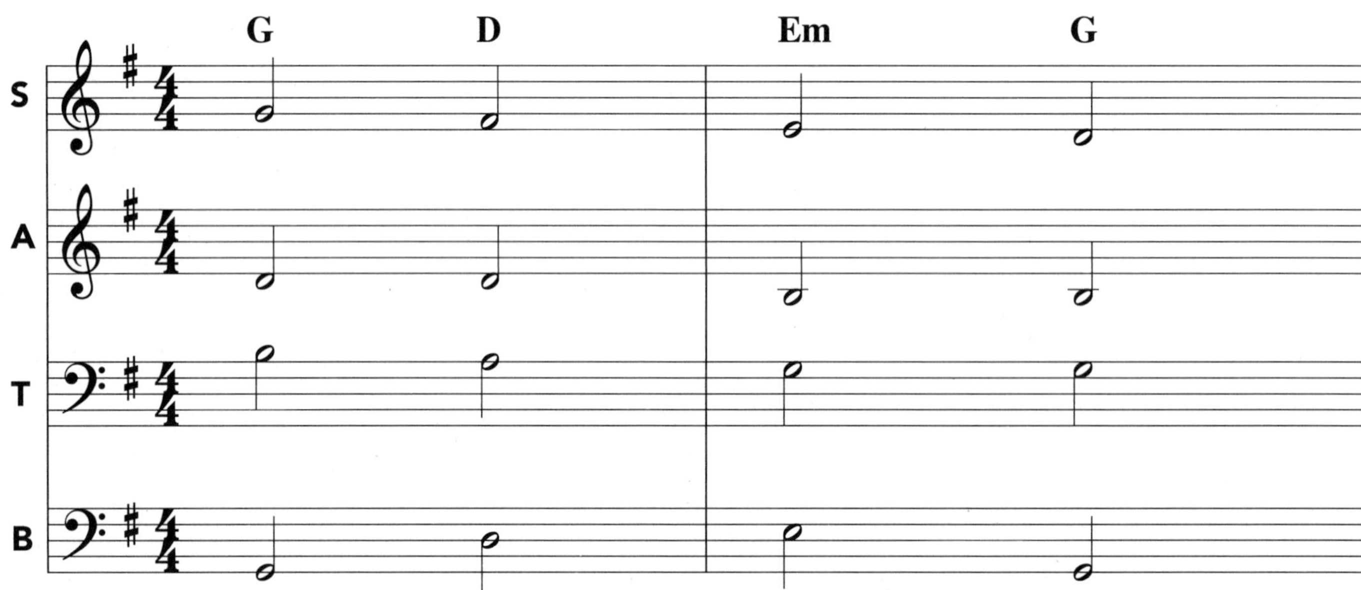

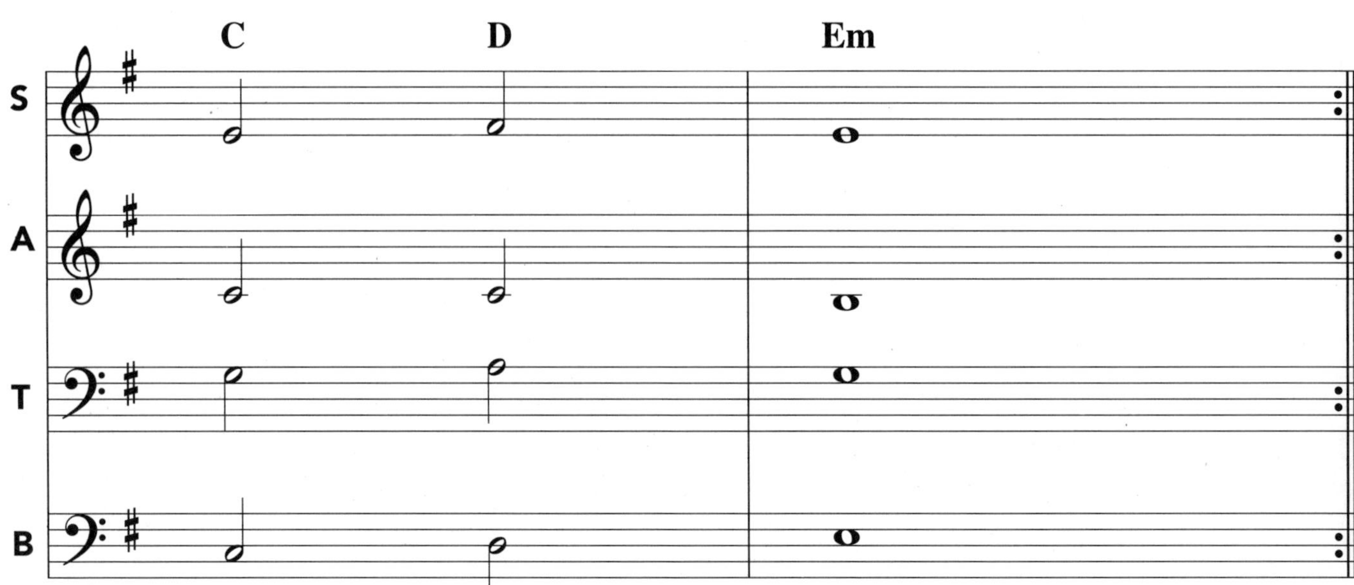

This song alternates between the keys of G major and E minor. It has two verses: the first expressing a longing for a lost love, and the second angrily rejecting the ex-partner. Listen to the recording and notice how the vocalist delivers each verse in a totally different way. This is partly done with dynamics, partly with range (verse 2 is sung an octave higher), partly with the way the words are expressed, and partly through the use of harmonies.

The harmony sung in the final four bars of each verse is based on the progression from the previous example. Listen to the impact the harmonies have by coming in at this point. Using harmonies only at points you wish to emphasise often works better than harmonizing the whole melody.

46. Where Are You Now?

Peter Gelling

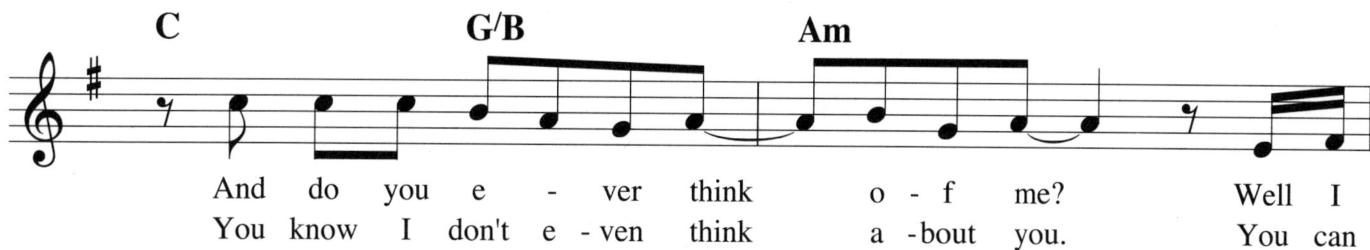

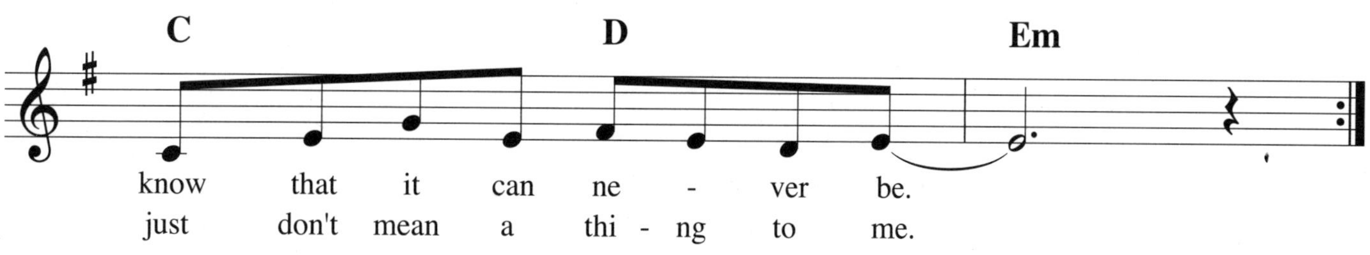

LESSON THIRTY THREE

SEVENTH CHORDS

Many songs contain chords made up of more than three notes. By adding more notes on top of the basic triads, it is possible to create many other types of chords. The most common of these are **seventh chords**. By adding another note either a major or minor third above the basic triad, **five** different types of seventh chords can be created. Here are formulas for the various types of seventh chords.

Major Seventh Chord Formula

Chord Symbol: **CMaj7**

1 3 5 7

Notes in Chord

C	E	G	B
1	3	5	7

Dominant Seventh Chord Formula

Chord Symbol: **C7**

1 3 5 ♭7

Notes in Chord

C	E	G	B♭
1	3	5	♭7

Minor Seventh Chord Formula

Chord Symbol: **Cm7**

1 ♭3 5 ♭7

Notes in Chord

C	E♭	G	B♭
1	♭3	5	♭7

Minor Seven Flat Five Chord Formula

Chord Symbol: **Cm7 ♭5**

1 ♭3 ♭5 ♭7

Notes in Chord

C	E♭	G♭	B♭
1	♭3	♭5	♭7

The final type of seventh chord is the diminished seventh. This chord is unusual in that it contains a **double flattened 7th** degree (𝄫7). This note is actually the same as the 6th degree (A) but it is technically called **B𝄫7** because the interval has to be some kind of seventh rather than a sixth because the chord is a type of **seventh** chord.

Diminished Seventh Chord Formula

Chord Symbol: **C°7**

1 ♭3 ♭5 𝄫7

Notes in Chord

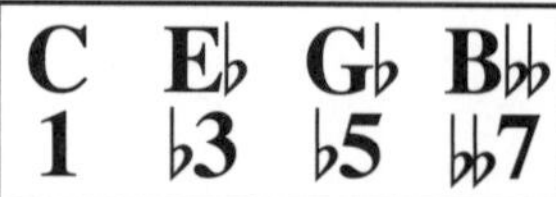

C	E♭	G♭	B𝄫
1	♭3	♭5	𝄫7

47.

Here is the notation for the five types of Seventh chords built on the note C.

Cmaj^7 C^7 Cm^7 Cm$^{7(\flat 5)}$ Cdim^7

All these seventh chord types are used in Jazz and other music, particularly from the Romantic era onwards. By far the most commonly used is the **Dominant 7th**. In Blues and Jazz, a dominant 7th often ends a song, rather than resolving to a major or minor ending. To learn more about the various types of 7th chords and how they can be used, see ***Progressive Complete Learn to Play Keyboard Manual.***

EXERCISES

✏ Write the correct chord symbols above each of the following seventh chords.

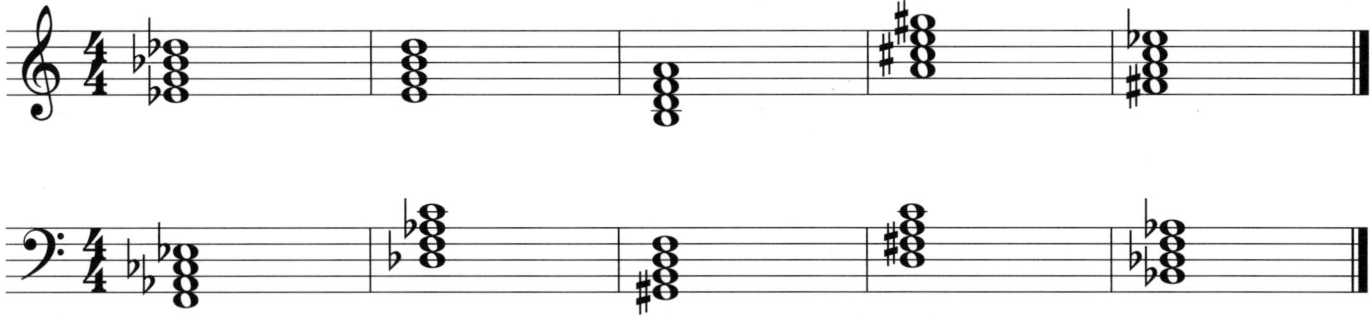

✏ Write the correct notes to create the chords below the symbols on the staves below.

Dmaj^7 A$\flat$m^7 Edim^7 F$\sharp^7$ B$\flat$m$^{7(\flat 5)}$

Gdim^7 D$\flat^7$ Fm$^{7(\flat 5)}$ Bmaj^7 G$\sharp^7$

SCALE TONE SEVENTH CHORDS

By applying the formulas for seventh chords to the C major scale, the following series of **scale tone seventh chords** is created.

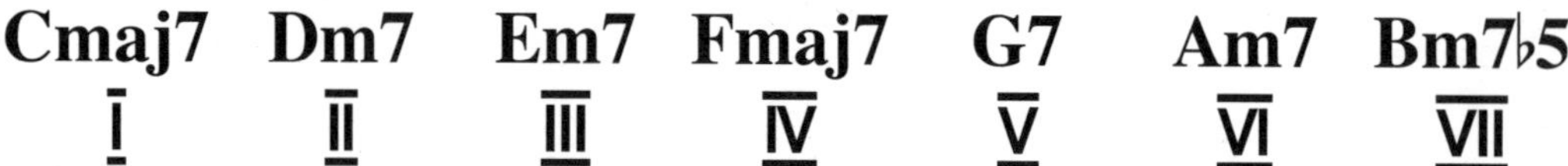

48.

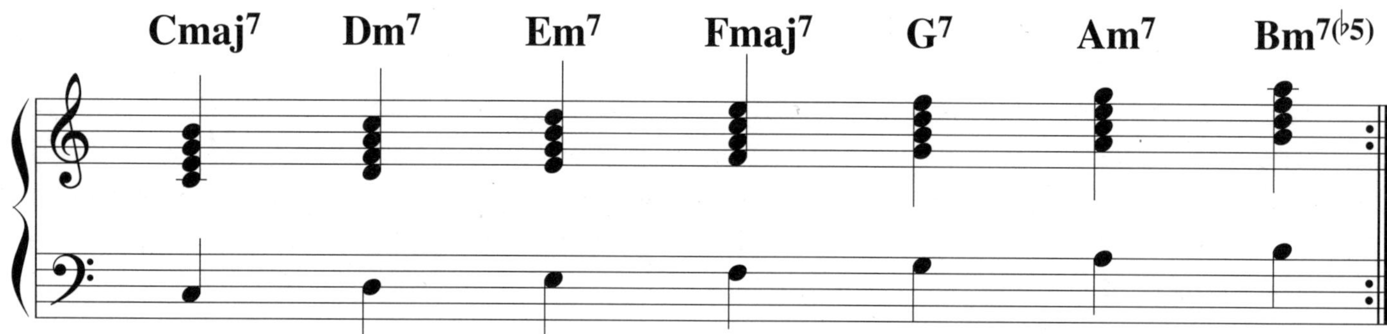

This table shows the scale tone 7th chords for every major key. If you wish to sing Jazz, it is essential to know these chords.

I	II	III	IV	V	VI	VII	VIII
Major7	**Minor7**	**Minor7**	**Major7**	**7**	**Minor7**	**Minor7♭5**	**Major7**
Cmaj7	Dm7	Em7	Fmaj7	G7	Am7	Bm7♭5	Cmaj7
Gmaj7	Am7	Bm7	Cmaj7	D7	Em7	F♯m7♭5	Gmaj7
Dmaj7	Em7	F♯m7	Gmaj7	A7	Bm7	C♯m7♭5	Dmaj7
Amaj7	Bm7	C♯m7	Dmaj7	E7	F♯m7	G♯m7♭5	Amaj7
Emaj7	F♯m7	G♯m7	Amaj7	B7	C♯m7	D♯m7♭5	Emaj7
Bmaj7	C♯m7	D♯m7	Emaj7	F♯7	G♯m7	A♯m7♭5	Bmaj7
F♯maj7	G♯m7	A♯m7	Bmaj7	C♯7	D♯m7	E♯(F)m7♭5	F♯maj7
Fmaj7	Gm7	Am7	B♭maj7	C7	Dm7	Em7♭5	Fmaj7
B♭maj7	Cm7	Dm7	E♭maj7	F7	Gm7	Am7♭5	B♭maj7
E♭maj7	Fm7	Gm7	A♭maj7	B♭7	Cm7	Dm7♭5	E♭maj7
A♭maj7	B♭m7	Cm7	D♭maj7	E♭7	Fm7	Gm7♭5	A♭maj7
D♭maj7	E♭m7	Fm7	G♭maj7	A♭7	B♭m7	Cm7♭5	D♭maj7
G♭maj7	A♭m7	B♭m7	C♭(B) maj7	D♭7	E♭m7	Fm7♭5	G♭maj7

EXTENDED CHORDS

In Jazz, Funk, Fusion, or Modern R&B, you will often find chords which extend past the 7th, notably various types of **9th**, **11th** and **13th** chords. These higher numbers come about by repeating the scale from which they are derived over two octaves. Thus, in the higher octave the 2nd becomes the 9th, the 4th becomes the 11th and the 6th becomes the 13th, as shown here in the key of C.

C	D	E	F	G	A	B	C	D	E	F	G	A	B	C
1	2	3	4	5	6	7	8	9	10	11	12	13	14	15

As you have already learned, most chords are made up of various 3rd intervals stacked one on top of the other. This means that by going through a scale in thirds (i.e. skipping every second note) it is easy to create chords up to a 13th.

Depending on the nature of the degrees of the chord, 9ths 11ths and 13ths may be either major, minor or dominant in quality. E.g. if you add a **9th degree** on top of a **dominant 7th** chord, you end up with a **dominant 9th** chord (usually just called a 9th chord). If you add a 9th degree on top of a **minor 7th** chord, you end up with **a minor 9th** chord, etc. The example below demonstrates the use of extended chords. If you wish to learn more about chords and their uses, see ***Progressive Complete Learn to Play Piano Manual***, or ***Progressive Complete Learn to Play Jazz Guitar Manual***.

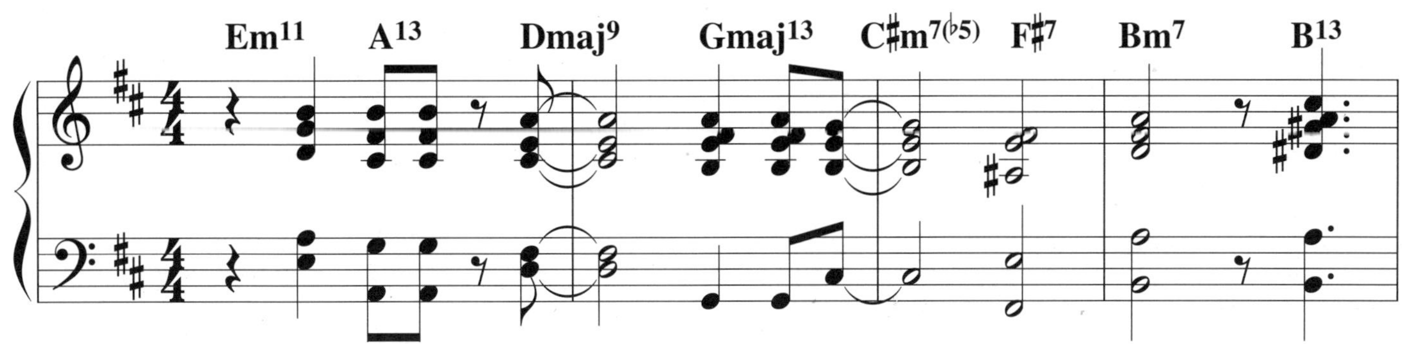

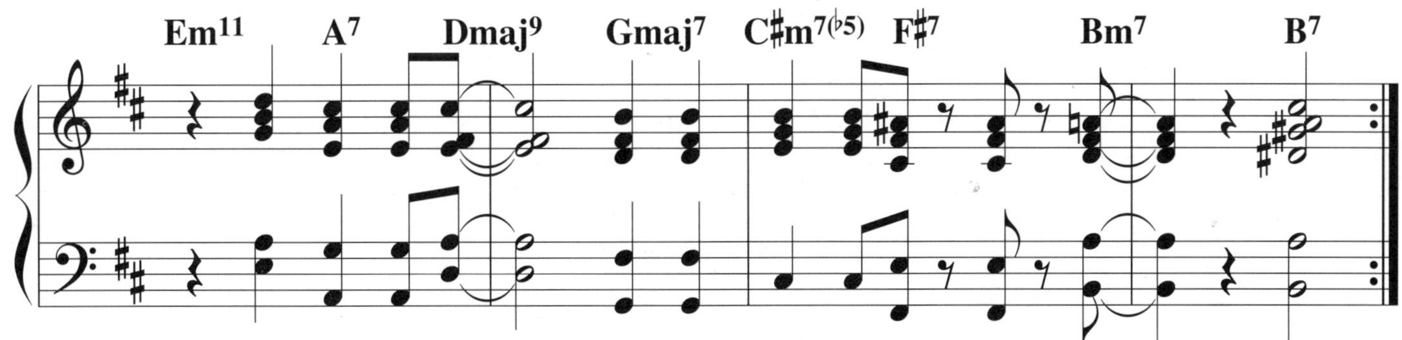

LESSON THIRTY FOUR

JAZZ SINGING

It takes three elements to sing Jazz well – vocal dexterity, a well trained ear and a knowledge of chords, scales, and arpeggios. All great Jazz singers have these elements. The best way to start singing Jazz is to imitate great vocalists and gradually add in more adventurous notes and techniques as you learn them. The following example is a Jazz style Blues sung with the wordless syllables of **scat singing**. Each phrase is followed by a space for you to repeat what you hear. Use the syllables shown here until you are comfortable with each phrase, then try using other syllables and improvise your own phrases.

CD 2 **50. Jazz Blues in B♭**

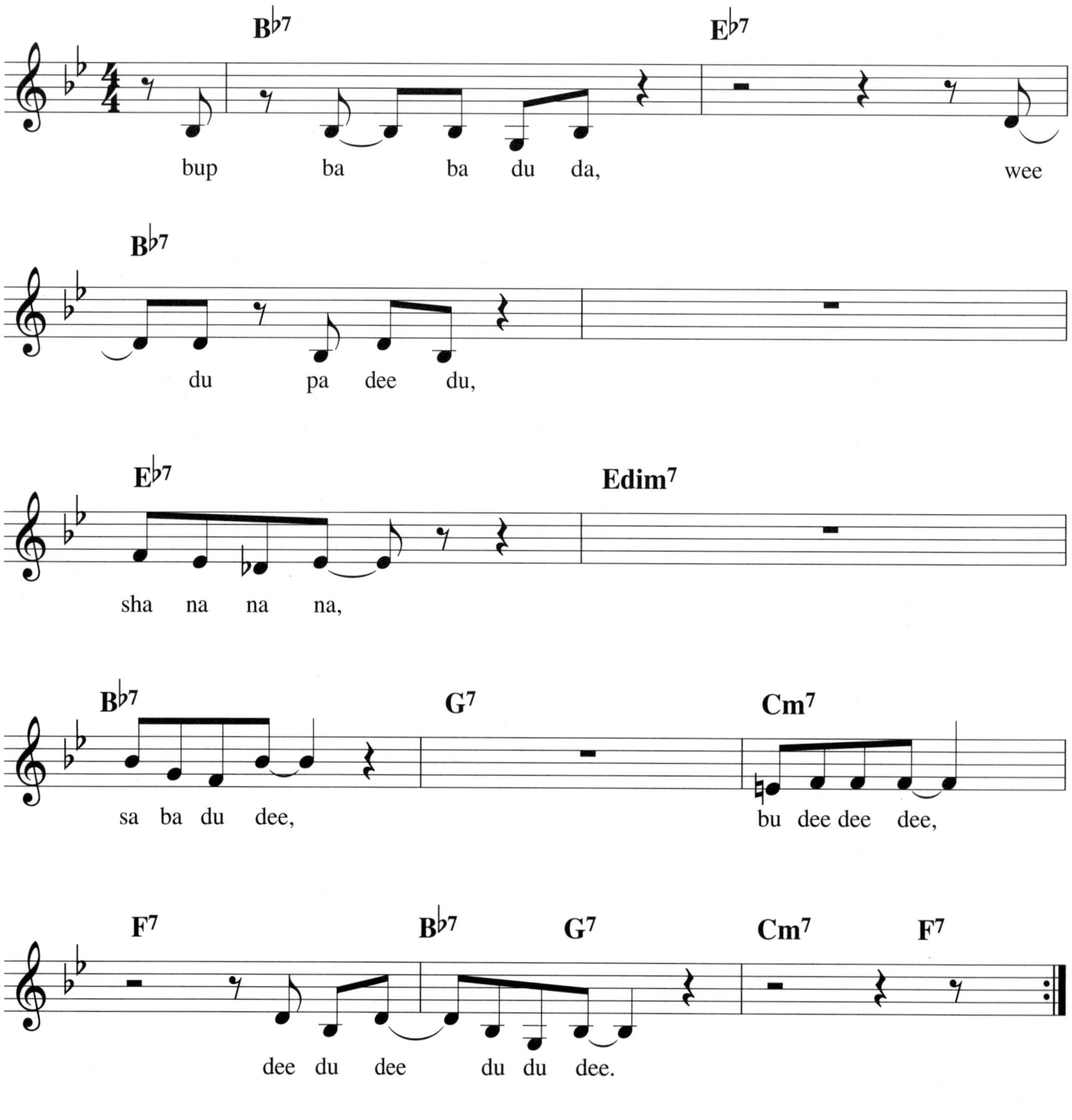
B♭7
E♭7
bup ba ba du da, wee
B♭7
du pa dee du,
E♭7
Edim7
sha na na na,
B♭7
G7
Cm7
sa ba du dee,
bu dee dee dee,
F7
B♭7
G7
Cm7
F7
dee du dee du du dee.

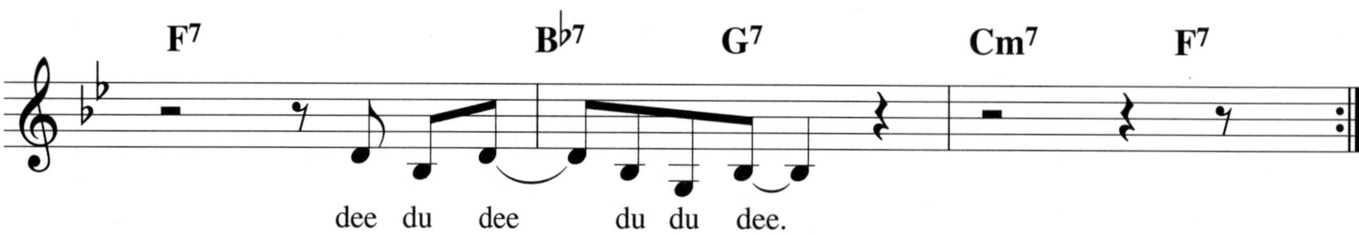

WHICH NOTES TO USE

Music theory is really only a way of explaining sounds. In reality, you can sing any note over any chord as long as it sounds good. It is only when a note is held that it either harmonizes or clashes with the accompaniment. The biggest step in learning to improvise is letting go and trusting your ear. You will obviously make mistakes as a beginning improviser, but the brain and the ear learn quickly and in time you will find more and more of the 'right' notes naturally, just by practicing singing by ear.

Having said that, the more you know about how chords, scales and arpeggios relate to each other, the more options you will have when improvising. Any time a band is playing a Blues progression, you can use the Blues scale in that particular key. The previous example was in the key of **B♭**. Here is the **B♭** Blues scale. Learn the notes and then sing it from memory.

51.

WHICH SOUNDS TO USE

The sounds you use are almost as important as the notes in scat singing, so it helps to practice them before you start improvising. If you listen to the singers like Ella Fitzgerald, Sarah Vaughan and Mel Torme, you will notice that they often imitate the sounds and musical lines played by saxophone and trumpet players. This includes slides, bends and all kinds of expressions. For beginners, however, it is best to start simply and then gradually add more complex sounds.

All the vowel sounds are commonly used in Jazz, but when it comes to consonants, 'hard' sounds like '**T**' or '**P**' are rarely used to begin a syllable, as they cause problems with microphones. 'Soft' consonants like '**D**' and '**B**' are much more suitable. Try syllables like **ba**, **bee**, **bu** and **bop**, along with **da**, **du**, **dee** and **dop**. The possibilities are endless, but these will help get you started.

Listen to the CD and try improvising short phrases using these syllables with the Blues scale over the backing to the **Blues in B♭**.

52. Sing with CD

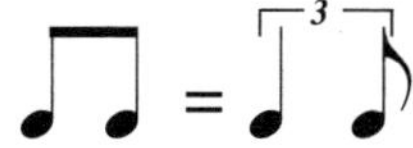

USING ARPEGGIOS

Another source of notes in Jazz songs is the arpeggios of the chords used by the accompaniment. Learning to sing arpeggios of all the various types of 7th chords is essential if you are serious about singing Jazz. However, this is a long term project and is best tackled in short bursts along with your regular practice. Concentrated work on arpeggios for ten minutes per day will bring great results after a few months.

This kind of study is best done with a teacher who knows Jazz theory, but here's something to get you started. Shown below is the same **Blues in B♭** but this time the arpeggios of all the chords have been added under the chord symbols. Learn each arpeggio individually and then try moving from one to another. Remember this is just an ear training exercise, not a melody you would sing when performing live.

CD 2 **53.**

LESSON THIRTY FIVE

ARTICULATIONS

There are many different ways in which a note can be sung or played, e.g. loud, soft, staccato, legato, etc. These are referred to as **articulations**. The way you articulate notes can make a dramatic difference to the way the music sounds.

In written music specific markings indicate the articulation desired by the composer. Two examples of this are shown below. For example, a short horizontal line directly above or below a note indicates that the note is to be held for its full written duration. This articulation is referred to as **tenuto**. Another common articulation which you may already know is **staccato**, which means the note is to be short and separate from other notes. Staccato is indicated by a dot directly above or below a note.

CD 2 54.0 Tenuto and Staccato

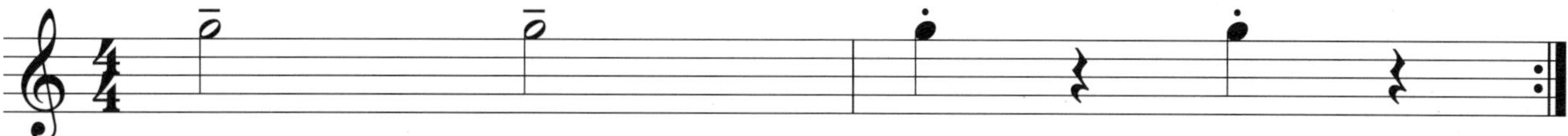

Listen to the CD to hear the effect produced by tenuto and staccato in this example. Experiment with these articulations by applying them to phrases you already know well and then try improvising with them. It is also important to listen to albums featuring your favorite vocalists. Pay careful attention to how they articulate notes in different styles and situations. If you do this for even a few minutes each day, you will soon begin to instinctively know how to articulate notes yourself.

CD 2 54.1

ACCENTS

Another important aspect of articulating notes is the use of **accents**. Accent markings are used to indicate notes which are to be sung or played louder than other notes. The most common are the tenuto accent (long), indicated by a horizontal wedge mark above or below the note, and the staccato accent (short), indicated by a vertical wedge above or below the note.

55.0

This example uses both types of accents. Try adding accents to phrases you already know and then try using them in your improvising.

55.1

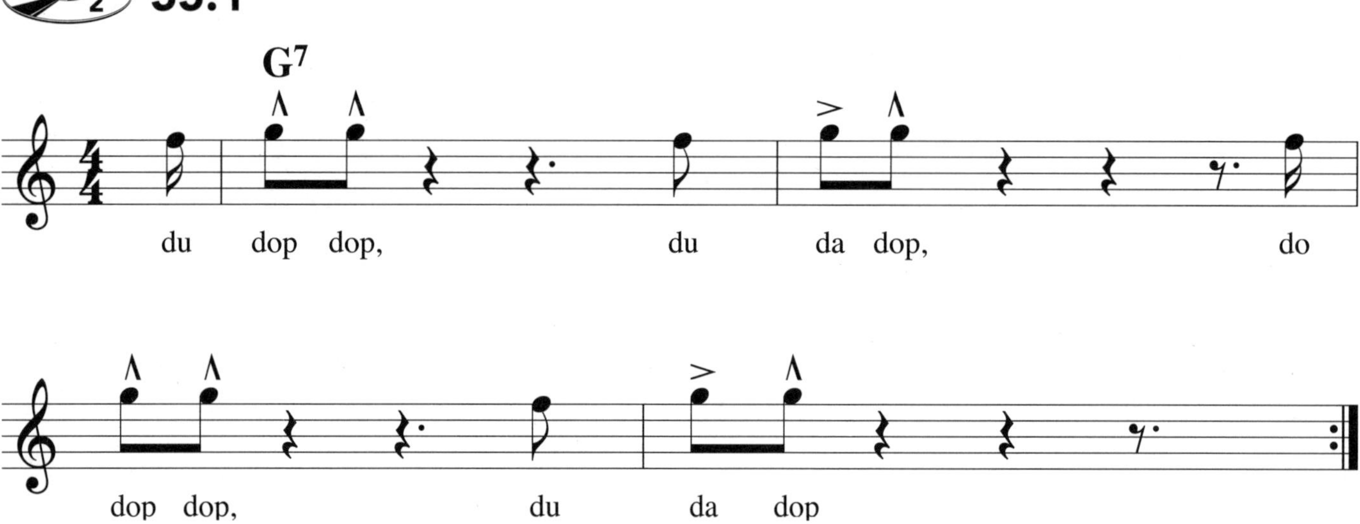

ACCENTS AND SWING

When singing swung eighth notes, it is common to give a slight accent to the notes which occur off the beat. Practicing this will help you develop a better feel for Jazz.

55.2

GHOST NOTES

A **ghost note** is a note sung or played more softly than other notes. It is often 'felt' more than heard. A ghost note is indicated by brackets placed either side of the note. The amount of 'ghosting' is up to the individual musician. A ghost note can be anything from about half the volume of unghosted notes right down to barely audible.

CD 2 56.0

Listen to the CD to hear the effect of ghost notes and then imitate what you hear. A space has been left on the repeat of the recording for you to sing this example with the band. Once you have the feel of ghost notes, try using them when improvising.

CD 2 56.1

As with other expressions and articulations, it is a good idea to practice ghost notes with scales and arpeggios. Here is the G Blues scale using ghost notes on the beat. Once again, there is space on the recording for you to sing on the repeat.

CD 2 56.2

This musical line also uses ghost notes on the beat. As with the previous examples, listen to the recording and imitate what you hear.

DEVELOPING RHYTHMIC CONTROL

To become a good Jazz singer it is essential to have control over exactly where in the bar you sing each note and also where you remain silent. A good way to develop this ability is to concentrate totally on rhythm by using only one note, and singing it in all different rhythmic positions within a bar. The following example begin with a pair of eighth notes on different beats within a bar, and then moves on to groups of four notes sung in various positions. The aim is to be able to instantly repeat a rhythm both by ear and from written music. On the recording, each bar is followed by a space for you to sing the rhythms in time with the band.

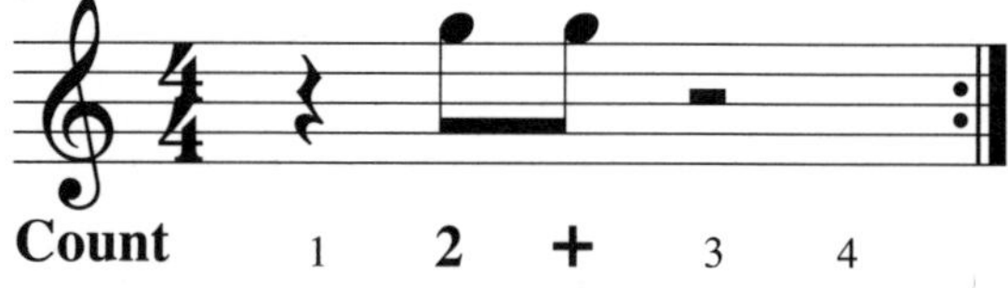

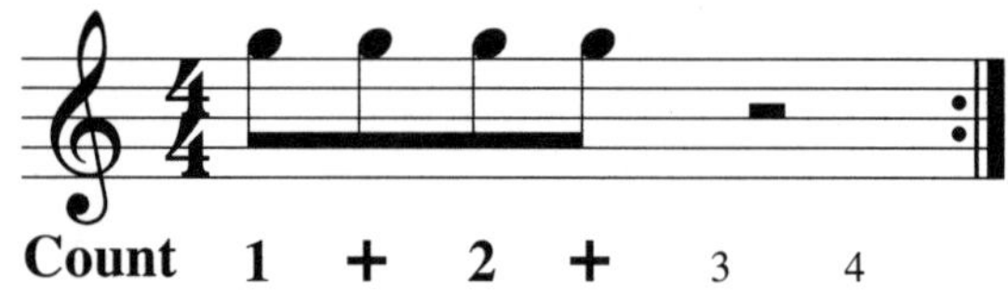

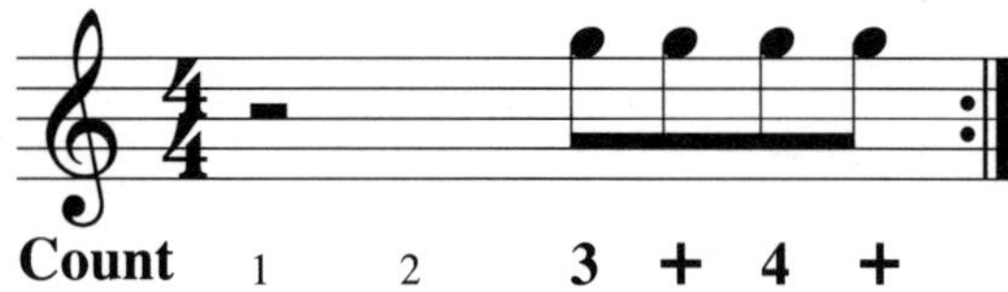

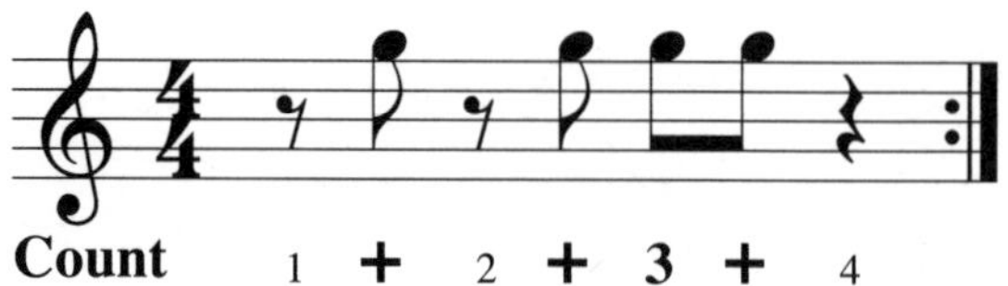

VOCAL SOLOING

Learning to sing Jazz well takes many years. We have only scratched the surface in this book. However, as long as you keep listening, imitating and improvising, you will see great improvements in your singing. To finish this section on Jazz, here is a 48 bar vocal solo sung over the **B♭** Blues we have been using. Learn it and then try writing some of the phrases and syllables on the staves below. Notice how the vocalist keeps coming back to the melody and lyrics as a springboard for improvisation. If you are singing several songs in succession and improvising on them, this technique helps make each song unique as well as giving you a context for improvised phrases and solos.

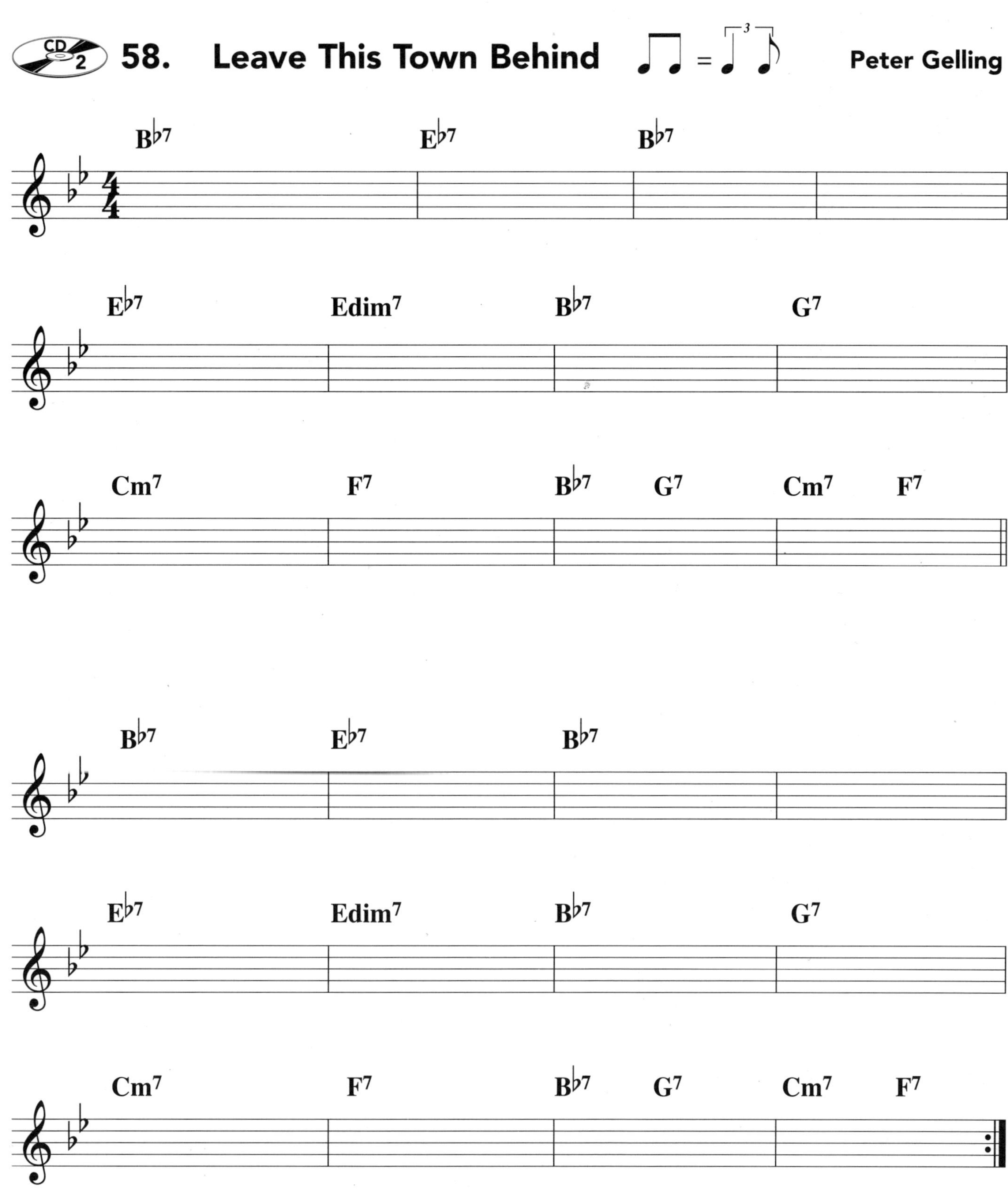

LESSON THIRTY SIX

MUSICAL FORM

The term **musical form** refers to the underlying structure of a piece of music. This could be a sequence of verses and choruses or a repeating chord pattern or bass line. The most common forms are **binary** (an A section followed by a B section - e.g. verse and chorus) and **ternary** (usually an A section followed by a B section, then a return to the A section, which is sometimes an exact repeat, and other times not).

The song **Greensleeves** is an example of **binary form**. The A section is played twice (first and second endings) and is then followed by the B section which ends the piece. The whole form can then be repeated with different lyrics for extra verses.

Greensleeves

Traditional

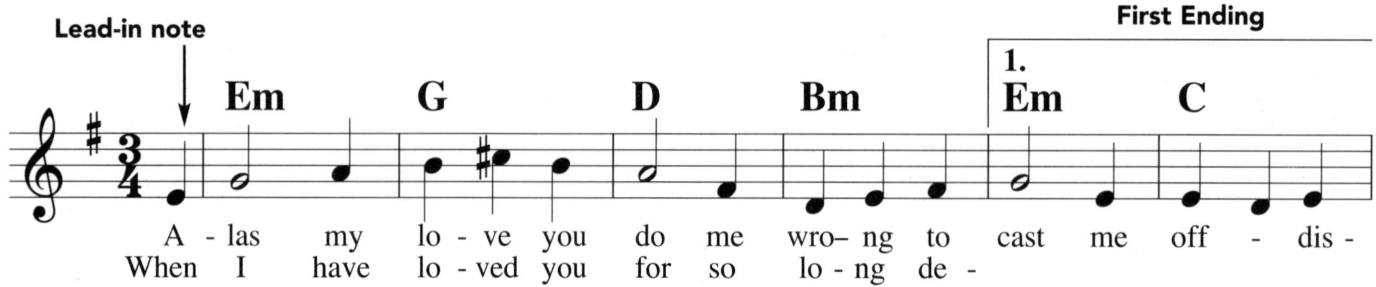

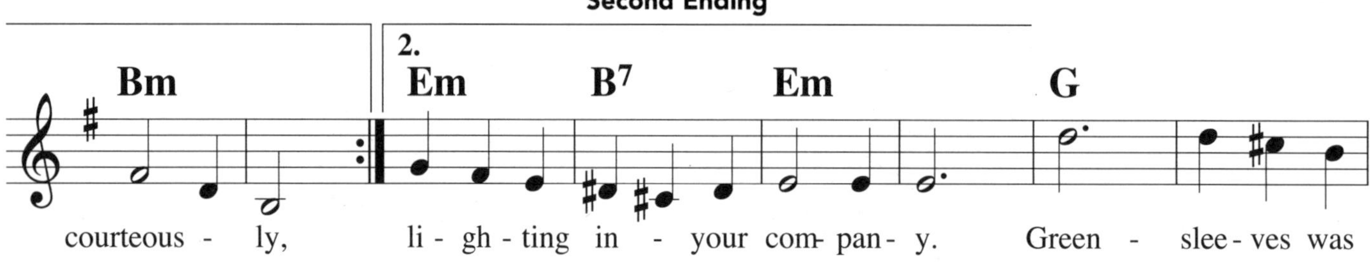

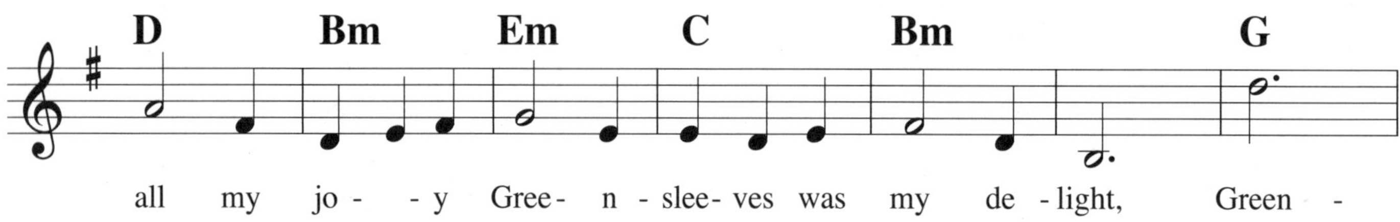

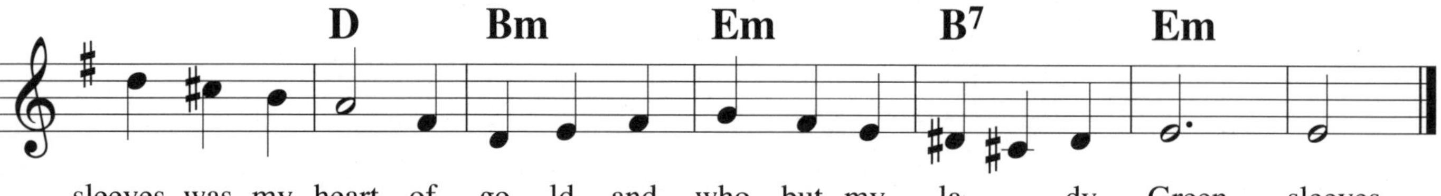

TYPICAL BLUES SONG FORMAT

Here is a common pattern of call and response which is found in many Blues songs. There are lots of variations, but memorising this pattern will enable you to play call and response very effectively with other musicians or vocalists. The first two responses are played over chord 1, while the third response is a turnaround. A good example of this format is the song *"Sweet Home Chicago"*. Listen to Blues albums for other examples.

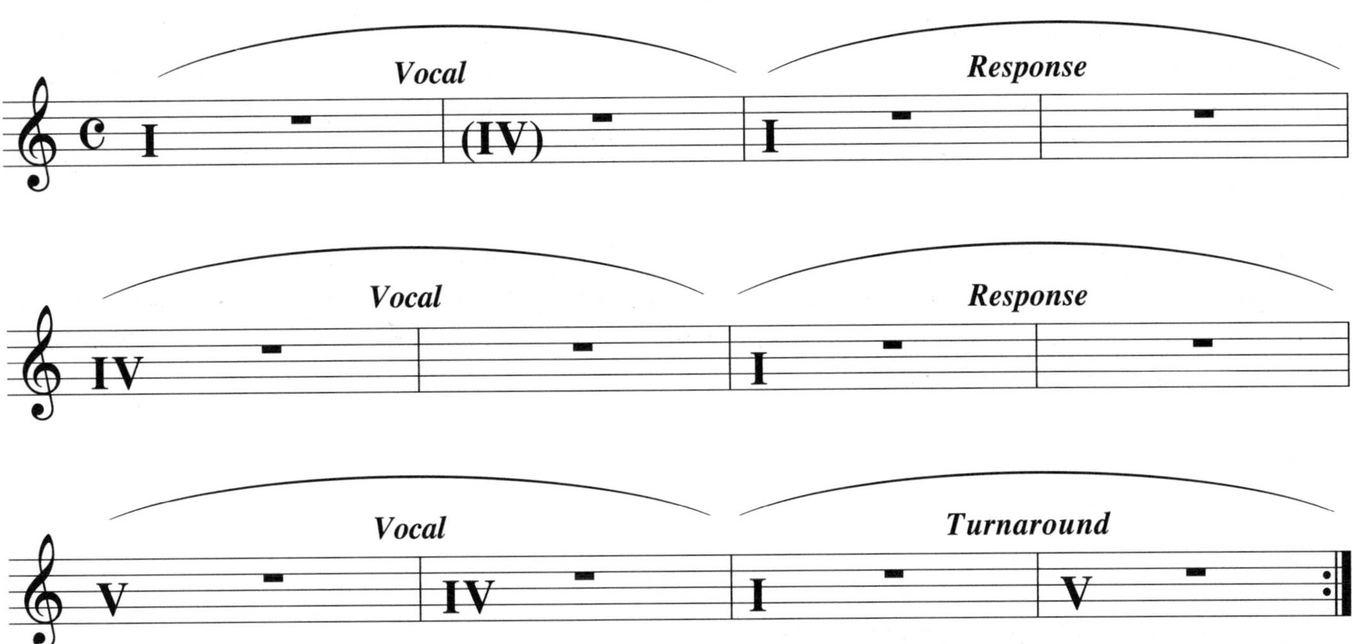

LEARNING SONG FORMS

With all that you have learned, you now have the knowledge and the tools to sing any style of music. It is recommended that you get together with other musicians as often as possible, as well as think about performing live. You should also be singing along with albums every day, sometimes copying what you hear and sometimes improvising, as well as learning melodies sung by your favorite vocalists, and analyzing them in terms of chord and note choices and use of rhythm.

To sing with other musicians, you need to build a repertoire. Get a book with a large collection of standards and start learning as many songs as you can. Make a habit of memorizing them and then transposing them to other keys that suit your voice. As you learn more songs, you will find that there are certain progressions which come up regularly, the most common being II V I. If you sing with Jazz musicians, there are certain song forms which they will assume you know from memory. These include **Rhythm Changes** (a chord progression based on George Gershwin's **I Got Rhythm**) and several variations on the **12 bar Blues** form.

Rhythm Changes is a typical example of **32 bar Song Form**, or **AABA form**. This **consists of an A section played twice**, followed by a **B section** (called a **bridge**) and then a return to the **A section** (or sometimes a variation of the A section). There are literally thousands of songs which use the **AABA** form.

PLAY-ALONG RECORDINGS

A great way to become familiar with the form of a song is to use a play-along recording of it. There are many **play along recordings** available which feature a rhythm section but no melody instrument. Many of them contain either standard songs or progressions which are very much like particular songs. Once you can sing the basic melody along with the rhythm section, you can start improvising phrases over the form until you are comfortable with it. By the time you can do this, you are ready to perform the song live.

SOME JAZZ TERMINOLOGY

Jazz musicians have added many new terms to the musical dictionary.

Tune - A song or composition used as the basis for improvisation.
Changes - The underlying chord progression of a song (a series of chord changes).
Head - The melody of a song, usually played at the start and finish, with solos in between.
Chorus - Once through the entire form of the piece.
Bridge - The B Section or 'middle eight'.
Blowing - Improvising, taking a solo.
Trading Fours - Musicians taking turns to improvise four bar phrases.
Bop - Bebop style (e.g. Charlie Parker, Dizzy Gillespie, Thelonious Monk).

There are many more, but these will help you out in Jam sessions.

RHYTHM CHANGES

The title **Rhythm Changes** refers to a progression based on the George Gershwin song **I Got Rhythm**. Over the years there have been many new melodies (or **heads** in Jazz terms) written on this progression and it is still routinely used by musicians jamming together or auditioning a new band member.

This example shows the basic progression in the key of **B Flat**. On the CD it is played without a melody. Try improvising along with the recording, using your knowledge of chords and keys, but also relying on your ear. This recording is quite fast (mm=220), so if you have trouble with it, practice with some slower songs first. In time, faster tempos will become easier. Ella Fitzgerald was amazing at improvising vocal solos at fast tempos.

LESSON THIRTY SEVEN

FORM, HARMONY AND DYNAMICS

Many songs have a simple one-part form which repeats. In this situation different sections can be created by thoughtful use of harmonies and variation in the instrumentation. The spiritual **Nobody's Fault but Mine** is a good example. Here are the first two verses.

60. Nobody's Fault But Mine

Trad, Arr. Peter Gelling

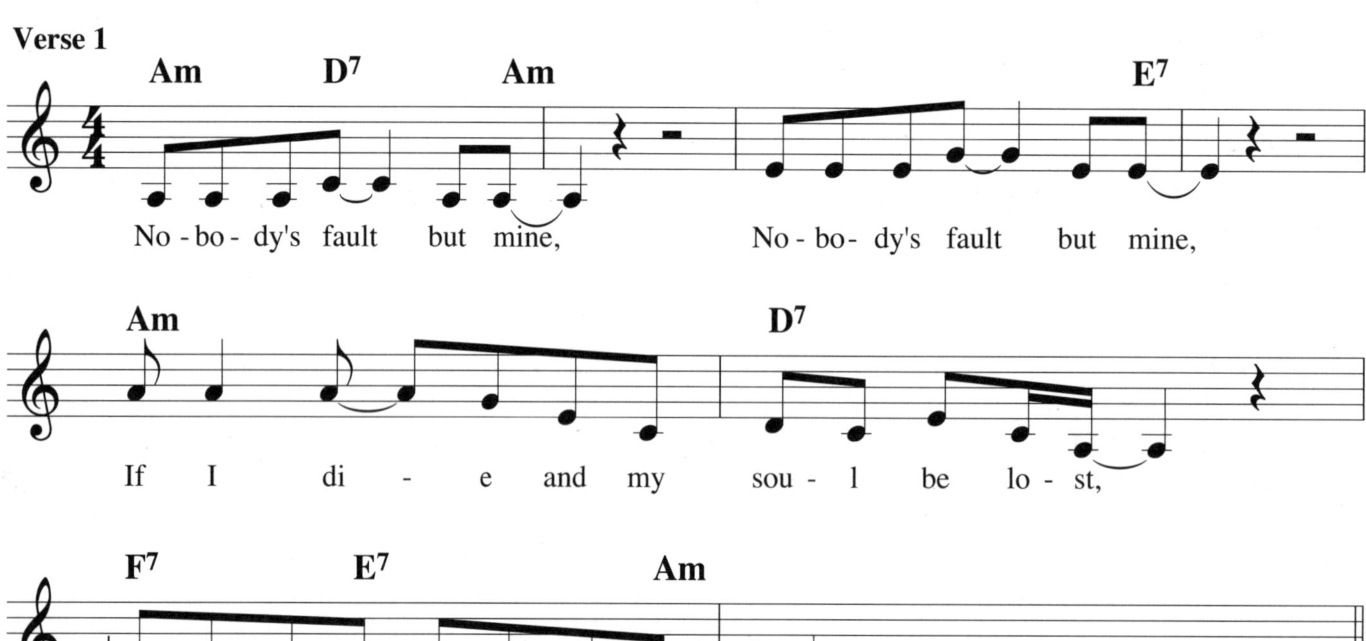

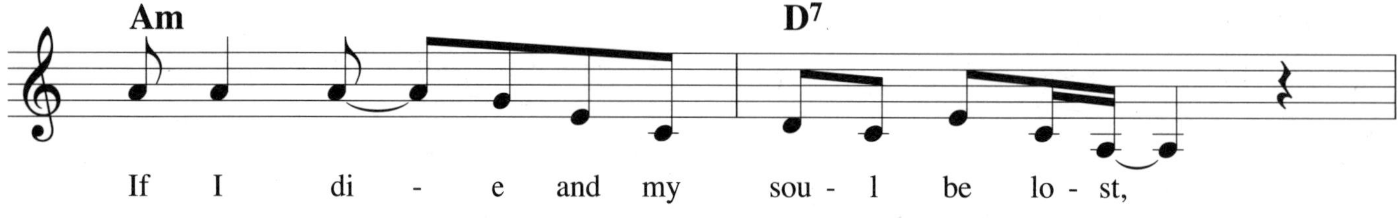

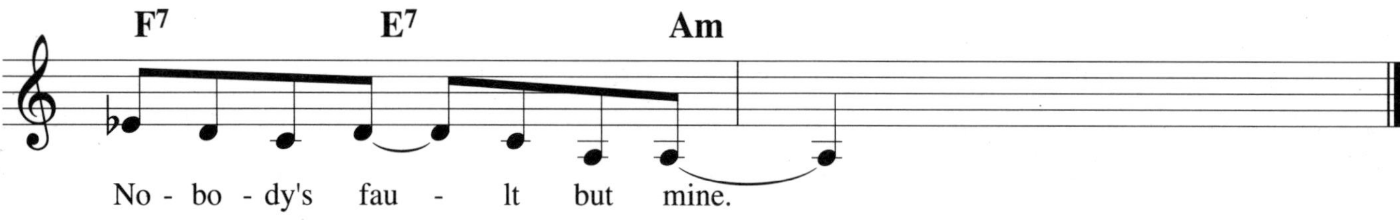

Because of the nature of the lyrics, a subtle arrangement with a single voice suits this song. However, after several verses, this may become rather dull. Other voices could be added, or the backing could be changed to add variety. On the recording, both these things have been done. A completely new instrumental section has also been added. This means that when the vocalist returns to the first verse, it feels fresh.

To build the dynamics, a choir has been added to the final section. The choir sings the melody in unison, while the lead vocalist improvises responses based on the lyrics. In the final verse, the choir breaks away from the melody and sings harmonies as a section. These harmonies are notated below. Notice the use of 7th and 9th chords here

Nobody's Fault But Mine – Harmonies

A FULL VOCAL SCORE

Here is an arrangement of another spiritual – **All my Trials** – arranged for four female voices accompanied by piano, cello and percussion. All the vocal parts are written out. Notice how each vocal part is busy sometimes and silent at other times. This kind of interplay and imitation is one of the things that makes choral arrangements spellbinding as well as creating drama and dynamics.

This arrangement is in the key of **F**, with a middle section in **D minor**. Analyze the score to see how the parts work with the chords. Try learning the parts one by one and try singing them with some friends. Male vocalists can sing the parts down an octave. Have fun with it! Once you know it well, try experimenting and create your own interpretation.

CD 2 61. All My Trials

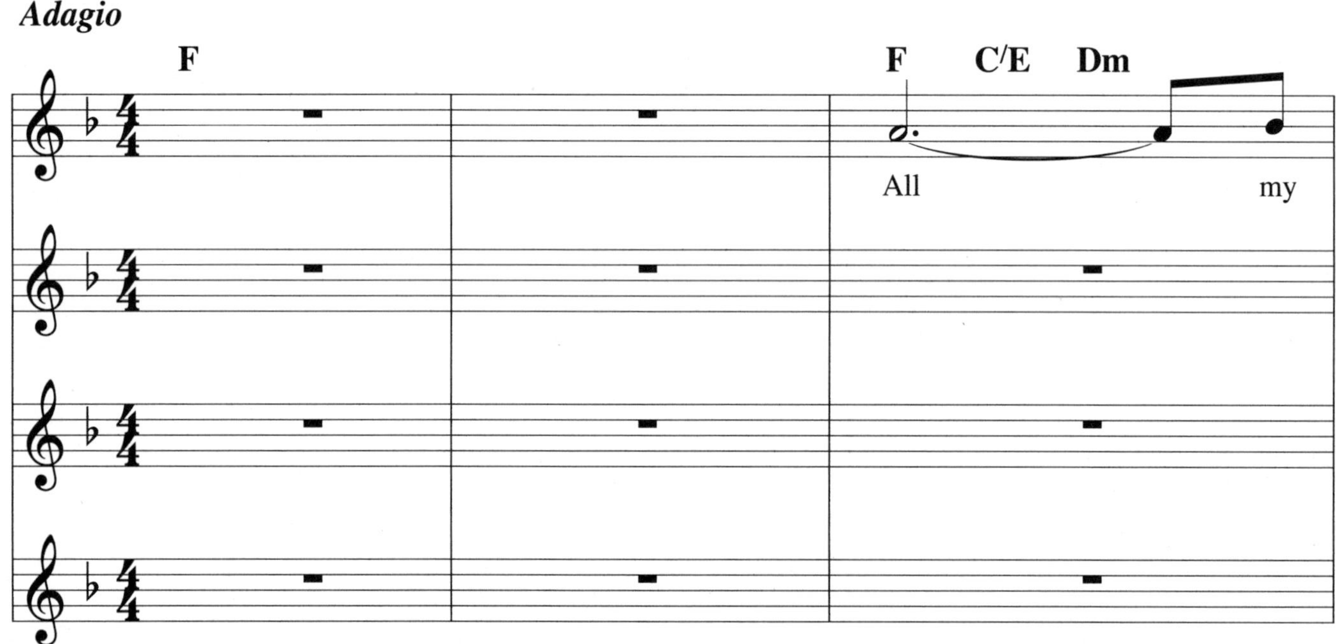

F
Cm
F
Am
had a lit - tle book was gi - ven to
me, and
ev - ry page spelt li - ber -
had a book give
me,
ev - ry pa - ge li - ber

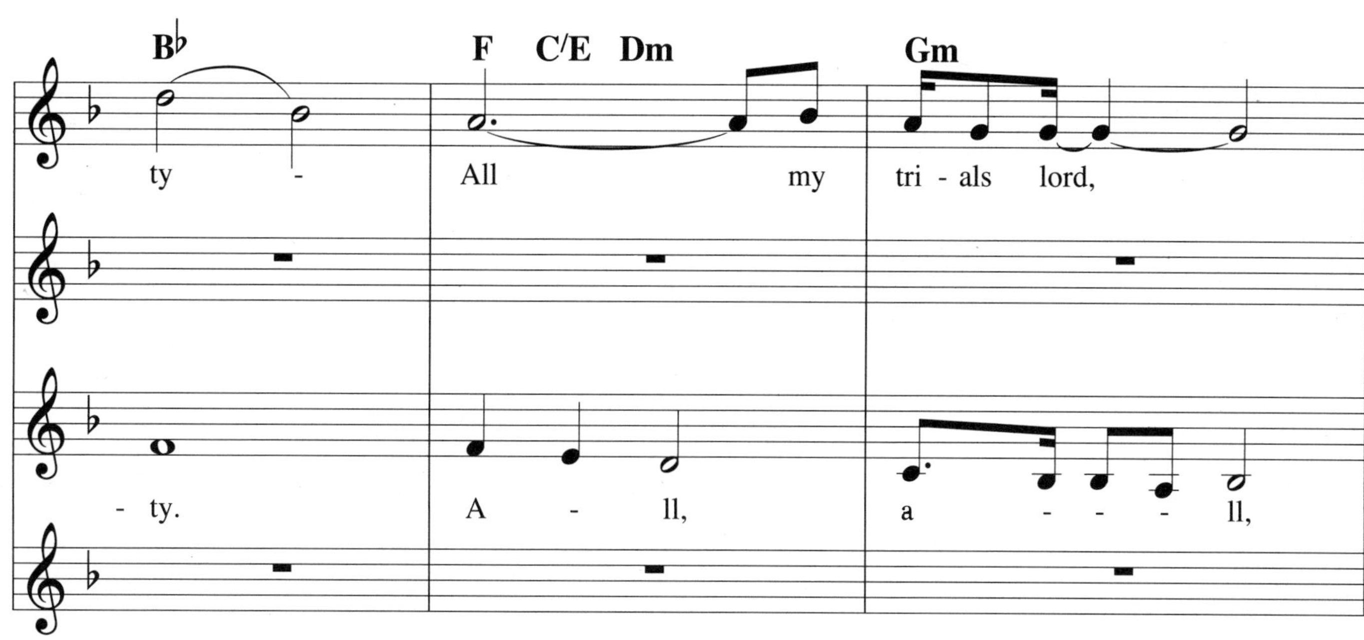
B♭
F C/E Dm
Gm
ty -
All my
tri - als lord,
- ty.
A - ll,
a - - - ll,

C7
Fsus4 F
soon be
o - ver. - If re
li -gion were athingthat mo- ney could
so - on be
o - ver
Ah -

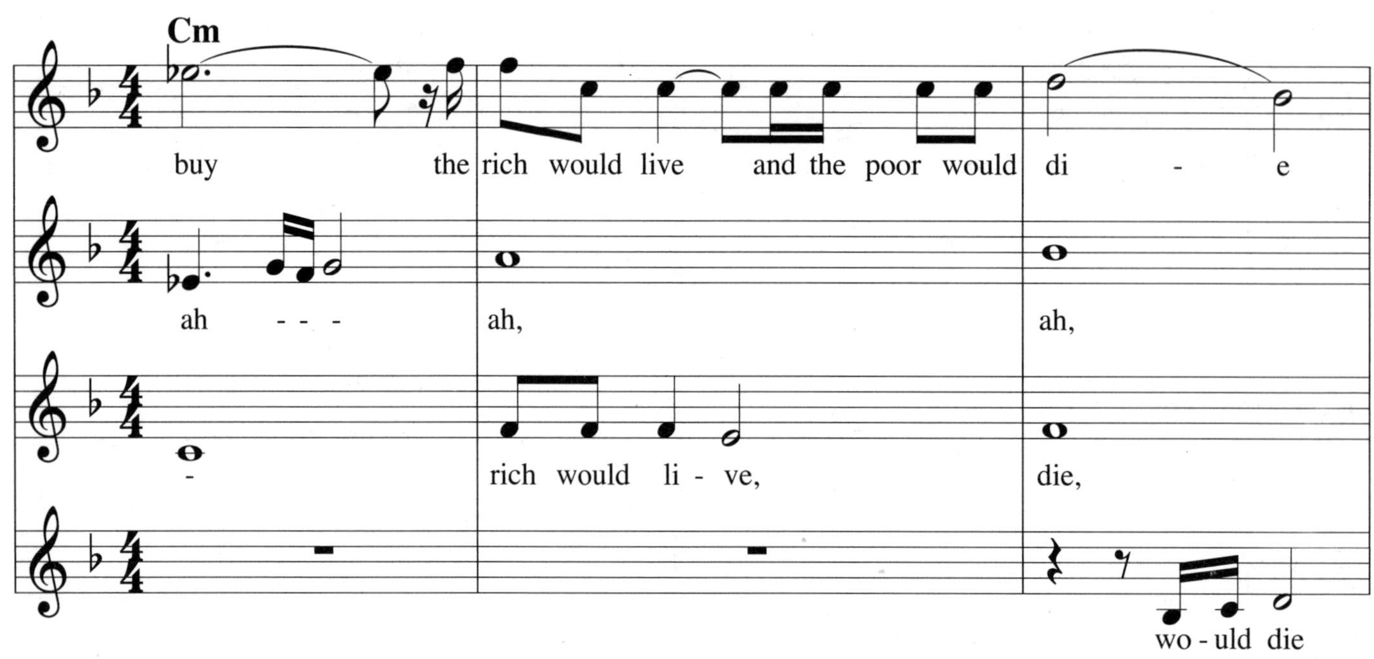
Cm
buy the rich would live and the poor would di - e
ah - - - ah, ah,
- rich would li - ve, die,
wo - uld die

F C/E Dm
Gm
C7
All my tri - als lord, soon be
Ah - - ah, ah - -
A - ll, a - - - ll, so - oon be

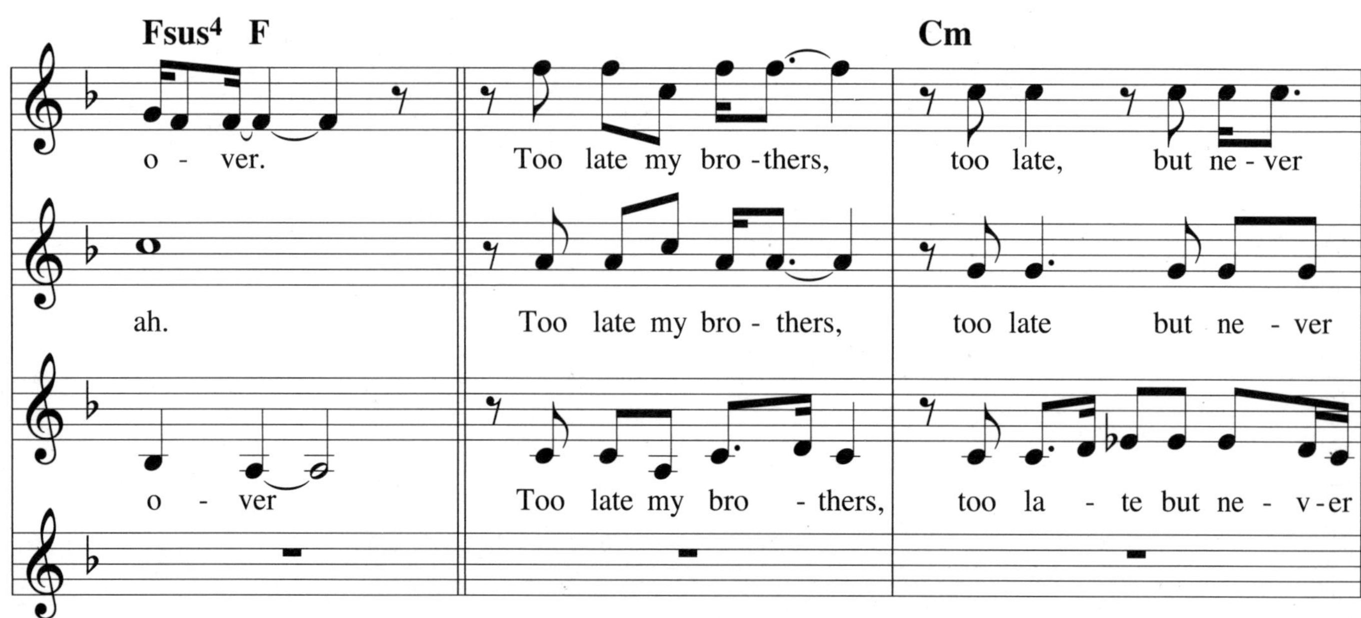
Fsus4 F
Cm
o - ver. Too late my bro - thers, too late, but ne - ver
ah. Too late my bro - thers, too late but ne - ver
o - ver Too late my bro - thers, too la - te but ne - v - er

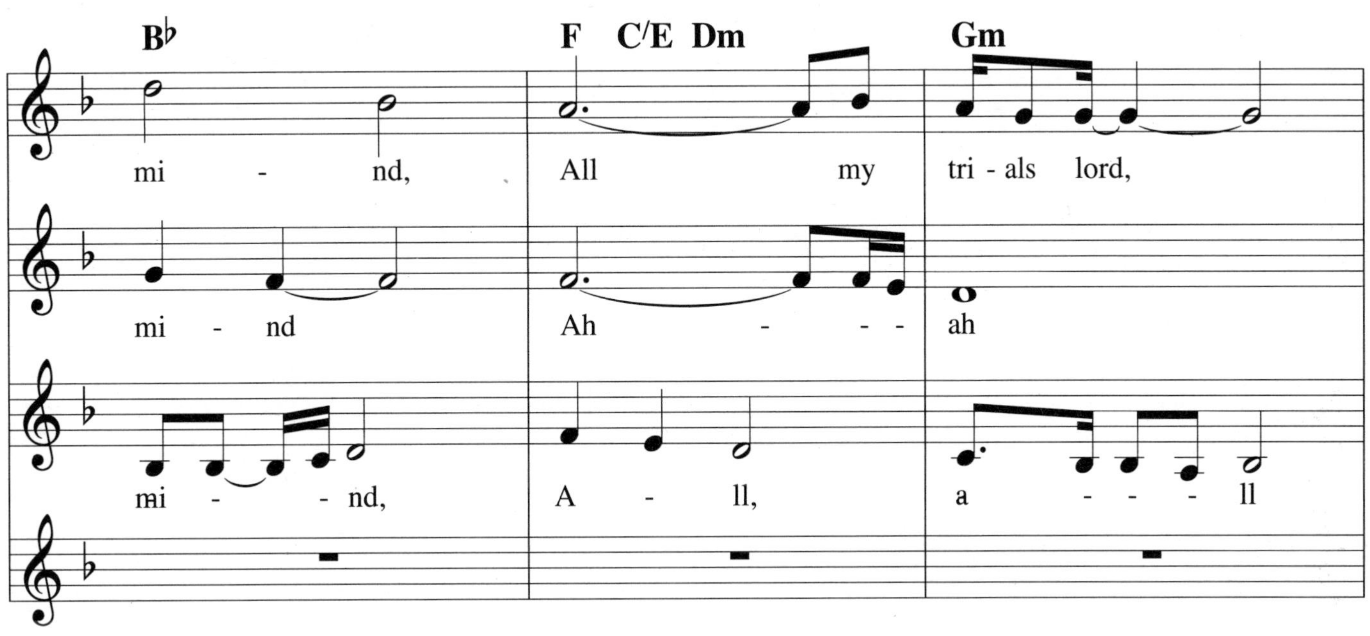
B♭
F C/E Dm
Gm
mi - nd, All my tri - als lord,
mi - nd Ah - - - ah
mi - - nd, A - ll, a - - - ll

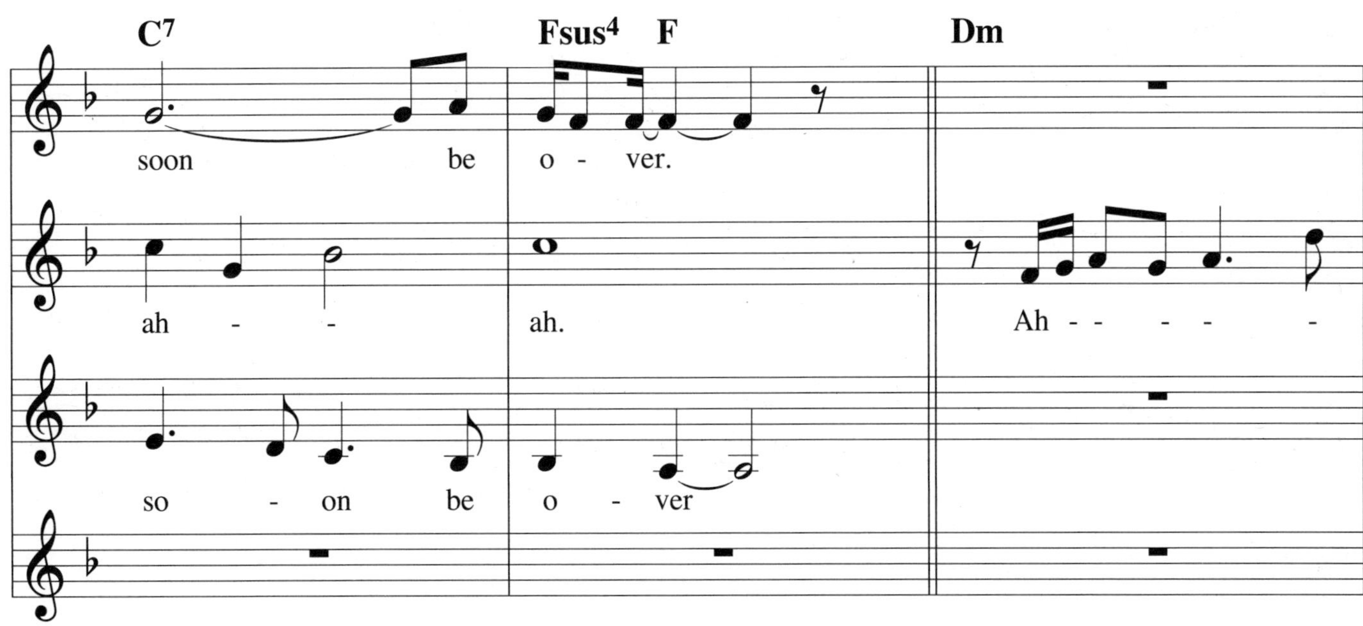
C7
Fsus4 F
Dm
soon be o - ver.
ah - - ah. Ah - - - - -
so - on be o - ver

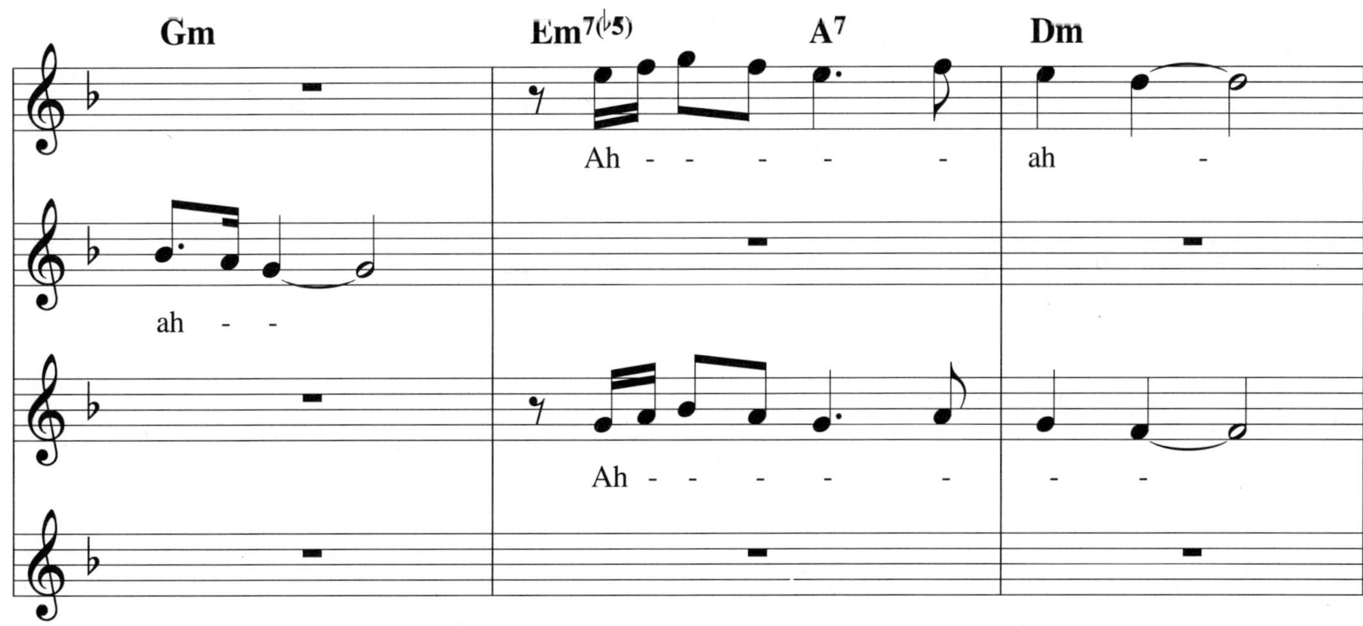
Gm
Em7(♭5)
A7
Dm
Ah - - - - - ah -
ah - -
Ah - - - - - - -

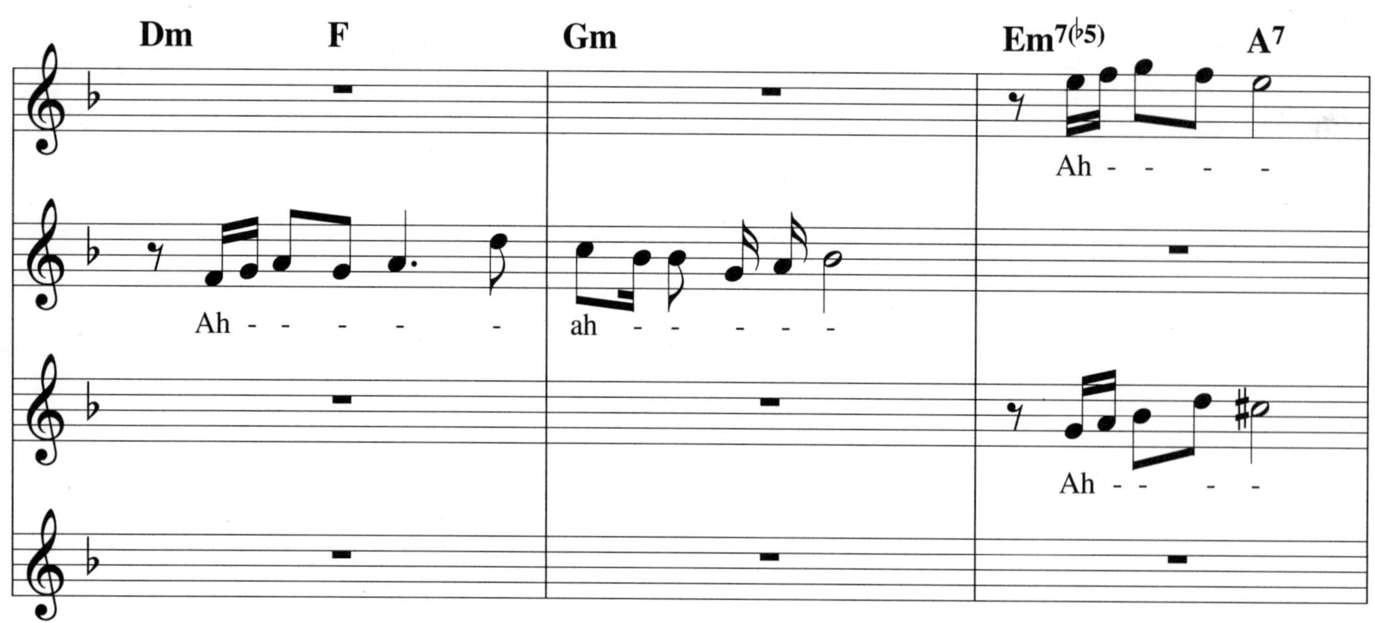

Dm F Gm Em7(♭5) A7
Ah - - - -
Ah - - - - - -
ah - - - - - -
Ah - - - -

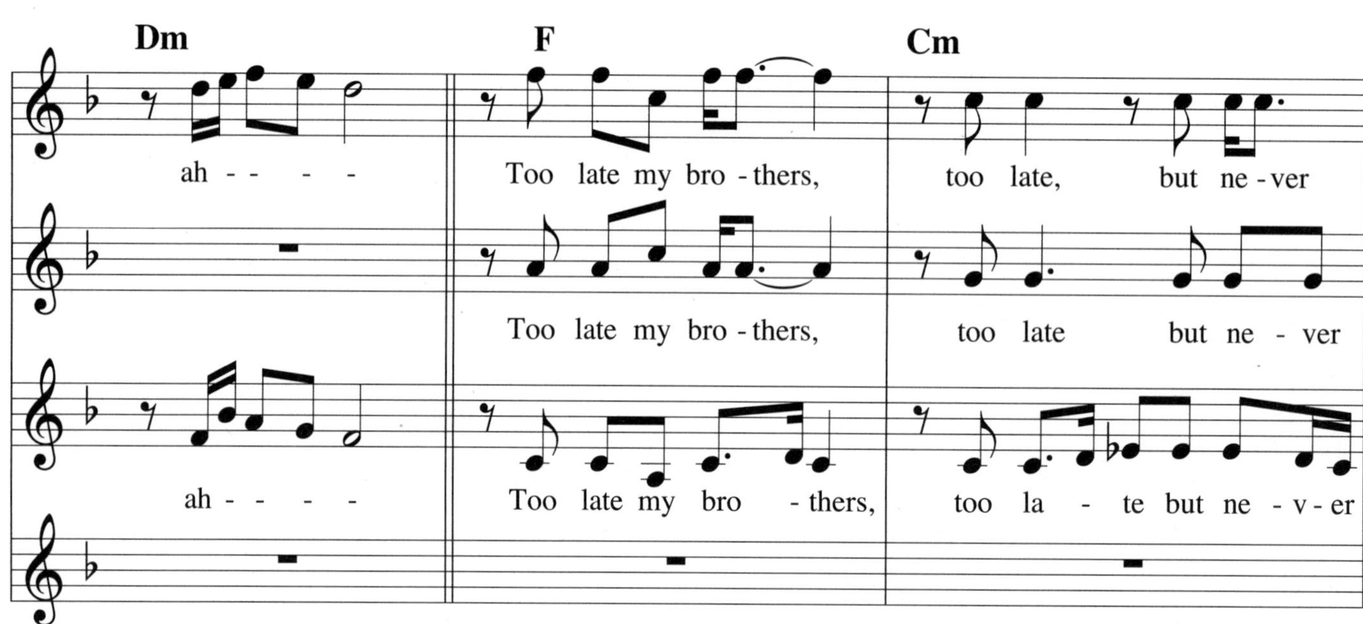

Dm F Cm
ah - - - -
Too late my bro - thers,
too late, but ne - ver
Too late my bro - thers,
too late but ne - ver
ah - - - -
Too late my bro - thers,
too la - te but ne - v - er

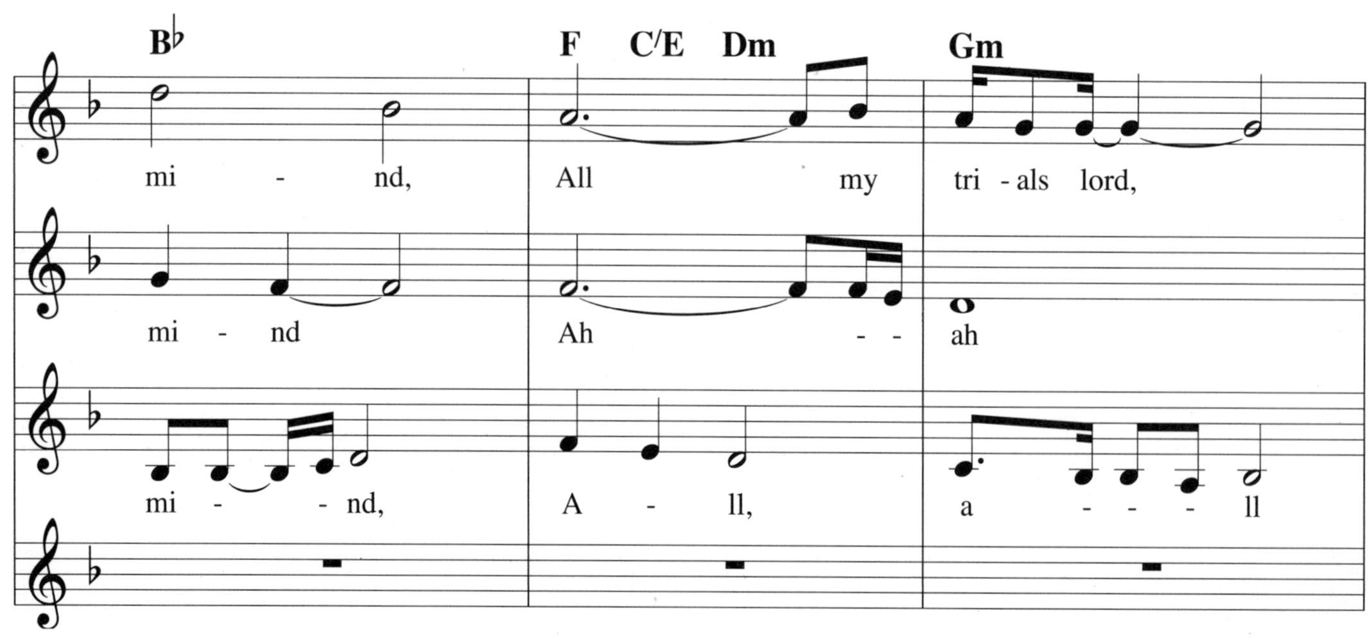

B♭ F C/E Dm Gm
mi - nd,
All my
tri - als lord,
mi - nd
Ah - -
ah
mi - - nd,
A - ll,
a - - - ll

C7
Fsus4
F
C/E Dm
soon
be
o - ver.
All
my
ah - -
ah.
so - on
be
o - ver

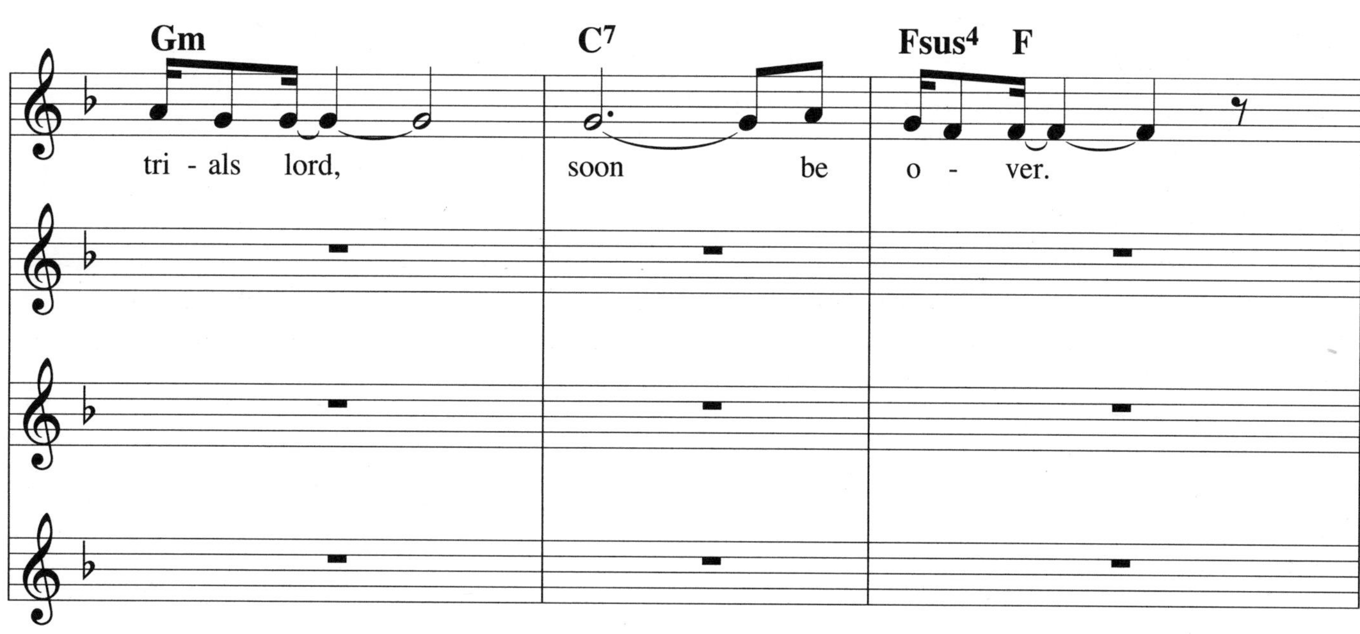
Gm
C7
Fsus4
F
tri - als
lord,
soon
be
o - ver.

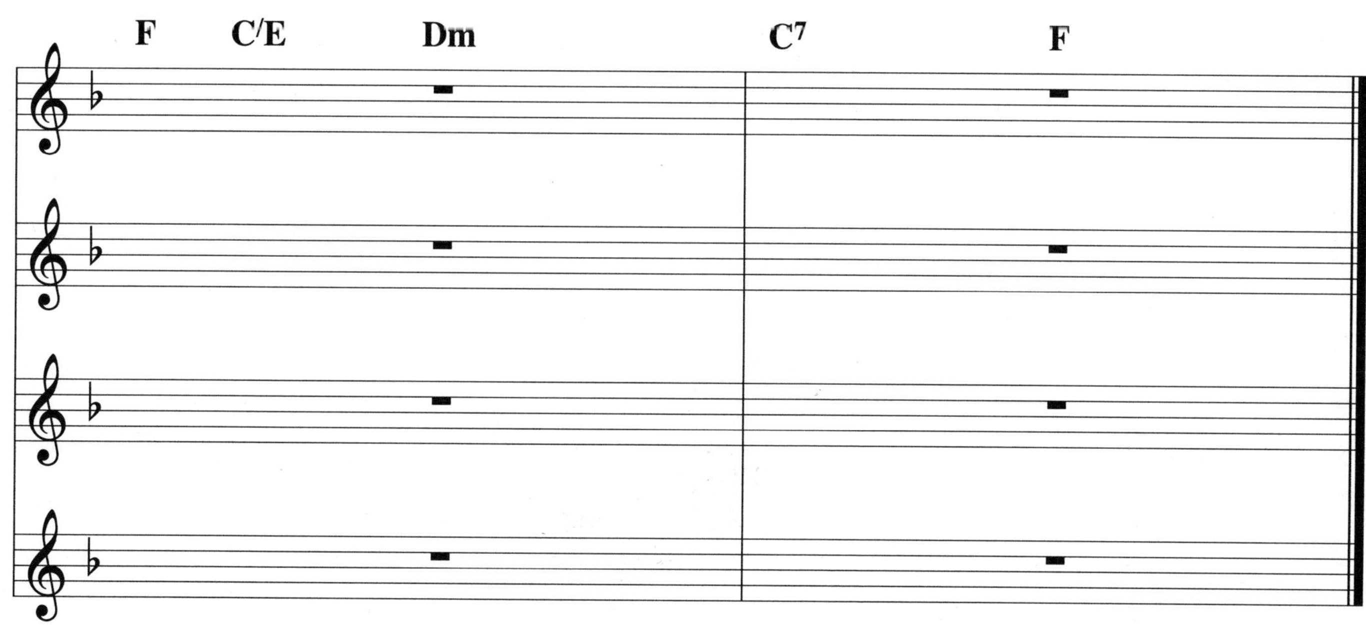
F
C/E
Dm
C7
F

LESSON THIRTY EIGHT

SINGING WITH A BAND

After you've worked on all the scales, rhythms, techniques and arpeggios, you need to be able to use them in a way that delivers the song well to the audience. When you are part of a band , the most important thing is to listen to each other and try to respond to each other. In this lesson, you will learn a bit about the roles of the various instruments.

BASS

Along with the drummer, the bass helps to keep solid time and provide the basic feel and drive. The bass and bass drum parts are often closely linked. The bass also spells out the chords and lays the foundation for the harmony of the song. Together, the bass and drums form the **rhythm section**. While a singer or horn player has time to breathe between phrases and a guitarist or keyboard player leaves space between lines or chords, the drummer and bass player have to play consistently to keep the groove going and feeling good. It is the job of the rhythm guitarist to 'lock in' with the rhythm section to keep the feel tight and drive the song forward.

Most electric basses have four strings which correspond to the bottom four strings of the guitar (**E**, **A**, **D** and **G**), but are tuned one octave lower. The strings are much thicker than guitar strings and the lower frets are wider apart. Like the electric guitar, the bass has pickups (usually two) and is played through an amplifier. The bass is usually played either with the index and middle fingers of the right hand, or 'slap' style with the thumb and index finger, but it can also be played with a pick.

BASS MUSIC NOTATION

Bass music is written on the **bass staff** and also uses Tablature – a notation system which uses lines to represent the strings of the bass and numbers to represent the frets.

TABLATURE

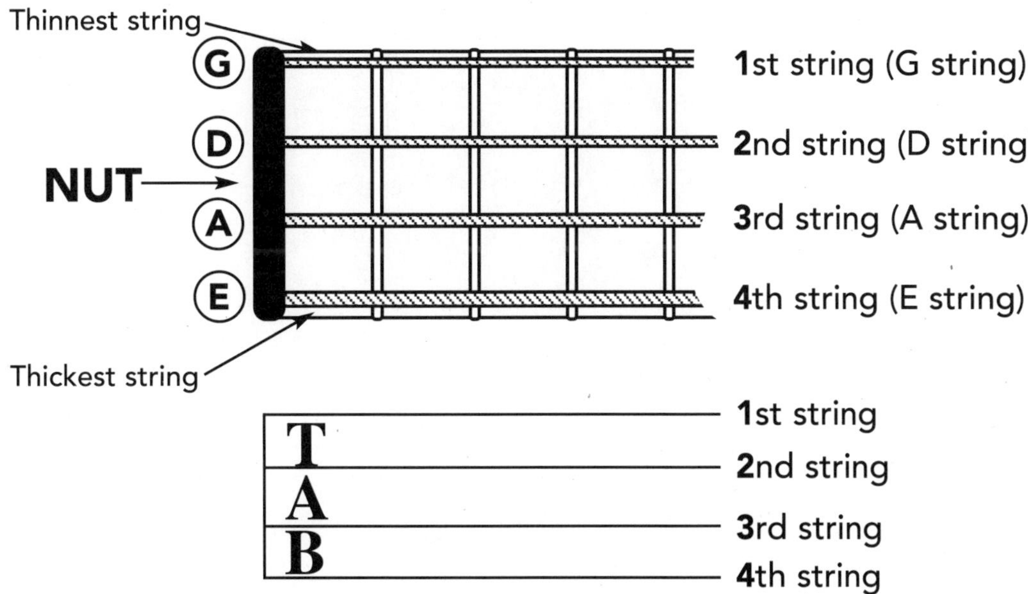

A number placed on a lines indicates the fret location of the note.

This indicates the 3rd fret of the second string (an F note).

This indicates the 7th fret of the 4th string (a B note).

This indicates the open third string (an A note)

62. Typical Blues Bass Line

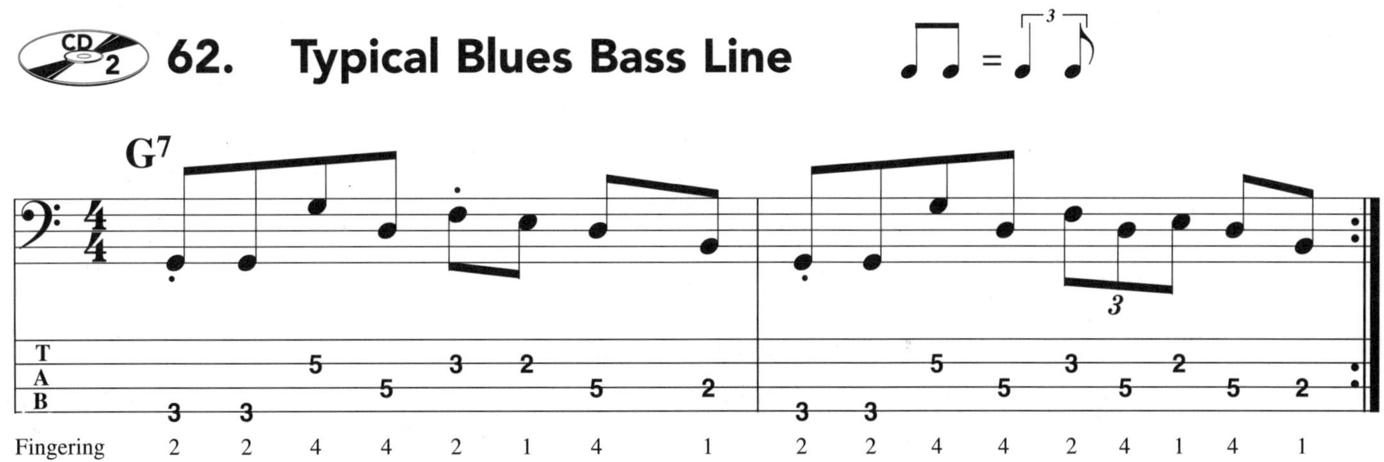

DRUMS

The drums set up and keep the basic feel of a song. They also drive the rhythm forward and provide endless rhythmic ideas for the other instruments through the use of accents, fills, and rhythmic patterns. The great thing about listening to the drummer is that you have three or four different parts that you can sing around or lock in with. Many musicians rely on the drummer to keep time for them, but in a good band everybody has a strong sense of time and no-one relies on anyone else. If you are not confident keeping time for yourself, work with a metronome or drum machine every day until you are confident.

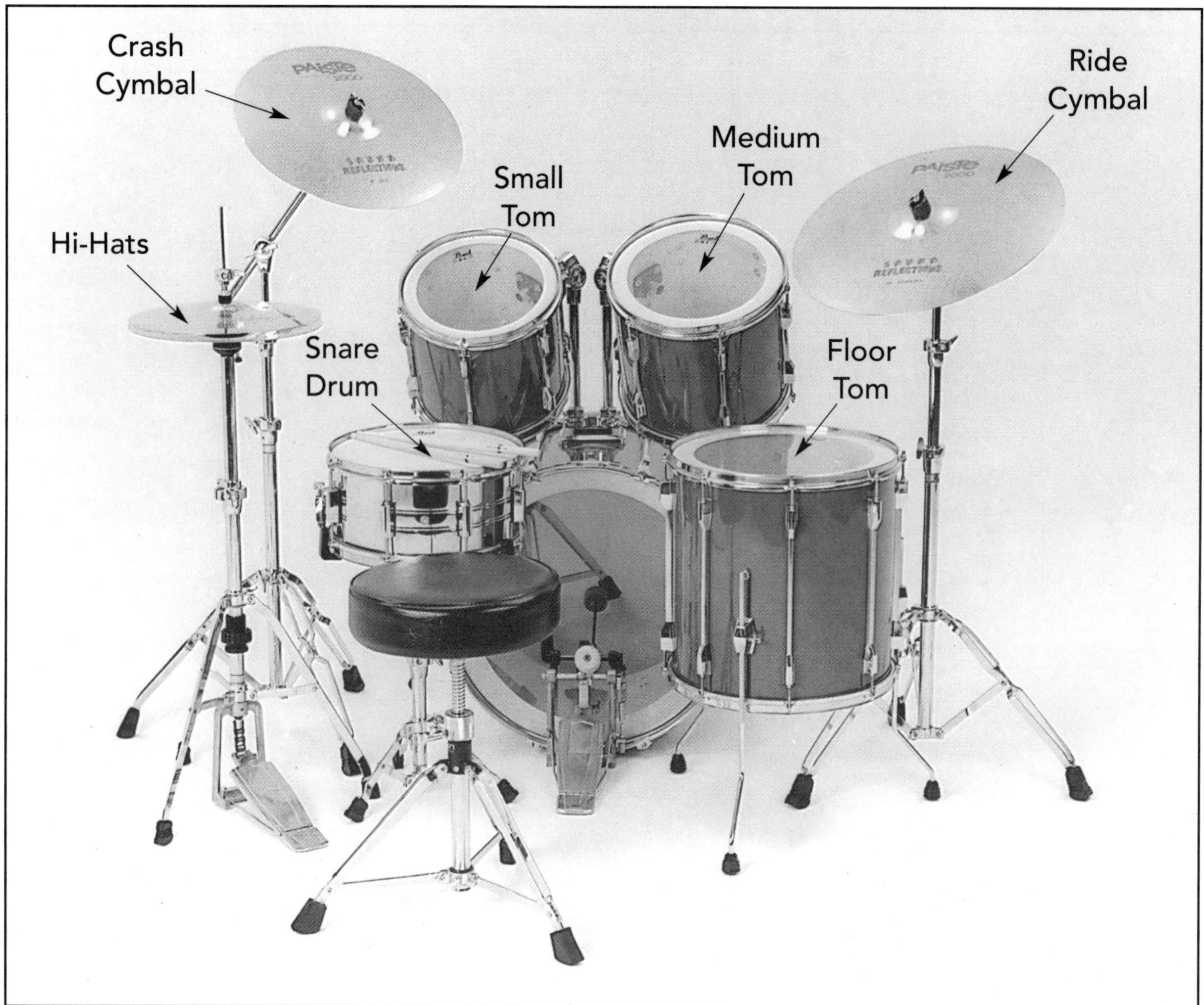

This drumkit contains three tom toms, but many drummers use only two, as these are probably the least necessary part of the kit. In fact, most drum parts can be played using only the snare drum, the bass drum and the hi-hat cymbals. The **bass drum** is played with the right foot and produces what is often called the 'bottom end' sound of the drums. The **snare drum** is usually played with the left hand, but the right hand is also used for certain beats as well as for playing fills. The **hi-hat and ride cymbals** are generally played with the right hand, but once again the left hand may be used in certain situations. The **crash cymbal** is played with either hand, depending on which one is most practical. The **tom toms** (toms for short) can also be played by either hand. **The hi-hat cymbals** can also be played by the left foot, or a combination of the right hand and the left foot.

DRUM NOTATION

Drum music is usually written in the spaces of the **bass staff**, plus the space above the staff. Each space represents a different part of the drum kit. The most commonly used system is shown below. Notice that cymbals are notated with an **X** instead of a notehead.

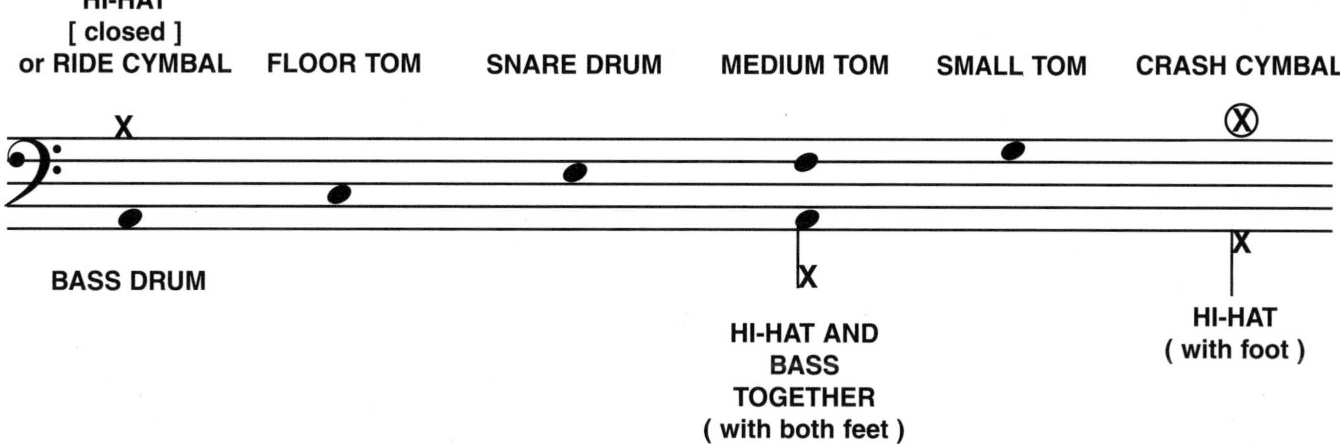

63.0 Rock Beat on Drums

Follow the notation as you listen to the recording and then try reading the notation without the recording, imagining the sounds of the drums as you follow the notes.

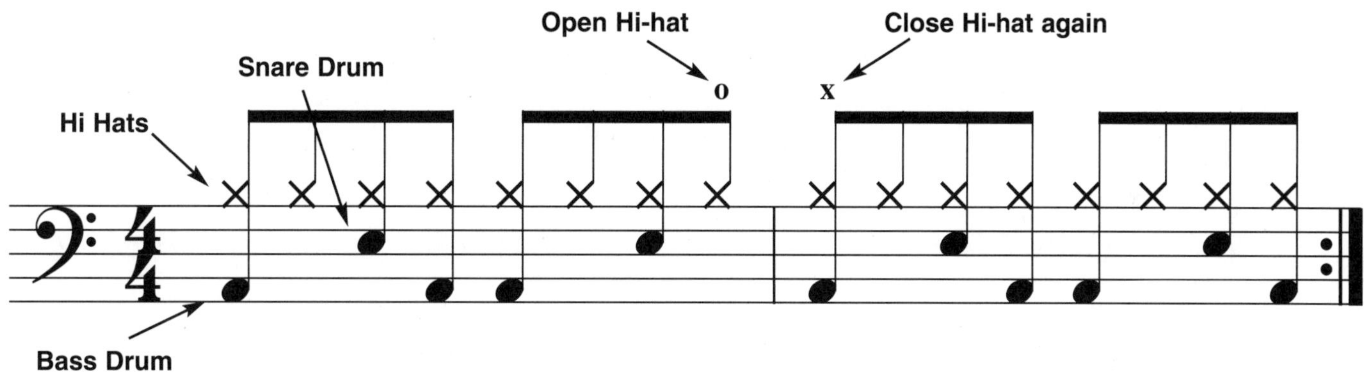

When a bass player is working out what to play with a drum part, the first thing they usually look at is where the bass drum falls. It is common for the bass and bass drum to play together.

63.1 Bass and Drums

GUITARS

Along with keyboards, guitars are usually responsible for playing chord progressions (rhythm guitar) and providing instrumental solos (lead guitar). The guitars also fill out the sound and punctuate the rhythms over the foundation laid by the rhythm section.

The role of a guitarist can vary widely depending on the style of music and the context. In Folk and World music, for example, acoustic guitars are more commonly used and there may be no drums involved. In this situation, the guitarist plays a percussive role as well as a harmonic one. In small intimate settings, the guitarist may even use fingerpicking and play intricate lines behind the vocalists.

In a Jazz group, the guitarist will improvise even when playing chord progressions. In fact, all the members of a Jazz band will improvise their parts, except for specific sections such as an intro or ending. Both acoustic and electric guitars are used in Jazz.

In a Rock band, electric guitars are by far the most common. In this situation there are usually clearly defined roles for rhythm and lead guitar. The **rhythm guitarist** locks in with the rhythm section and helps drive the momentum of the band, while the **lead guitarist** plays riffs (repeated patterns) and melodies in between lyrics, as well as improvising solos and playing responses to the vocalist. If you have a good lead guitarist, you can have lots of fun with call and response. Audiences like this too.

Electric guitars contain **pickups** which are like built in microphones that send the signal to the amplifier. The volume can be adjusted on both the guitar and the amplifier. When singing with a band using electric instruments, you may want to protect your hearing by using ear plugs, unless the band plays quietly. You could try using the old joke: How do you get a guitarist to turn down their Amp? (Put a sheet of music in front of them). But be prepared for the guitarist to retort: And how do you know when a singer is at your door? (They can't find the key and they don't know when to come in) – which is all the more reason to work on your theory and ear training.

Solid Body Electric

Hollow Body Electric (semi acoustic)

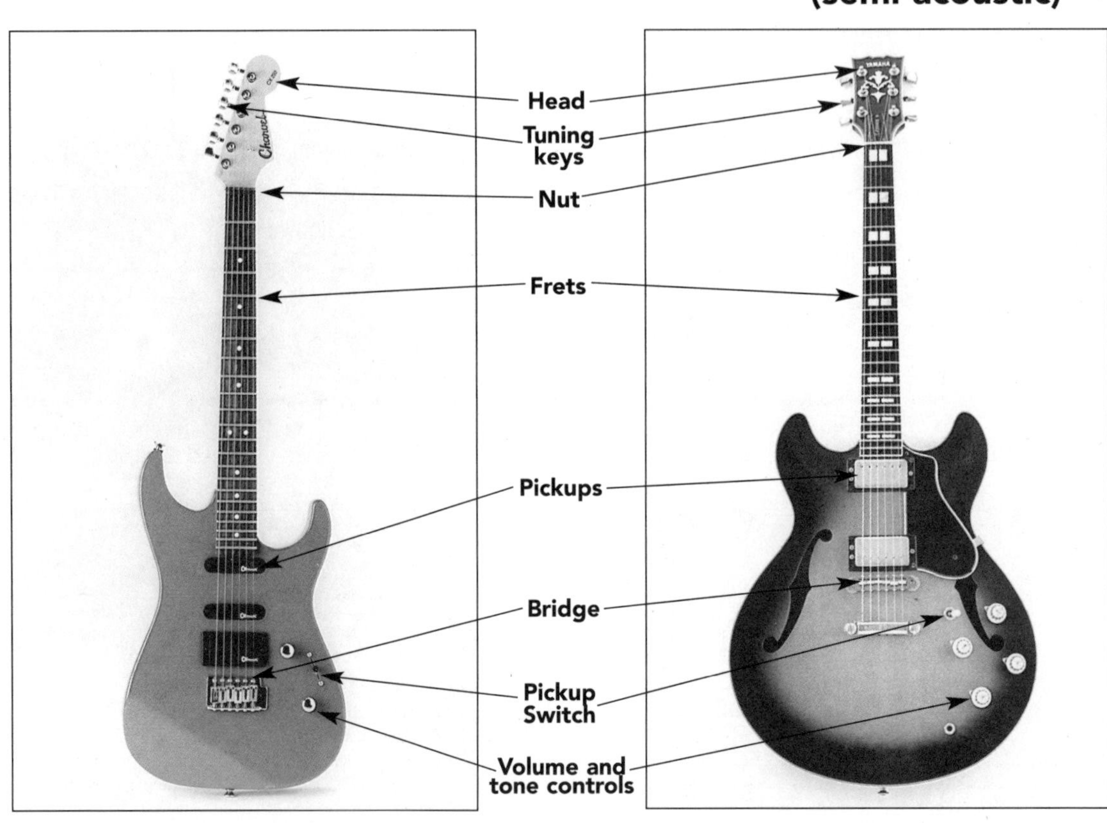

GUITAR NOTATION

Guitar music is written on a treble staff in standard notation. It also uses tablature, consisting of **six** lines representing the six strings of the guitar.

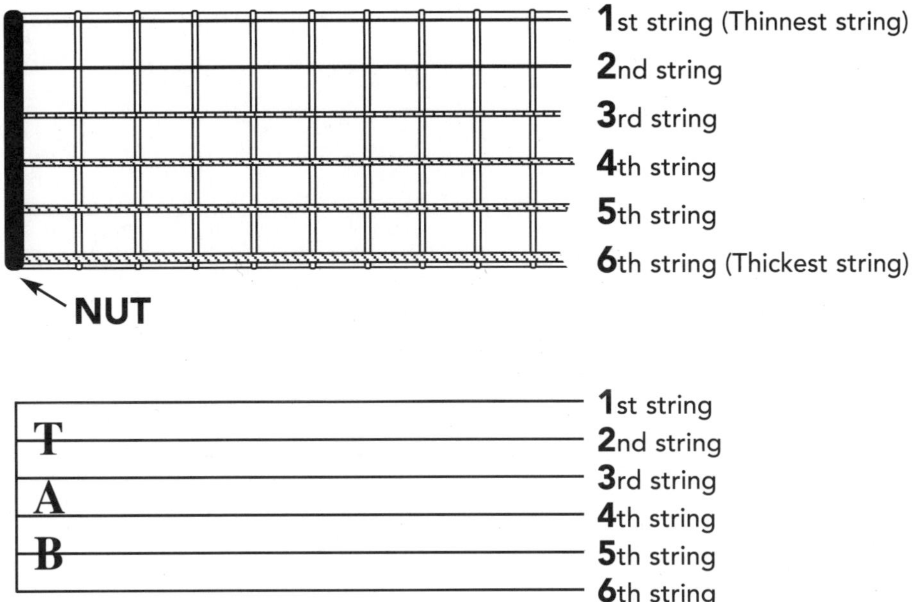

THE LEFT HAND

The left hand fingers are numbered as such:

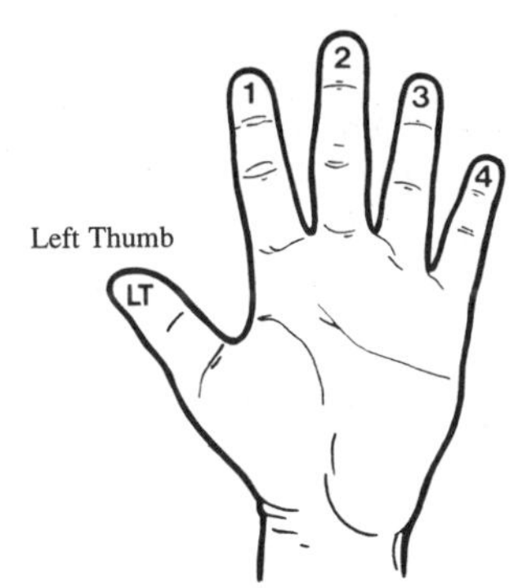

As in bass notation, a number placed on a lines indicates the fret location of a note.

T A B 0 — This indicates the open (unfretted) 3rd string (a G note).

T A B 3 — This indicates the 3rd fret of the 5th string (a C note).

T A B 1 — This indicates the 1st fret of the 1st string (an F note).

CD 2 64. Rhythm Guitar

Here is an example of guitar music written in both standard notation and tablature.

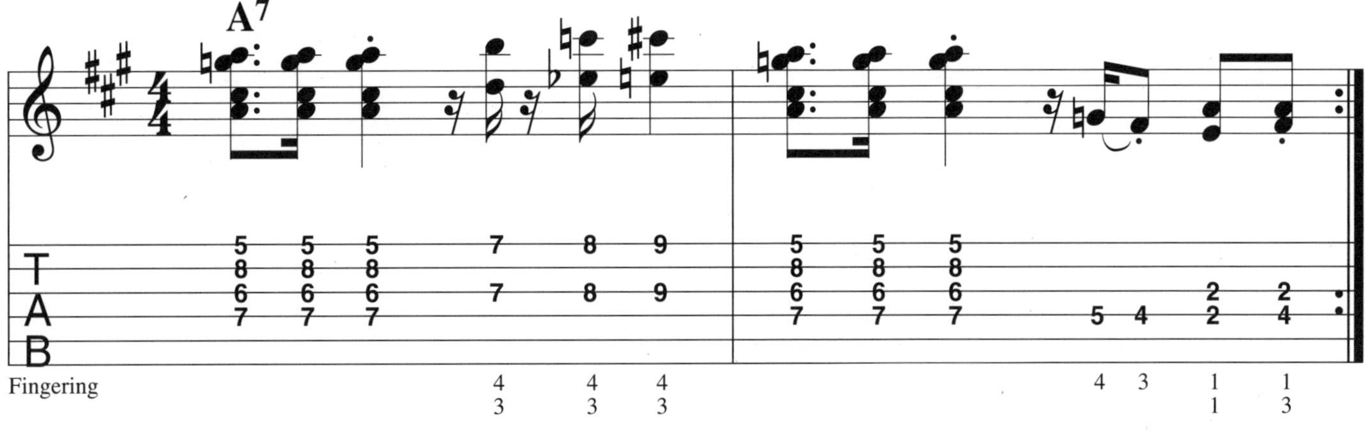

THE WHOLE BAND

With bass, drums and guitar, you have the basis of a band. Once they have worked out their parts, all three can lock in together and provide the momentum that makes you want to jump up and sing with them. Listen to the following examples and notice where notes are played together and where one instrument leaves space for the others. A good general principle to use is: if one part is busy, it is best to have something simple played with it, rather than all the parts being active.

65.0.

65.1.

Just as more than one melody can be created from a scale, a guitarist has a wide choice of chords and chord sequences. Listen to the following example. This time the guitarist plays along with some of the bass line and some of the drum part, but also leaves space for other instruments to be heard. The bass and drum parts are the same as the previous example – only the guitar part has changed.

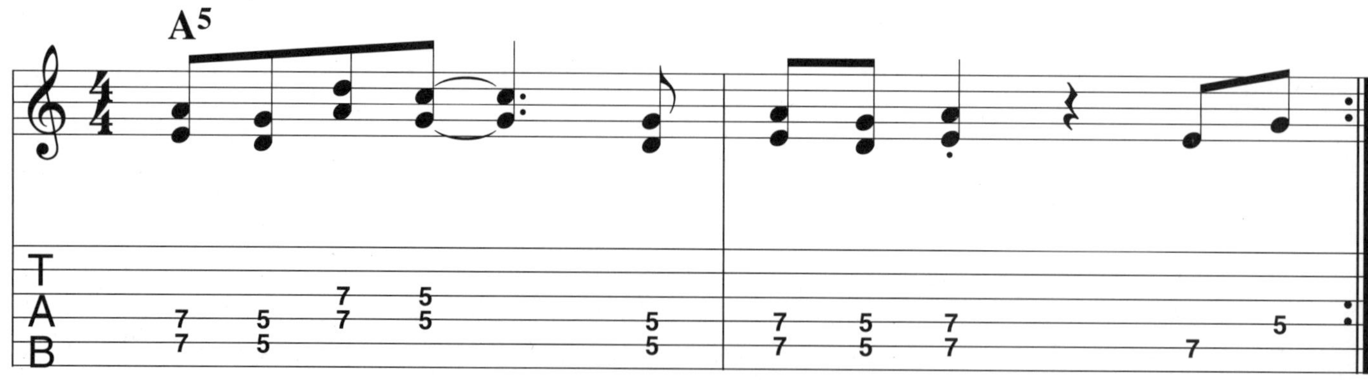

The next example features two guitar parts. Listen to how one leaves space for the other and how they connect at certain points to keep the sound tight. When you have two guitarists in a band, it is important to work out clearly defined parts so that they complement each other, rather than clashing. Careful listening, discipline and lots of rehearsal is the key. Listen to bands like ACDC, Lynyrd Skynyrd, and Metallica to hear great examples of two guitarists working together. For guitar and keyboards, check out Little Feat, Steely Dan, The Neville Brothers, The Eagles, Booker T and the MG's, B.B. King and the Amazing Rhythm Aces.

66. Two Guitars

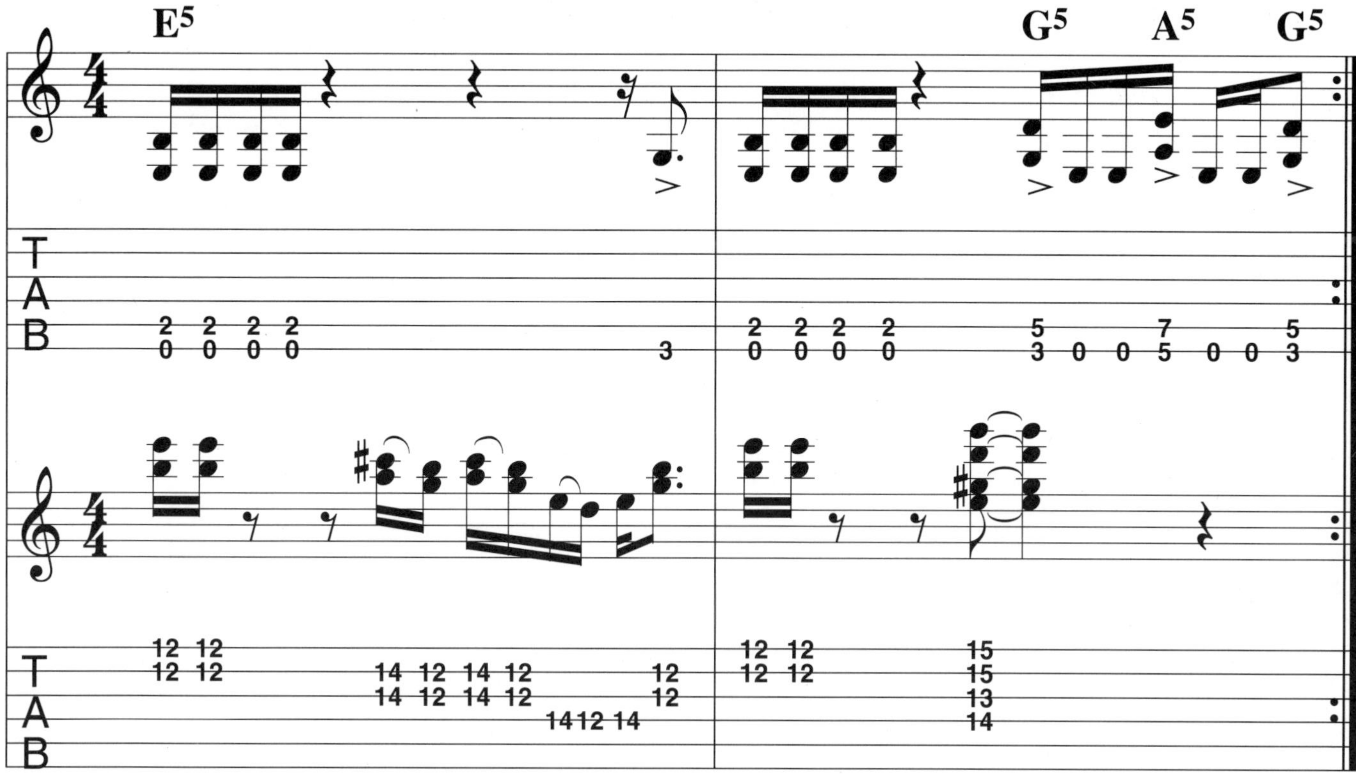

67. Guitar and Keyboards

In this example, the keyboard locks in with the drums and the guitar plays a complementary rhythm and then leaves space for the keyboard to be heard, before doubling the keyboard part just before it repeats. Once you understand how the instruments work together, you can feel much more involved in songwriting and arranging.

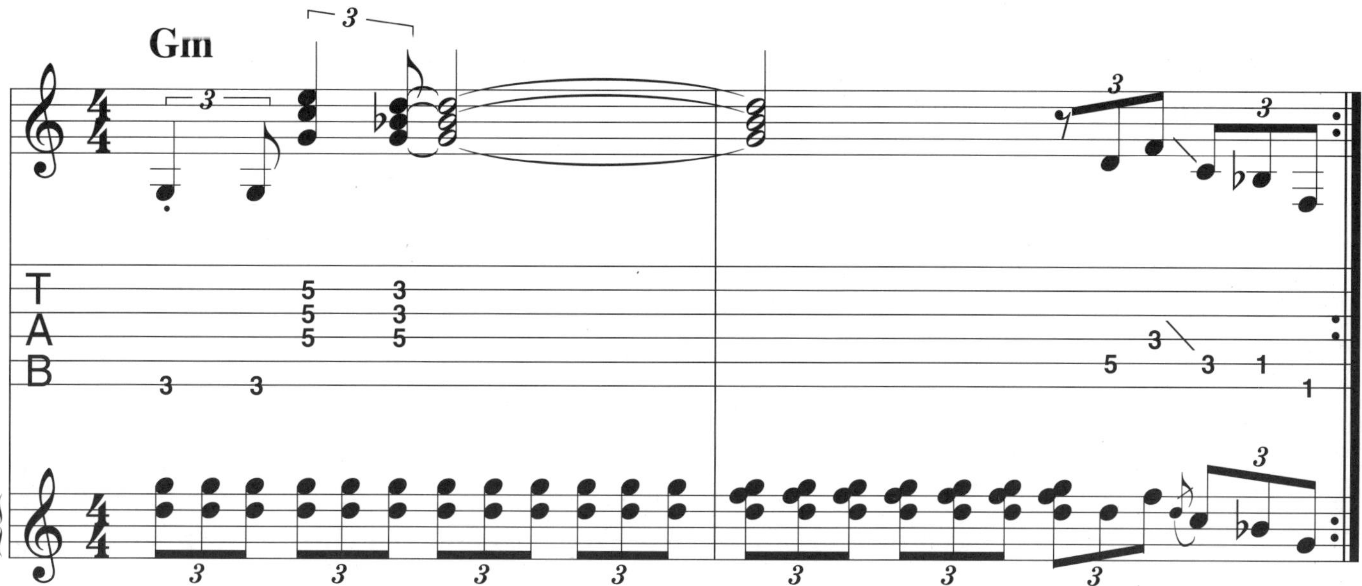

LESSON THIRTY NINE

PERFORMING IN PUBLIC

Performing in public can be both exciting and frightening for any new performer, whether they are a singer, an instrumentalist, an actor or simply someone giving a speech on a social occasion. Many people who are shy at first develop into dynamic performers who can entertain and captivate an audience. Like any other skill, performing in public takes time to develop and there is much to be learned from watching other performers. To begin with, the best approach can be to simply take a deep breath, walk on, smile, look the audience in the eye and begin with a song you are very familiar with. If you are nervous, concentrate on the sound you and your accompanist(s) are making and move your body to the music in any way that feels good. If you are able to enjoy yourself, this will communicate itself to the audience. Nervousness can be turned into excitement and positive energy and can actually make your natural reactions and responses to the music quicker.

OVERCOMING NERVES

There are three essential elements in overcoming nervousness and turning it into a positive. The first of these is **knowing your material well**. This means thoroughly rehearsing all aspects of each song before you even consider performing them. If you are unsure of the words, or the notes or timing of either the melody or the accompaniment, it is not surprising that you would be nervous. The more certain you are of these things, the more you are free to concentrate on expressing the meaning of the lyrics and making great music.

The second element is **being comfortable with your equipment and your environment**. Most public performances involve the use of microphones. Using a microphone will be discussed later in this lesson. When you are on stage, it is important to be comfortable using the microphone and to not be startled by hearing yourself through the PA system or foldback speakers. If possible, have a sound check before members of the public arrive. Most professional ensembles have a thorough sound check in which all the equipment is tested individually and together at least an hour (preferably more) before the show. This allows everybody to become comfortable with the sound of the room as well as the equipment. If you learn a bit about PA systems you can also communicate your requirements and preferences to the person operating the sound system. Talk to the sound engineer and take an interest in the settings used for the various instruments as well as your voice

The third element is **trusting yourself**. If you are considering singing in public, you are probably fairly confident that you are making a good sound when you sing and you have probably received compliments from friends as well. In this case, you should be able to sing equally well or better in public, particularly once an audience begins to respond. Your body instinctively knows every aspect of producing a good vocal sound, so it is usually just a case of 'letting go' and becoming part of the music. The more you can become the character in each song (like an actor) the more convincing your performance will be and the better you will be able to deliver it.

EYE CONTACT

When you sing, you are telling a story to the audience. Look at them as you tell this story and they will respond. Obviously you cannot look at everybody, but you can pick out certain people (e.g. someone wearing bright clothing or someone with a bald spot). Another option is to look towards the people in the middle of the audience. Change your focus from time to time to include all sections of the audience. Everybody will feel you are communicating with them personally and will enjoy your performance more. Remember that when people go to hear a public performance, they are looking forward to having a good time. This means they are automatically prepared to like you even before they see or hear you, so the performance should be no problem. Another important aspect of any performance is eye contact between the performers. The fact that an ensemble are communicating well and obviously enjoying themselves makes the audience feel good too.

STAGE PRESENCE AND STAGE CRAFT

Most great performers have what is commonly known as good **stage presence**. Stage presence is the overall impression created in the minds and emotions of the audience by the performer. This impression is created partly by the drama of the music and the visual experience, but largely by the individual personality of the performer. As always, there is much to be learned by watching other performers. It is essential for aspiring performers to see professional singers, musicians, actors or other entertainers perform live as often as possible. You can do this by going to shows or watching performances on DVDs or television. Notice how each performer communicates with both their ensemble and the audience. Analyse their use of both spontaneous and choreographed movement. Watch how the music is expressed through their bodies and facial expressions, as well as through their sound. Notice whether they use humour or not, or any other elements of public performance you can think of. All these things can be learned and developed and can be described as various aspects of stage craft.

DEVELOPING YOUR OWN STYLE

Many performers learn their stage craft and their ability to express their vocal or instrumental technique by copying other performers at first, and then adapting what they have learned to develop their own style and presence. Ray Charles studied Nat King Cole's style of singing and playing early in his career, but later developed his own intensely personal style which had little in common with Nat King Cole. This is similar to the way students of visual art are taught to copy the works of masters early in their development. By doing this, students learn about color, form, design, balance, etc. as well as technique. However, this is only the first step in the process. The idea is to master the practical elements in order to be able to express your own feelings, ideas and personality through your own work. Copying a Rembrandt or Picasso painting is a valuable exercise for an art student, but it is not an end in itself. So it is with singing and performing. Learn all you can from performers you admire, whether it is their vocal technique, their musicianship or their stagecraft. Study them in detail and work diligently on everything you learn, particularly in the early stages of your development. However, there is no point in slavishly copying any particular person's style over a long period of time (unless you want to be a comedy act). As your confidence develops along with your personal feeling for the music you are performing, your own style will begin to emerge by itself if you let it. As you practice and perform, notice the things that you feel most intensely about. These are the seeds which will grow into your own vital style if you are true to them and develop them properly.

MICROPHONES

All singers need to know how to use a microphone. Even if you mainly sing in a choir or in small rooms with only a piano accompaniment, it is likely that you will be required to use a microphone at some stage. If you sing with a band, you will use a microphone every time you perform. It is a good idea to have your own microphone that you are comfortable with, even if the venue you are performing at provides them along with the PA system.

MICROPHONES FOR PERFORMING LIVE

There are several different types of microphones. Each of them is best suited to a different musical situation (e.g. live band performance, or recording session). The type most commonly used for live performances is the **dynamic microphone**. These microphones contain a diaphragm and a coil which is activated when the voice causes it to vibrate. They are normally **uni-directional**, or 'front sensitive' which means that sounds entering from the sides of the microphone are amplified less than sound entering from the top or front. Because of their resistance to feedback (the piercing sound made when a microphone picks up the sound coming from the speakers and amplifies it again) uni-directional microphones are particularly useful in a live band environment.

Omni-directional microphones receive sound equally from all sides of the microphone. This makes them useful for back-up vocals in situations where two or more singers share one microphone, but they are not recommended for a lead singer in a live band situation.

Before you buy a microphone it is advisable to visit a music store and try some out. The Shure SM58 microphone in the photo below is a typical professional quality uni-directional dynamic microphone and is one of the most common used by bands. There are also other good microphones available of a similar design. If you intend to perform in public regularly, it is worth spending a little extra on a good microphone as it will make you sound better, which will add to your confidence and make you more comfortable with your sound on stage.

Shure SM58 - A Typical Dynamic Microphone

MICROPHONE TECHNIQUE

When using a uni-directional microphone, there are some important fundamentals to remember:

• Hold the microphone in the palm of your hand with your fingers curled loosely around it, just tightly enough to avoid dropping the microphone, but not tightly enough to cause tension.

• Sing directly into the microphone. Many beginning performers unintentionally move sideways away from the mic as they are singing. This means that the sound is lost to the audience and they can't understand what is being sung. Practice moving around and singing into the microphone. Make sure that when you move sideways your hand keeps the mic in relatively the same position, so that your voice goes directly into it at all times. The best position for the mic is just below your mouth at about a 45 degree angle, so that the centre of the head of the mic is aimed directly at your mouth.

• Depending on the natural volume of your voice along with the sensitivity of the equipment being used, the distance between your mouth and the microphone should vary between one and ten centimetres. During loud passages the microphone should be pulled back slightly in order to balance the overall volume. This will also reduce the chances of 'PEE POP', which is the term used to describe the effect created by 'hard' consonants such as **b, d, g** and particularly **p** exploding out of the singer's mouth and onto the microphone (articulating consonants lightly can also help avoid this problem).

• Avoid touching the microphone with your mouth, as the sound will distort and unwanted sounds produced by the contact will be amplified along with your singing.

• If you are moving around while you are singing, stay away from the 'front of house' speakers or you may experience feedback problems. As long as you are somewhere behind or – at the most – level with the front of house speakers but a reasonable distance from them, you shouldn't have any feedback problems.

STUDIO MICROPHONES

In a recording studio, a **condenser microphone** is often used. These microphones are much more sensitive than dynamic microphones. Since the singer in the studio is usually hearing the accompaniment through headphones, the microphone can afford to be more sensitive at a much lower volume. They pick up many more subtleties and provide a deeper and more detailed sound than dynamic mics. Condenser mics also contain a capacitor and therefore need electric power to run. When singing into a condenser mic, you can afford to be a little further back from it. However, there is generally a best position or 'sweet spot' where your voice will sound best. This varies from one voice to another and from one condenser microphone to another, so when you are in a recording situation and are unsure of the sound, it is best to try a few different mics and experiment with the positioning of each one before deciding what sounds best. The recording engineer will usually be able to hear your voice and choose a microphone which will complement it.

WARMING UP

Before you begin a performance, it is a good idea to go through some kind of warm up routine. This will help loosen your muscles and help you relax, as well as getting your blood flowing and helping to focus your mind for the performance. The first steps in any warm up routine are usually breathing and stretching exercises. Start with the breathing exercise explained on page 14. Then do some gentle movements and gradually stretch more as your body begins to feel more flexible. The next step is to sing some sustained notes using an open vowel sound such as **ah**. Gradually move your voice around higher and lower pitches and then sing a couple of scales. The exercise for moving between registers (sliding between octaves) on page 56 is particularly useful. Next try some exercises using various vowel sounds, such as the one given on page 46. The final stage is to sing a verse from the song you intend to begin the performance with. Include any physical movements you normally use when performing the song. This should get you in the mood for the performance and make you keen to get out there and begin.

LOOKING AFTER YOUR VOICE

It is important for a singer to keep fit. All the muscles, ligaments, tendons, etc. used in singing and stage movement require regular exercise to keep them flexible and in the best condition for performing. It is also important not to strain your voice, as this can lead to poor technique along with a lessening of the sound quality. In extreme cases such as repeated shouting, this can lead to vocal nodules. These are growths on the vocal cords which can cause permanent damage.

Nodules usually occur in Rock singers who sing with a rough technique at high volume (shouting) over extended periods, often in an attempt to compete with the volume of electric guitars played through large amplifiers. If you are singing with a band, it is essential to have adequate foldback. Foldback speaker are ones aimed at the performers rather than the audience. They are there so the performers can hear themselves properly when amplified through a PA system. If you are having trouble hearing yourself, you should never sing louder to try to overcome the situation. Instead, you will need to either turn the foldback up or get the instrumentalists to turn their amplifiers down, or both. Many beginning electric guitarists and drummers are not used to playing at quieter volumes, but it is essential that they learn. Otherwise you may end up with vocal damage.

When rehearsing songs, don't forget that dynamics are an essential part of music. If you always play and sing too loud, you have nowhere to go. Get the musicians accompanying you to play at a comfortable 'middle' volume and work out the best places in the song to increase or decrease the volume for dramatic effect. When performing, everything you do either as a singer or an ensemble should have the sole purpose of communicating the song to the audience. This means moving them emotionally rather than deafening them.

Another aspect of looking after your voice is drinking plenty of water. Other liquids can adversely affect the sound of your voice, but water keeps the throat and larynx lubricated without affecting the sound. It also has the added bonus of preventing dehydration if you are using a lot of energy on stage. As well as this, a sensible diet and regular exercise will help keep your body in the best possible condition for singing and performing.

THE IMPORTANCE OF LISTENING

As mentioned earlier, your most important source of information as a singer is **recordings**. Singing is an aural art, so you need to do a lot of listening to get all the subtleties of phrasing, articulations and vocal inflections available to you as a singer. Listen every day to albums which feature great vocalists.

All music is an extension of what has come before it, so you need to be aware of the development of singing throughout the history of music. Studying **Classical** harmony will give you a solid grounding in ear training and music theory which can be used in any style of music. There is also a whole tradition of Classical singing, from the songs of Schubert and Schumann to the Choral music of J.S. Bach, to the operas of Mozart, Verdi and Puccini.

For more recent styles such as Jazz, Blues and Rock, it is essential to listen to a wide variety of singers, some of whom are listed below. There is a lot of crossover between styles which come under the headings of Rock, Pop, Jazz, Blues, R&B and Funk. There are many great singers in these styles, but the following list is a good start.

Blues:
Bessie Smith, Ma Rainey, Robert Johnson, Son House, Howlin' Wolf, Muddy Waters, Magic Sam, Bobby Bland, BB King, Jimmy Witherspoon, Koko Taylor, Ruth Brown, Etta James, Robert Cray, John Lee Hooker and Lightnin' Hopkins.

Soul/Gospel:
Mahalia Jackson, Aretha Franklin, The Five Blind Boys of Alabama, Ray Charles, Johnny Adams, Wilson Pickett, Otis Redding, Patti LaBelle, O.V Wright, Ann Peebles, The Jackson Five, The Neville Brothers, Earth, Wind and Fire, James Brown and Stevie Wonder.

Rock/Pop:
Elvis Presley, Little Richard, The Beatles, The Beach Boys (great harmonies), The Bee Gees, Joe Cocker, Janis Joplin, Led Zeppelin, Pink Floyd, Lynyrd Skynyrd, Atlanta Rhythm Section, Little Feat, Steely Dan, ACDC, Van Halen, Freddie Mercury (Queen), Jeff Buckley, Bruce Springsteen, The Eagles, The Doobie Brothers, Sting, George Michael, Madonna, Prince, Celine Dion and Whitney Houston.

Jazz:
Louis Armstrong, Billie Holiday, Big Joe Turner, Ella Fitzgerald, Frank Sinatra, Sarah Vaughan, Jon Hendricks, Bobby McFerrin, Mel Torme', Tony Bennett, Diana Krall and Cassandra Wilson.

Country:
Patsy Cline, Hank Williams, Merle Haggard, Loretta Lynn, Johnny Cash, Dolly Parton, Charley Pride, Willie Nelson, Emmylou Harris, The Amazing Rhythm Aces, Alison Kraus/Union Station, Don Williams, Dwight Yoakam, Tammy Wynette, and George Jones.

Folk/Acoustic:
The Weavers, Harry Belafonte, Peter, Paul and Mary, Joan Baez, Indigo Girls, Christy Moore, Planxty, The Chieftans, The Dubliners, Enya, Steeleye Span, The Roches, Tom Paxton, James Taylor, Carole King, Crosby, Stills, Nash and Young, Cat Stevens, Jackson Browne, Joni Mitchell, K.D. Lang, Edith Piaf.

There are also many great exponents of World music and various ethnic folk traditions which are not mentioned here. Ask other singers who they listen to to get some ideas.

RECORDING

After learning all the techniques, scales, exercises, stage craft and everything else, the best thing you can do when it comes to recording is just relax and sing. Trust that you have done everything you can to prepare and become the character in the song. Let the recording engineer take care of the technical and electronic side of things and let the music happen.

Listen to this recording and notice how the vocalist is having fun with the band while telling the story. In the end music is about having pleasure. The more you can relax and just be the music, the better your performance will be.

 68. Tell Me Blues

Peter Gelling

This song comes from the author's album ***Fortune***. The vocalist is Doug Williams, who grew up in Chicago. For recordings by peter Gelling visit ***www.bentnotes.com***

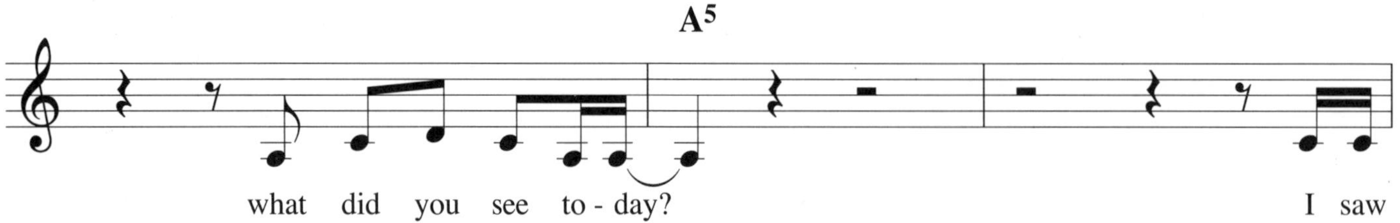

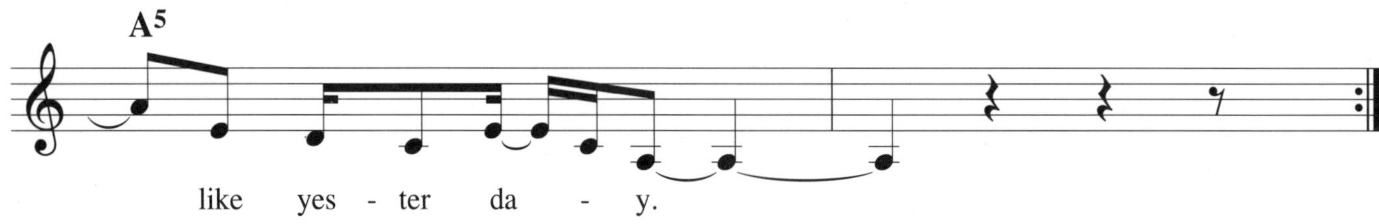

CYCLE OF FIFTHS

All major keys can be summarised in the following diagram known as the **Cycle of Fifths** (or the Cycle of Fourths).

CYCLE OF FIFTHS

If you start at the top of the cycle, **C**, and go in a clockwise direction, each new key and each new sharp is a fifth higher than the previous key or sharp. The key of **F♯** contains six sharps. After **F♯**, the next logical key would be **C♯** (containing seven sharps). However, this is not practical, and rather than using the key of C♯, you would use the enharmonic name for this key, i.e. **D♭** (which contains five flats).

CYCLE OF FOURTHS

If you start at the top of the cycle, **C**, and go in a counter clockwise direction, each new key and each new flat is a fourth higher than the previous key or flat. The key of **G♭** contains six flats. After **G♭**, the next logical key would be **C♭** (containing seven flats). However, this is not practical, and rather than using the key of **C♭**, you would use the enharmonic name for this key, i.e. **B** (which contains five sharps).

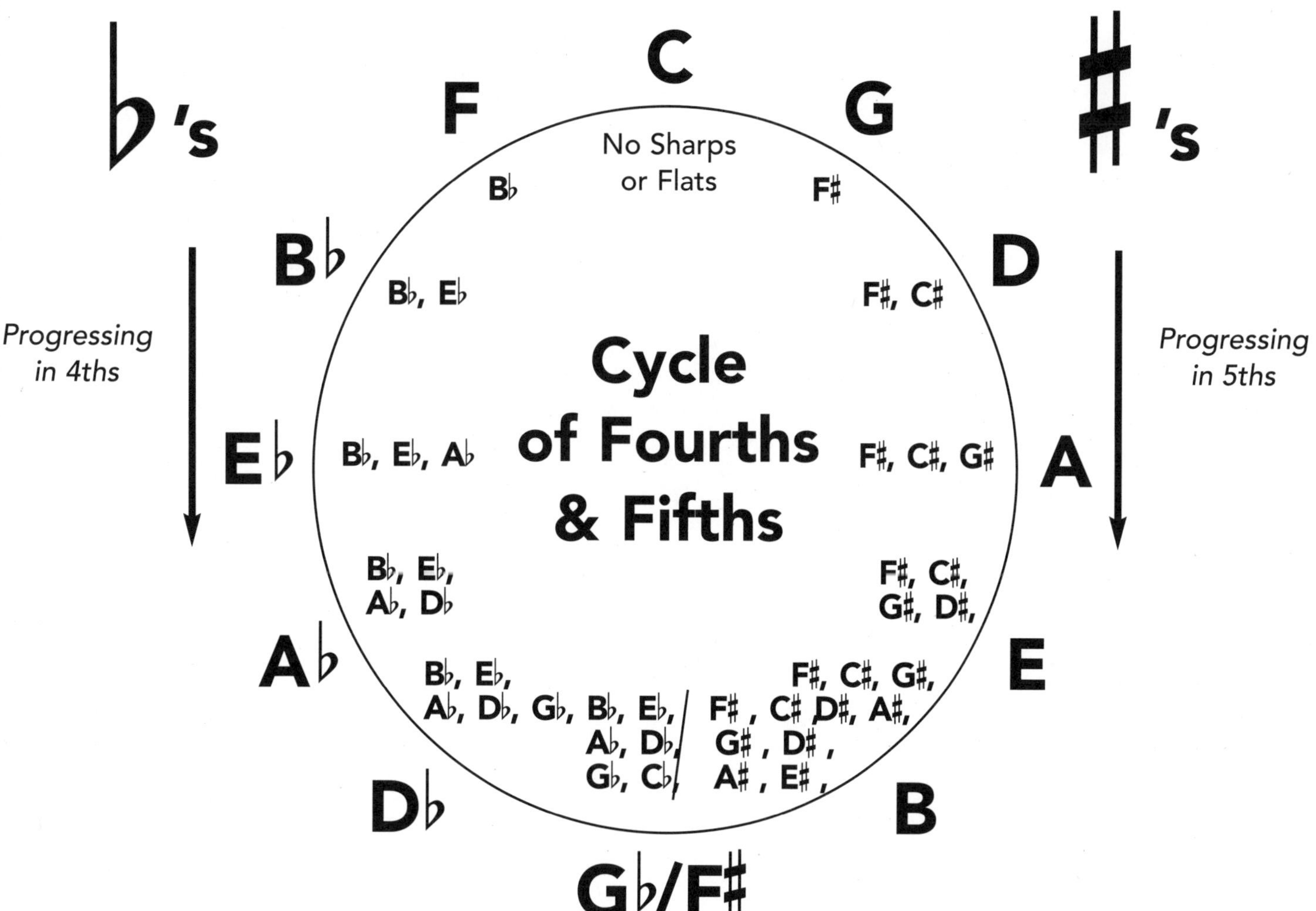

Notes on the

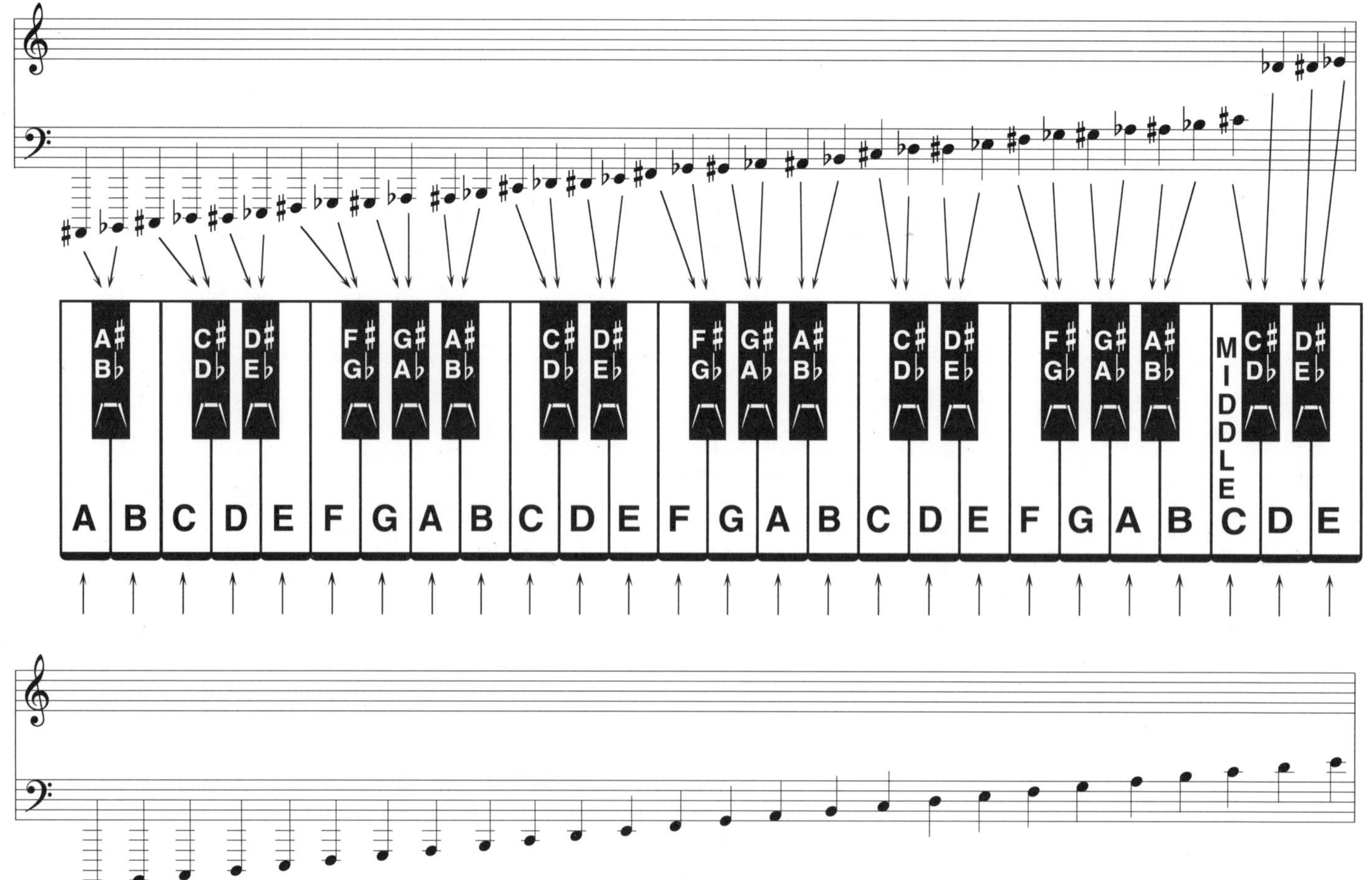

A♯ B♭
C♯ D♭
D♯ E♭
F♯ G♭
G♯ A♭
A♯ B♭
C♯ D♭
D♯ E♭
F♯ G♭
G♯ A♭
A♯ B♭
C♯ D♭
D♯ E♭
F♯ G♭
G♯ A♭
A♯ B♭
MIDDLE
C♯ D♭
D♯ E♭
A B C D E F G A B C D E F G A B C D E F G A B C D E

Keyboard

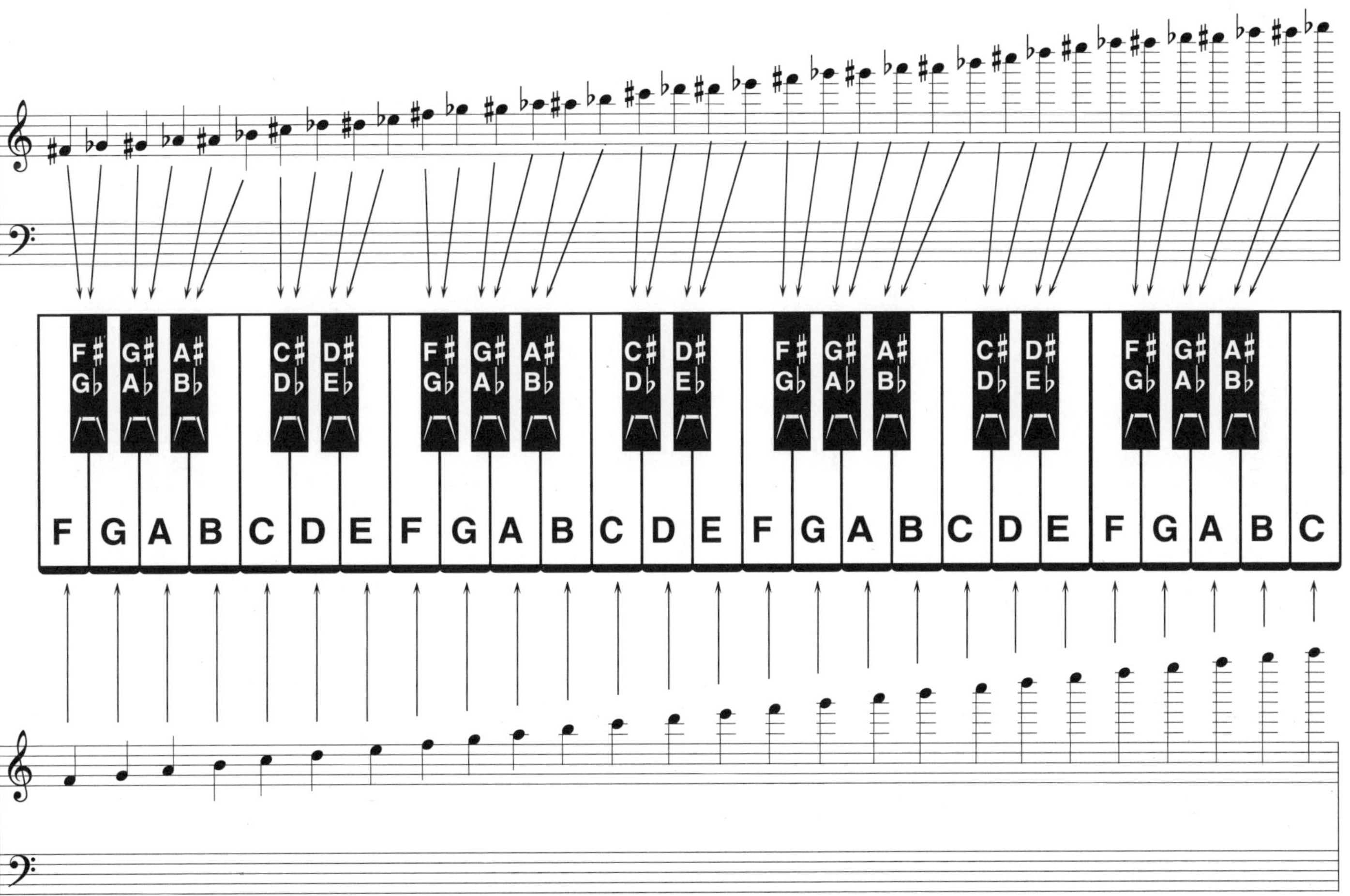
F♯ G♭
G♯ A♭
A♯ B♭
C♯ D♭
D♯ E♭
F♯ G♭
G♯ A♭
A♯ B♭
C♯ D♭
D♯ E♭
F♯ G♭
G♯ A♭
A♯ B♭
C♯ D♭
D♯ E♭
F♯ G♭
G♯ A♭
A♯ B♭
F G A B C D E F G A B C D E F G A B C D E F G A B C

Written below is a summary of all major scales and key signatures.

MAJOR SCALES AND KEY SIGNATURES

Key	Key Signature	♯'s/ ♭'s	Scale
C		0	
G		F♯	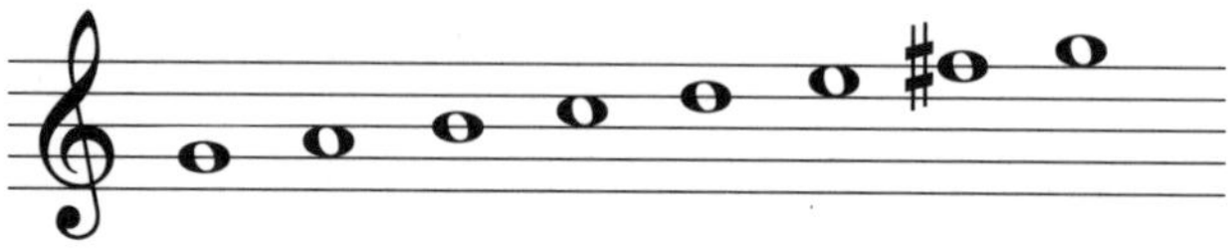
D		F♯ C♯	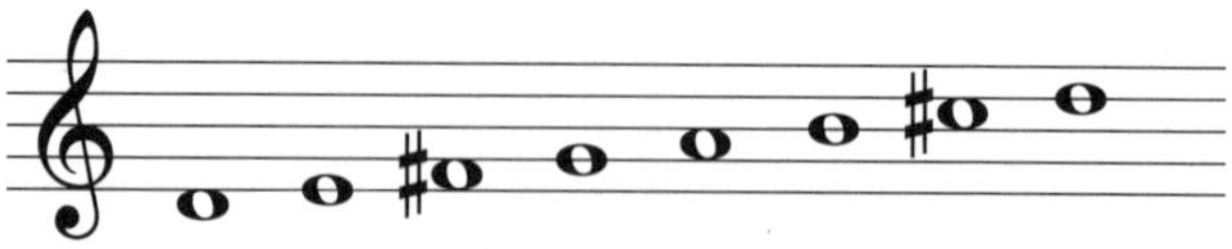
A		F♯ C♯ G♯	
E		F♯ C♯ G♯ D♯	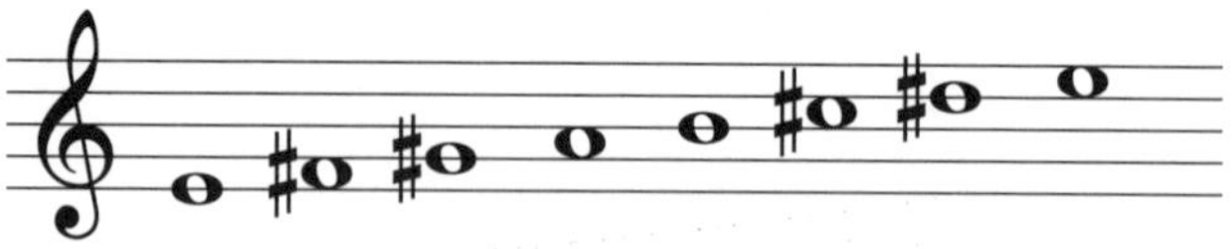
B		F♯ C♯ G♯ D♯ A♯	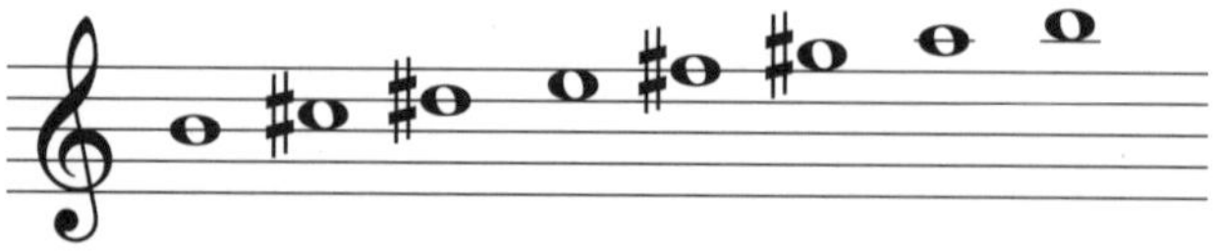
F♯		F♯ C♯ G♯ D♯ A♯ E♯	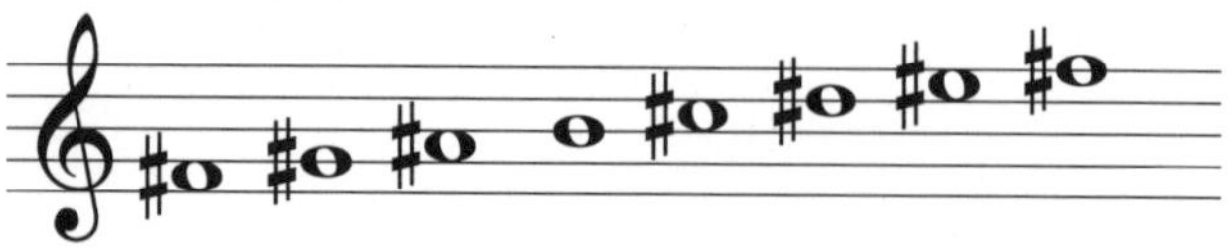

Major Scales and Key Signatures (cont.)

Key	Key Signature	♯'s/ ♭'s	Scale
F		B♭	
B♭		B♭ E♭	
E♭		B♭ E♭ A♭	
A♭		B♭ E♭ A♭ D♭	
D♭		B♭ E♭ A♭ D♭ G♭	
G♭		B♭ E♭ A♭ D♭ G♭ C♭	

It can be seen that each key signature is a shorthand representation of the scale, showing only the sharps or flats which occur in that scale. Where an additional sharp or flat occurs, it is not included as part of the key signature, but is written in the music, e.g. in the **key of G**, if a **D♯** note occurs, the sharp sign will be written immediately before the **D** note, **not** at the beginning of the line as part of the key signature.

To determine whether a song is in a major key or the relative minor key, look at the last note or chord of the song. Songs often finish on the root note or the root chord. E.g., if the key signature contained one sharp, and the last chord of the song was **Em**, the key would probably be **E minor**, not **G major**.

MINOR SCALES AND KEY SIGNATURES

Minor Key	Relative Major Key	Key Signature	♯'s/ ♭'s	Scale
Am	C		0	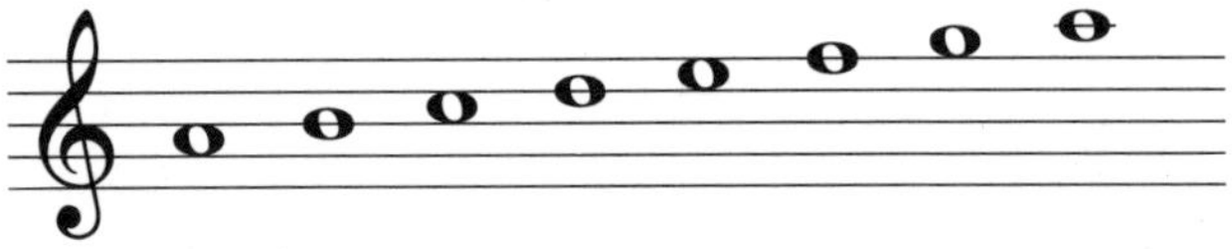
Em	G		F♯	
Bm	D		F♯ C♯	
F♯m	A		F♯ C♯ G♯	
C♯m	E		F♯ C♯ G♯ D♯	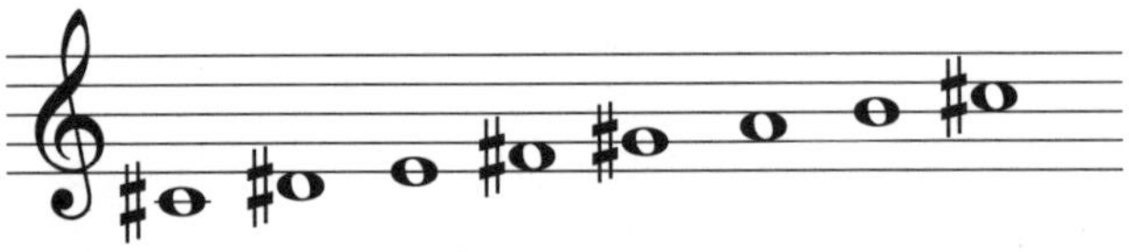
G♯m	B		F♯ C♯ G♯ D♯ A♯	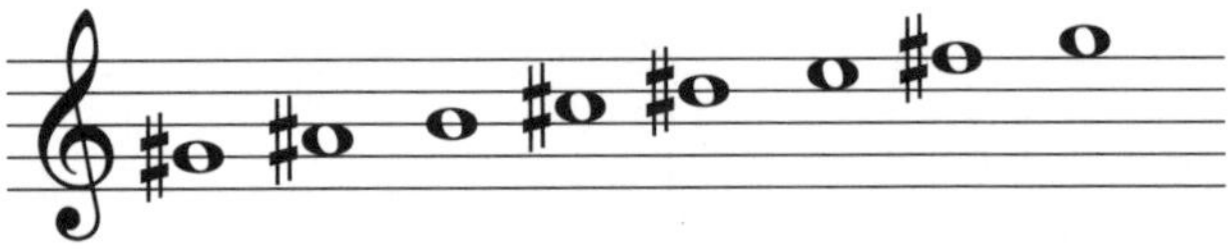
D♯m	F♯		F♯ C♯ G♯ D♯ A♯ E♯	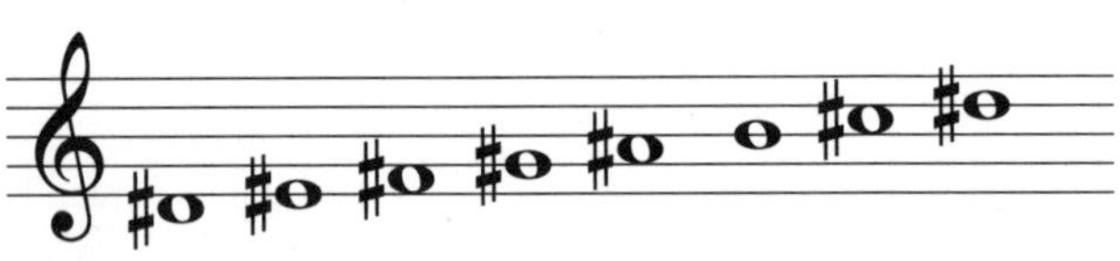

Minor Scales and Key Signatures (cont.)

Minor Key	Relative Major Key	Key Signature	♯'s/ ♭'s	Scale
Dm	F		B♭	
Gm	B♭		B♭ E♭	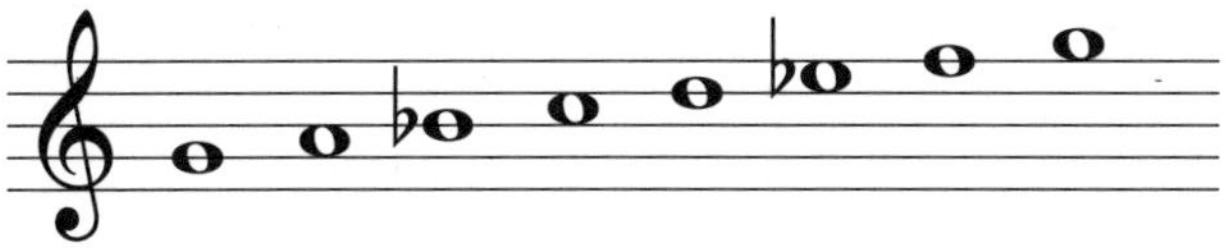
Cm	E♭		B♭ E♭ A♭	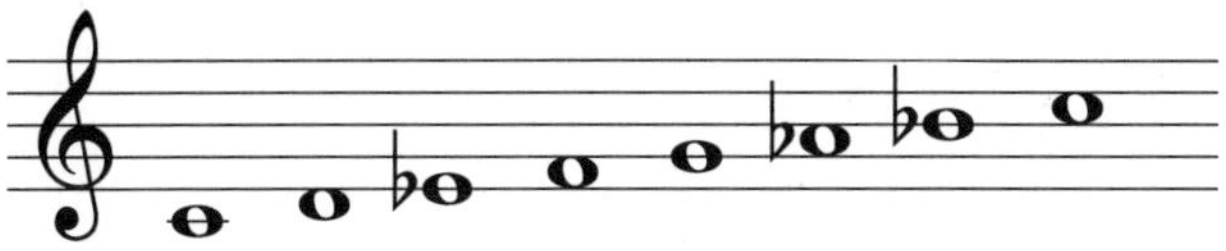
Fm	A♭		B♭ E♭ A♭ D♭	
B♭m	D♭		B♭ E♭ A♭ D♭ G♭	
E♭m	G♭		B♭ E♭ A♭ D♭ G♭ C♭	

BLUES SCALE SUMMARY

The Blues scale consists of the **1 ♭3 4 ♭5 5 ♭7** notes of the Chromatic scale. Written below is a summary of all Blues scales.

C Blues Scale

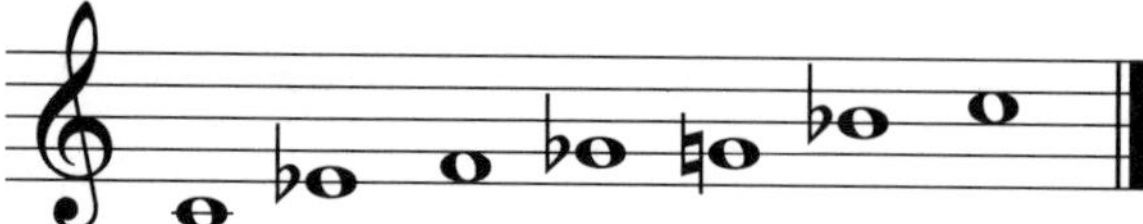

G Blues Scale

D Blues Scale

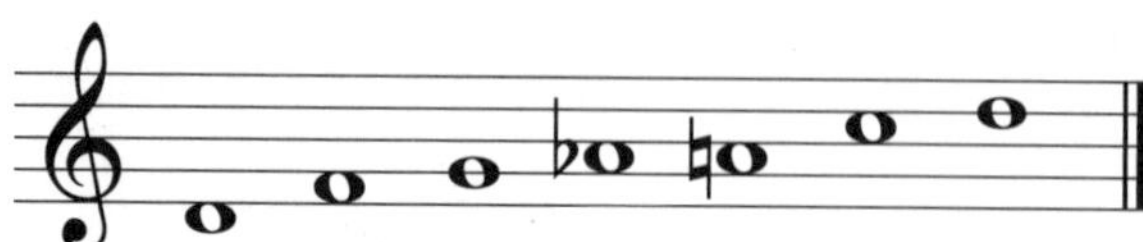

A Blues Scale

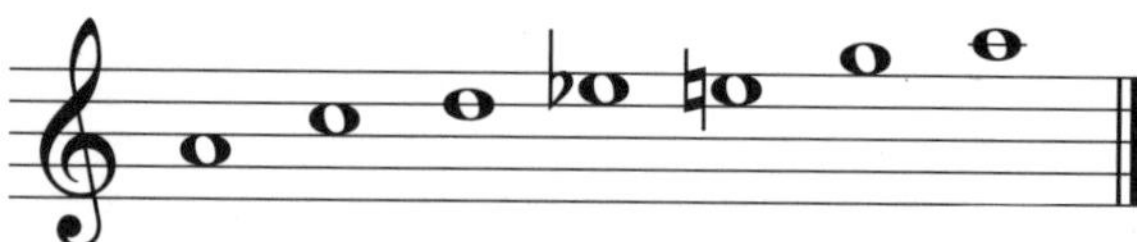

E Blues Scale

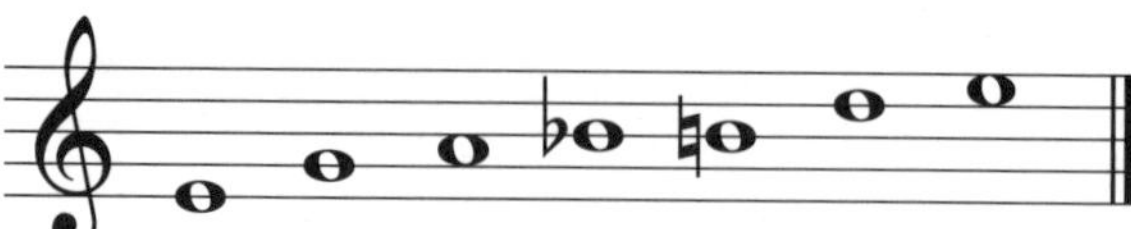

B Blues Scale

F♯ Blues Scale

F Blues Scale

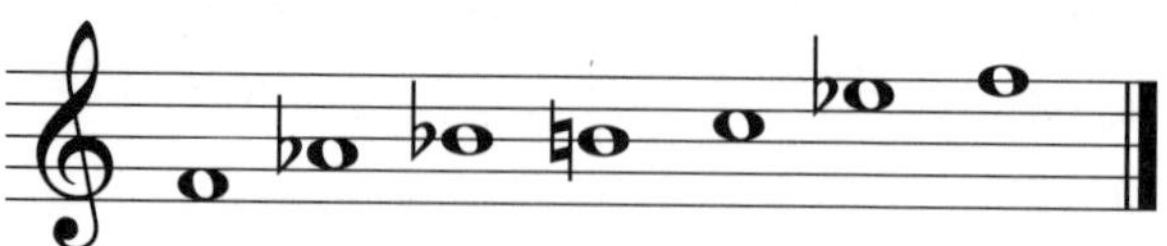

B♭ Blues Scale

E♭ Blues Scale

A♭ Blues Scale

D♭ Blues Scale

G♭ Blues Scale

GLOSSARY OF MUSICAL TERMS

Accidental — a sign used to show a temporary change in the pitch of a note (i.e. sharp ♯, flat ♭, double sharp 𝄪, double flat 𝄫, or natural ♮). The sharps or flats in a key signature are not regarded as accidentals.

Ad lib — to be played at the performer's discretion.

Allegretto — moderately fast.

Allegro — fast and lively.

Andante — an easy walking pace.

Arpeggio — the playing of a chord in consecutive single notes.

Bar — a section of music occurring between two bar lines (also called a measure).

Bar chord — a chord played with a left hand finger depressing all six strings on the guitar.

Bar line — a vertical line across the staff dividing the music into equal sections called bars.

Bass — the lower regions of pitch in general.

Chord — a combination of three or more different notes played together.

Chord progression — a series of chords played as a musical unit (e.g. in a song).

Clef — a sign placed at the beginning of each staff of music which fixes the location of a particular note on the staff, and hence the location of all other notes.

Coda — an ending section of music, signified by the sign 𝄌.

Common time — an indication of $\frac{4}{4}$ time — four quarter note beats per bar (also indicated by 𝄴).

D.C. al fine — repeat from the sign 𝄋 to the word 'fine'.

Dynamics — the varying degrees of volume in music, e.g. 'piano' (soft) and 'forte' (loud).

Eighth note — a note with the value of half a beat in $\frac{4}{4}$ time, indicated thus ♪ (also called a quaver).

Eighth rest — half a beat of silence indicated thus: 𝄾

Enharmonic — describes a difference in notation, but not in pitch, of two notes.

Fermata — a sign (𝄐) used to indicate that a note or chord is held to the player's own discretion.

Flat — a sign (♭) used to lower the pitch of a note by one semitone.

Forte — loud, indicated by the sign *f*.

Half note — a note with the value of two beats in $\frac{4}{4}$ time, indicated thus: 𝅗𝅥 (also called a minim).

Half rest — indicating two beats of silence, is written: 𝄼 on the third staff line.

Harmony — the simultaneous sounding of two or more different notes.

Interval — the distance between any two notes of different pitch.

Key — describes the notes used in a composition in regards to the major or minor scale from which they are taken; e.g. a piece 'in the key of C major' describes the melody, chords, etc., as predominantly consisting of the notes, **C, D, E, F, G, A,** and **B** — i.e. from the **C** scale.

Key signature — a sign, placed at the beginning of each staff of music, directly after the clef, to indicate the key of a piece. The sign consists of a certain number of sharps or flats, which represent the sharps or flats found in the scale of the piece's key.

Leger lines — small horizontal lines upon which notes are written when their pitch is either above or below the range of the staff.

Legato — smoothly, well connected.

Lick — a short musical phrase.

Major scale — a series of eight notes in alphabetical order based on the interval sequence tone tone - semitone - tone - tone - tone - semitone, giving the familiar sound **do re mi fa so la ti do**.

Melody — a group of notes of varying pitch and duration, and having a recognizable musical shape.

Metronome — a device which indicates the number of beats per minute, and which can be adjusted to any desired tempo.
Moderato — at a walking pace.
Natural — a sign (♮)used to cancel out the effect of a sharp or flat. The word is also used to describe the notes **A**, **B**, **C**, **D**, **E**, **F** and **G**; e.g. 'the natural notes'.
Note — a single sound with a given pitch and duration.
Octave — the distance between any given note with a set frequency, and another note with exactly double that frequency. Both notes will have the same letter name.
Open voicing — a chord that has the notes spread out between both hands on the keyboard.
Pitch — the sound produced by a note, determined by the frequency of vibrations. The pitch relates to a note being referred to as 'high' or 'low'.
Plectrum — a small object (often of a triangular shape) made of plastic which is used to pick or strum the strings of a guitar, bass, mandolin or banjo.
Quarter note — a note with the value of one beat in $\frac{4}{4}$ time, indicated thus ♩ (also called a crotchet).
Quarter rest: 𝄽 indicating one beat of silence.
Repeat signs — used to indicate a repeat of a section of music, by means of two dots placed before a double bar line.
Rhythm — the aspect of music concerned with duration and accent of notes.
Riff — a repeating pattern which may be altered to fit chord changes.
Semitone — the smallest interval used in conventional music. On guitar, it is a distance of one fret.
Root note — the note after which a chord or scale is named (also called 'key note').
Sharp — a sign (♯) used to raise the pitch of a note by one semitone.
Staccato — to play short and detached, indicated by a dot placed above the note.
Staff — five parallel lines together with four spaces, upon which music is written.
Syncopation — the placing of an accent on a normally unaccented beat.
Tempo — the speed of a piece.
Tie — a curved line joining two or more notes of the same pitch, where the second note(s) is not played, but its time value is added to that of the first note.
Timbre — a quality which distinguishes a note produced on one instrument from the same note produced on any other instrument (also called 'tone colour'). A given note on the guitar will sound different (and therefore distinguishable) from the same note on piano, violin, flute etc. There is usually also a difference in timbre between two instruments of the same type (e.g. two pianos).
Time signature — a sign at the beginning of a piece which indicates, by means of figures, the number of beats per bar (top figure), and the type of note receiving one beat (bottom figure).
Tone — a distance of two semitones.
Transposition — the process of changing a piece of music from one key to another.
Treble — the upper regions of pitch in general.
Treble clef — a sign placed at the beginning of the staff to fix the pitch of the notes placed on it. The treble clef (also called 'G clef') is placed so that the second line indicates as G note.